Charles Plummer

Elizabethan Oxford

Reprints of Rare Tracts

Charles Plummer

Elizabethan Oxford
Reprints of Rare Tracts

ISBN/EAN: 9783337252786

Printed in Europe, USA, Canada, Australia, Japan

Cover: Foto ©Thomas Meinert / pixelio.de

More available books at **www.hansebooks.com**

ELIZABETHAN OXFORD

Reprints of Rare Tracts

EDITED BY

CHARLES PLUMMER, M.A.

FELLOW AND CHAPLAIN OF CORPUS CHRISTI COLLEGE, OXFORD

Oxford

PRINTED FOR THE OXFORD HISTORICAL SOCIETY

AT THE CLARENDON PRESS

1887

TABLE OF CONTENTS.

PREFACE.

THE late appearance of the present volume, which completes the issues of the Oxford Historical Society for the year 1886, is due to the fact that it was not originally intended to form part of the issues of that year. But when the work which was to have occupied that position had to be laid aside, owing to the absence from England of one of the persons responsible for its appearance, it was resolved by the Committee of the Society that the present work should be substituted for it, because, consisting as it does entirely of reprints, it could be more easily produced than works based mainly on manuscript authorities. And the present Editor undertook to see the volume through the press, not because he had any special qualifications for the task, but merely because he had more leisure than many others for the labour of correcting the proof sheets.

To this humble function his work has been almost entirely restricted. And it only remains for him in these few prefatory words, to give a brief account of the contents of this volume, and of the authors of the several tracts contained in it, so far as he has been able to discover anything about them. For the selection of the contents of the volume he is not responsible. That was the work of more capable hands.

The first tract contained in the volume is the 'Oxoniensis in Anglia Academiæ Descriptio' by Nicholas Fitzherbert, or, as he here calls himself, Nicolaus Fierbertus. This modification of his name was probably a concession to Italian ears, for in a list of the household of Cardinal Allen drawn up after the death of the latter in 1594, he appears under the name of Nicolo Fierberti[1]. In his later tract 'De Antiquitate et Con-

---

[1] Letters and Memorials of Cardinal Allen, p. 375.

tinuatione Catholicæ Religionis in Anglia,' to which is appended the 'De Alani Cardinalis Vita Libellus,' published at Rome in 1608, he calls himself Nicolaus Fizerbertus. The tract here reprinted was originally published at Rome in 1602, and addressed ' ad perillustrem et Reverendissimum Dominum Bernardinum Paulinum S. D. N. Clementis VIII Datarium[1].' It was reprinted by Hearne with notes in the ninth volume of Leland's Itinerary. It is here reprinted from the original edition, without any alteration beyond the correction of one or two obvious misprints and mistakes in punctuation. A few notes, chiefly borrowed from Hearne, are added at the end. The tract is a rare one. Hearne declares that he had ·not seen more than two or three copies of it, though he 'had made diligent search after it[2].' There are two copies of it in the Bodleian, and for the present edition I have had, through the kindness of the owner, the use of a copy belonging to Mr. F. Madan of Brasenose College, Sub-Librarian of the Bodleian.

The author, Nicholas Fitzherbert, belonged to a family which suffered greatly for its constancy to the older faith. According to the document quoted above[3] his father and one of his uncles died in prison after languishing there the one twenty-six, the other thirty-two years 'for the faith.' His cousin Thomas Fitzherbert spent, like himself, the greater part of his life in exile for the same cause[4]. Nicholas was the second son of John, the second son of Sir Anthony Fitzherbert, the well-known lawyer and legal writer, to whose dying exhortations, according to a story, which has, it must be confessed, a somewhat legendary complexion, the religious constancy of his descendants was largely due[5]. According to his epitaph

---

[1] 'Datarius: Primus Cancellariæ Romanæ minister.' Du Cange. The arms on the title-page, which are here omitted, are not however those of the person to whom the book is dedicated, but those of the Cardinal Bartolommeo Cesi, who died in 1621 or 2, v. Ciacconius. iv. coll. 306, 307.

[2] Preface to Leland, vol. ix.

[3] Letters and Memorials, p. 375.

[4] Biographia Britannica. Vol. III. pp. 1940, 1941.

[5] Ib. 1938, 1939.

as given by Hearne[1] he was fifty years old at his death in
1612; according to another account he was sixty-three years
old when he died[2]. The latter version seems to throw his
birth too far back, the former to bring it too far forward.
For according to Wood[3] he entered Exeter College about
1568, and his name occurs in a list of the members of Exeter
of the year 1572[4], he being then, according to Wood, the
senior undergraduate of the college. I can find no record of
his having graduated at Oxford ; so that he probably, like his
cousin Thomas[5], left Oxford on account of his religion without
taking a degree[6]. He withdrew to the continent, and it is
probable that he went in the first instance to the English
Seminary at Douay, which had been founded by Dr. (afterwards Cardinal) William Allen in the year 1568. The description in his biography of Allen of the mode of life and study
in the Seminary reads like that of an eye-witness[7]. And this
presumption is converted into practical certainty by the fact
that his name, with the double epithet of *nobilis* and *pauper*[8],
occurs in a list of Englishmen who matriculated at the University of Douay[9]. It would probably be here too that he
first formed his friendship with Cardinal Allen, who had left
Oxford in 1561. In 1578 political troubles caused the re-
moval of the Seminary to Rheims[10]; and this may have led
Fitzherbert to withdraw to Italy. Pits, who knew him per-
sonally, met him for the first time at Bologna in 1580, where
he was engaged in studying the civil law[11]. Shortly after he

---

[1] Adam de Domerham, II. 720, 721.

[2] Biogr. Brit. u. s. p. 1941.

[3] Ath. II. 120, [I. 382].

[4] Clark, Register, p. 32 ; Boase, Reg. Coll. Exon. p. 185. It is probably from a
misunderstanding of this list that some have spoken of N. Fitzherbert as having
been *Fellow* of Exeter about 1572. Ib. 208.

[5] Biogr. Brit. u. s. p. 1940.

[6] He says himself that he left Oxford 'adolescens admodum.' Inf. p. 28.

[7] Letters and Memorials, pp. 7-9.

[8] In his Preface (inf. p. 5) he speaks of himself as 'a fortunæ bonis egentissimus.'

[9] Douay Diaries, p. 275.

[10] It returned to Douay in 1593, and was dissolved in 1793.

[11] Pits, p. 814.

proceeded to Rome, where Gregory XIII (1572–85) who had recently founded the English Seminary at Rome, gave him a monthly pension of ten gold crowns to enable him to study [1]. He took orders in the Roman Church [2], but when or where I have not discovered.

In April 1583, Allen, writing from Rheims to the Rector of the English Seminary at Rome, speaks with gratitude of Fitzherbert's exertions on behalf of the Seminary at Rheims, and from this and another letter of July 1583 it appears that he had been making a collection for it in the kingdom of Naples [3]. In 1585 Allen proceeded to Rome, and in 1587 was made a Cardinal. In the same year Fitzherbert became a member of his household [4]. The account which he gives of the domestic life of the Cardinal [5] is evidently based on personal knowledge. I have found but few notices of him subsequent to the death of Allen in October 1594. He seems to have continued to reside in Rome, where all his works were published; his translation of the Galateo of Giovanni della Casa, Bishop of Benevento [6] in 1595 [7], the Description of Oxford in 1602, and the tract on the Antiquity of the Catholic religion in England, with the life of Cardinal Allen appended, in 1608 [8]. He perished by drowning at Florence in

---

[1] 'Per studiare.' Letters and Memorials, p. 375. Cf. Douay Diaries, p. 302, where 'Master Fytharberte' appears as receiving a pension of 'x crownes by monthe' from the Pope.

[2] 'E clerigo.' Letters and Memorials, p. 375.

[3] Ib., pp. 189, f., 201.

[4] Pits, u. s. With this agrees the statement that at the time of Allen's death in 1594, 'e stato sette anni in servitio del signor Cardinale.' Letters and Memorials, p. 375. The office which he held was that of 'coppiero' or 'cupbearer.' Ib.

[5] Ib., pp. 17, 18.

[6] Giovanni della Casa, 'Il Galatheo, overo trattato de' costumi e modi che si debbono tenere ò schifare nella commune conversatione,' &c. Vinezia, 1562. 8vo. On the original work see Hallam, Lit. of Europe, ii. 128.

[7] We find a 'Mr. Fitzherbert' mentioned as being in Rome in Jan. 1597, Douay Diaries, p. 390; but this might be Thomas Fitzherbert.

[8] The Preface is dated Rome, May 17, 1608. The life of Allen has been reprinted in Letters and Memorials, pp. 1–20; and it is this reprint which is cited in the foregoing account. He is said to have written a longer life of Allen which never saw the light. Biogr. Brit. u. s. p. 1941.

1612, and was buried in the Church of the Benedictines there[1]. Pits describes him as a man of piety and urbanity, learned both in the canon and civil law, and well versed in the humaner letters; while the document so often quoted speaks of him as a noble and excellent gentleman [2].

As to his work here reprinted Hearne in his Diaries [3] speaks of it as 'libellus non magni momenti'; but in a note added subsequently he confesses: 'Fallor. Multa notatu digna, alibi frustra quærenda, habet Fitz Herbertus.' And he speaks to much the same effect in the Preface to the ninth volume of Leland's Itinerary.

After a brief description of England generally, in which he notes among other things the decline of the culture of the vine, and the extinction of the wolf in England; the fondness of the English for country life, hospitality, and hunting [4], the author comes to the two Universities Oxford and Cambridge, of which he briefly gives the mythical history [5]. Modern readers may perhaps be a little surprised at the stress which Fitzherbert lays on the healthiness of Oxford [6]. He estimates the number of students at three thousand, which is almost certainly an exaggeration [7]; and he gives a very ideal picture of their 'modesty, taciturnity, obedience, and zeal for study,' which caused Erasmus to compare the colleges to well-ordered monasteries [8]. They rise at five o'clock in the morning; the college gates are closed for the night at nine in summer and eight in winter. The proctors

---

[1] Hearne, Adam de Domerham, ii. 720, 721.

[2] 'Gentilhuomo assai nobile; da bene.'

[3] Ed. Doble, ii. 260, 261. [4] Infra, p. 8.

[5] Ib. pp. 10, 11. It is told at greater length by Hutten; inf. pp. 37 ff. On the mythical history of Oxford, see Parker, Early History of Oxford, chap. ii.

[6] Infra, pp. 9, 12.

[7] Ib. p. 15. In 1568, the very year in which Fitzherbert is said to have entered Exeter, the number of Students and Servitors is given as 1842. Infra, p. 205. Harrison, 'Description of Britaine,' Book II. ch. 3, says, speaking of Oxford and Cambridge, 'there are about three thousand students nourished in them both, as by a late surveie it manifestlie appeared.' But whether this means 3000 in each, or 3000 in the two together, I do not feel sure.

[8] Infra, p. 16.

'take no excuse,' if they find any one outside his college walls after those hours [1]. In addition to the sixteen colleges, there are eight halls, frequented mainly by the sons of the rich and noble, the discipline in them being laxer than in the colleges; though the colleges also, in addition to members of the foundation, receive a number of noble youths who live at their own expense [2]. Entrance to the University is through the 'gymnasia' and public schools of England, of which the most noted are Winchester, Eton, Durham, and London [3]. The disputations which precede the degrees of B.A. and M.A. are then described; those undergraduates who fail in the former are 'sent down' by the stricter colleges [4]. The object of the University is to furnish a 'supply of persons duly qualified for the Service of God in Church and State [5].' As Chancellor, some noble high in the royal favour is chosen; as 'Pro-chancellor,' some head of a college [6]. The Proctors have to entertain any great men who may visit the University, and to transact the affairs of the University at Court; and thus, unless they are 'utterly brainless' (an impossible supposition, let us hope), have many opportunities of securing their future promotion [7]. Then, after enumerating some of the heroes of the Catholic faith which England and Oxford had produced in days gone by [8], he concludes with an impassioned address to Oxford, in which he adjures her by the example of these, and of the Catholic Martyrs and Confessors of his own day, the Fishers, Mores, Allens, Campians, Bristols, to abandon the error of her ways and return to the path of truth [9]. It may be safely said that this appeal, however worthy of respect, would have but little effect on those to whom it was addressed, seeing that it begs every question that was at issue between them and the author of it.

Of the author of the next piece, 'The Antiquities of Oxford by Leonard Hutten,' I have found very little beyond what is

[1] Infra, pp. 16, 17. [2] Ib., p. 16. [3] Ib., p. 17.
[4] Ib., p. 18. [5] Ib., p. 19. [6] Ib., p. 20.
[7] Ib., pp. 20, 21. [8] Ib., pp. 22-25. [9] Ib., pp. 25-28.

recorded by Wood[1]. He entered Christ Church as a West-minster Student in 1574, became canon in 1599, being then Bachelor of Divinity. 'The year after he proceeded in that faculty. His younger years were beautified with all kind of polite learning, his middle with ingenuity and judgement, and his reverend years with great wisdom in government, having been often sub-dean of his house. He was also an excellent Grecian, well read in the fathers and Schoolmen, . . . and not meanly versed in the histories of our own nation.' He had also a hand in the translation of the Bible under James I. He died May 17, 1632, and was buried in the Divinity (or Latin) Chapel of Ch. Ch. Cathedral. Besides his canonry at Ch. Ch. he held at various times other pieces of ecclesiastical preferment. He wrote, 'An Answer to a treatise concerning the Cross in Baptism.' Oxon. 1605, 4to.; 'Historia Funda-tionum Ecclesiae Christi Oxon.[2]' which has never been printed. · According to some he was the author of a play called 'Bellum Grammaticale,' which was performed at Oxford before Queen Elizabeth in 1592[3], but Wood on chronological grounds denies this[4]. The work here printed was first published by Hearne at the end of his edition of the Textus Roffensis (Oxford 1720), from a Manuscript belonging to Dr. Robert Plot[5]. Wood, who had seen four copies of it, describes it as a slight performance, mostly taken from Brian

---

[1] Ath. Ox. II. 532-4, [I. 570, 571].

[2] The hope expressed by Hearne (Diaries, II. p. 261) that the MS. of this work might be found in the Archives of Ch. Ch. was not realised when Dr. Kitchin catalogued the Ch. Ch. MSS. Wood (u. s.) once saw a copy which belonged to Dr. Fell.

[3] Infra, p. 255.

[4] This authorship is however assumed in the Bodleian Catalogue. The play has been twice printed; London, 1635, 8vo; ib., 1726. In the latter edition it is stated to have been 'ab eruditissimis Oxoniensibus adinventa.' It is said to be based on the prose tract of the same name by Andrea Guarna of Salerno.

[5] Text. Roff. p. xxxvii. It is a wonder that Dr. Plot should have ventured to lend his MS. to a brother antiquary like Hearne, seeing that he himself, when asked to return a remarkable stone which had been lent to him, laid down the maxim: 'y[t] 'twas a Rule amongst Antiquaries to receive, and never restore.' Hearne's Diaries, Ed. Doble, I. pp. 66, 67. This principle has been often acted upon, but seldom stated with such frankness.

Twyne's 'Apologia Antiq. Acad. Oxon.' But Hearne both in his Diaries[1] and also in the Preface to the Textus Roffensis[2] denies this with some vivacity. I must leave it to others better versed than myself in the antiquities of Oxford to decide this question of the merits of Hutten as an antiquarian. I shall only here call attention to one or two miscellaneous matters of interest mentioned by him.

One point of some interest, especially to a Corpus man like the present editor, is the public spirit shown towards the city by Dr. John Claymond the first President of C. C. C. The road which enters Oxford from the South 'haveing in it above 40 Arches of Stone, [was], I will not saie first founded, but very well repaired and restored by the charge of Doctor John Claymond[3].' Further, the Corn Market was by him 'builded att his owne charge, and covered with lead[4].' The mention of the 'House upon the left hand' as we enter Oxford from the South 'called Childswell in the ascent of an Hill where old traditions Saie was . . . a Well, which . . . had a vertue to make Women that were barren to bring forth Children, and soe gave name to that Place[5]' may interest readers of Matthew Arnold; though the name has got corrupted in the course of time[6]. So too it is interesting to learn that the Conduit at Carfax (now in Nuneham Park) was the work of Mr. Otho Nicholson, a Gent. of London, and that every College had 'from thence a Cock to their kitchins, and the whole Towne recourse thereunto for their Water[7].' The work breaks off just as the author is beginning

---

[1] II. p. 261.   [2] P. xxxviii.   [3] Infra, pp. 83, 84

[4] Ib. pp. 86, 87. I may here note that at p. 84, the original MS. of Shepreve's life of Claymond has *Claymondi nummis*; and at p. 87 it has: ut possit *siccum*, as was kindly pointed out to me by Mr. Herbert Hurst. I may add that this MS. belonged originally to C.C.C. but is now among the Wood MSS. in Bodley. Another illustration of the risks of lending.

[5] Ib. p. 83.

[6] 'Runs it not here, the track by *Childsworth* Farm.' Matthew Arnold, Thyrsis, stanza 2. Hearne in the 5th vol. of Leland's Itinerary (1st ed.) speaks of 'Chilswell Farm at the West End of a great Field commonly called Hincksey Field on the North Side of Foxcombe Hill,' p. 134. The name Chilswell is still in local use.   [7] Infra, p. 86.

to describe the existing colleges and halls. But this, according to Hearne[1], is due not to the mutilation of the MS. but to the prudence of the author, who was afraid that he might perhaps excite ill-feeling if he meddled with the private affairs of the different Colleges. The work is composed in the form of a letter; but I have found no hint as to the person to whom it was meant to be addressed. It is printed here from Hearne, without any alteration beyond the correction of a few obvious misprints. The two appendices which follow it are likewise borrowed from Hearne.

The next group of tracts has to do with the visit of Queen Elizabeth to Oxford in 1566. First in order come the 'Commentaries' of John Bereblock. These were first published by Hearne at the end of his edition of the History of the life and reign of Richard II by the Monk of Evesham (Oxford 1729), from a manuscript given to the Editor by Thomas Ward, of Warwick, Esquire. From Hearne it was borrowed by Nichols in the first edition of his Progresses of Queen Elizabeth. It is here reprinted from Hearne. But while I was engaged upon this volume Mr. Madan pointed out to me a MS. (Bodl. Add. A. 63) which evidently referred to this visit of Queen Elizabeth, and a very brief inspection showed me that it was a copy of Bereblock's Commentaries. It is not the MS. used by Hearne, as the pagination of the two MSS. is quite different. But they evidently have some common origin, as they often agree in their least rational blunders, and even in the little flourishes with which the text in one or two places is adorned, and which Hearne has reproduced. On the other hand this MS. (which I have called B) has enabled me to improve Hearne's text in many points, and I have given the more important variations in the notes. In the matter of spelling I have frequently followed B, as it is more uniform than Hearne's text in this respect. The MS. is written in a good engrossing hand of the period[2].

[1] Text. Roff., p. xl.

[2] Tanner mentions a MS. of Bereblock's Commentaries, belonging to Dr. Rivers, Fellow of All Souls.

Bereblock[1] was born in Kent near Rochester. He became Fellow of St. John's in 1558, was admitted B.A. in March 1561; and M.A. in Feb. 156⅝. In June 1566 he was admitted Fellow of Exeter, and the same year he was made Dean[2]. He was Senior Proctor in 1569, his colleague being Thomas (afterwards Sir Thomas) Bodley, the founder of the Bodleian Library. In 1570 Sir William Petre, who in 1564 had practically refounded Exeter College[3], gave him leave of absence for four years, and during this absence he took the degree of B.C.L. in some Continental University in 1572. The same year his name occurs in a list of the members of Exeter College, next but two after the sub-rector[4].

Next to the Commentaries of Bereblock comes the ' Topographical Delineation' of Oxford by Thomas Neale. This, which was presented to Queen Elizabeth by the author, is in the form of a dialogue in Latin Verse between the Queen and her favourite Robert Dudley, Earl of Leicester, Chancellor of the University. The illustrations (which are here omitted) were drawn by the above mentioned Bereblock, as he himself tells us[5]. He also tells us that the Queen never received any present with greater pleasure; I fear the modern reader will not derive very much pleasure either from Neale's verses or Bereblock's drawings[6]; though a faint gleam of unconscious prophetic humour lights up the account of All Souls[7]; and the hint that Christ Church could do with a little more money, is amusing as coming from a Christ Church man[8].

[1] For this account of Bereblock, cp. Tanner, p. 82; Boase, Reg. Coll. Exon. pp. 45, 207; Id., Reg. Univ. p. 244.

[2] In Reg. Coll. Exon. p. 181 we find 12ˢ. paid for a bed-post (fulcrum) in his bed-chamber (cubiculum). July–Nov. 1566.

[3] Boase, Reg. Coll. Exon. p. xx. Sir Wm. Petre is one of the persons to whom Bereblock addressed his Commentaries. See the title-page.

[4] Clark, Register, p. 32.

[5] Infra, pp. 140, 183. He is said also to have made drawings of his native town of Rochester. Tanner, u. s.

[6] The drawings, however, look much better in the original MS. than in any of the reproductions.

[7] Infra, pp. 160, 161.   [8] Ib., 158.

The original MS. is in Bodley[1]. (MS. Bodl. 13.) That portion of the verses which contains the descriptions of the Colleges and Halls was printed by Miles Windsor in his 'Academiarum Catalogus.' (London 1590.) But the work was first published in its entirety by Hearne at the end of his edition of Dodwell's Dissertation 'De Parma Equestri Wood-wardiana.' (Oxford 1713.) It was embodied by Nichols in both editions of his Progresses of Queen Elizabeth. From the former of these it is here printed; but I have compared the text throughout with the facsimile reproduction of the original MS., made by Mr. Guggenheim (Oxford 1882), with a preface by Mr. Madan. Besides these verses Neale also wrote an account of Queen Elizabeth's visit, from which the 'Brief Rehearsal' by Richard Stephens[2] was abridged. But of Neale's original work I have found no trace[3].

Thomas Neale was born in the year 1519 or 1520 at Yate in Gloucestershire, and educated at Winchester. Thence he entered New College as a Probationer in 1538, and two years later became perpetual fellow. The dates of his degrees are as follows; B.A. May 1542, M.A. July 1546, B.D. July 1556. Under Mary he was chaplain to Bishop Bonner, and Rector of Thenford in Northamptonshire. On the accession of

[1] It was given to the Bodleian by John More in 1630. Whether this is the actual copy presented to the Queen I cannot say. Hearne is of opinion that it is. 'Illud ipsum esse existimo quod Serenissimæ Reginæ donavit Auctor.' (Preface to Dodwell, p. vii.) It might be questioned whether what was presented to the queen was a book, or a map with Bereblock's views and Neale's verses in the margin. I think that Bereblock's own words (infra, p. 140) imply the former; though Wood says that a map was hung on the door of St. Mary's during the Queen's visit. Robinson, who also mentions the map (charta), distinctly speaks of Neale's present to the Queen as *hunc librum*. Infra, pp. 183, 185.

[2] Infra, pp. 197 ff.

[3] I was at first inclined to suspect that Stephens might have confused Neale and Bereblock, owing possibly to their co-operation in the 'Delineatio.' But there are some things in Stephens which are not in Bereblock's Commentaries. My own opinion is that Neale's work must be practically embodied in Wood's account of this visit in the History and Antiquities, ed. Gutch II. pp. 154 ff. This account agrees closely and even verbally with that of Stephens. And the scribe who made the Harleian Copy of the latter omits the report of the Queen's speech to the University, because it is 'almost exactly the same as printed in Wood's Hist. et Antiq. Univ. Oxon.' Infra, p. 205.

Elizabeth he returned to Oxford and was made Regius Professor of Hebrew in 1558 or 1559[1]. This post he resigned in
1569. Prior to this date he had entered himself as a member
of Hart Hall[2]; and he built himself a lodging opposite the
Hall which was long known as Neale's House. Ultimately
he retired to Cassington, fearing molestation on account of his
religion. He erected a monument to himself in Cassington
Church in the year 1590 being then in his seventy-first year.
How much longer he survived is not certainly known. But
there is evidence which suggests that he died that very year.
Pits regards him as a steady Catholic, though he admits that
he was of a very timid nature. He is said to have been
the inventor of the story of the consecration of Archbishop
Parker at the Nag's Head Inn in Cheapside; Pits, indeed,
roundly asserting that Neale was present at the ceremony.
Besides the works already mentioned he translated into Latin
the Commentaries of Rabbi David Kimchi upon the twelve
Minor Prophets. Of these the first nine were presented by
him to Queen Elizabeth in 1566[3], the remaining three having
been already dedicated to Cardinal Pole[4]. These last were
printed at Paris, 1557, 4to. In the Dedication he praises Pole
for his services to the restoration of religion, and says that
he undertook the work chiefly at the solicitation of his friend,
Jean Mercier, Regius Professor of Hebrew at Paris. This
Dedication is dated Paris, March 1, 1556.

We now come to the account of Queen Elizabeth's visit,
compiled by Nicholas Robinson, who about this time[5] became
Bishop of Bangor; and to the 'Brief Rehearsal' by Richard
Stephens, which has been already mentioned. These were

---

[1] His name occurs in that position in a list of members of Ch. Ch. belonging
to the year 156⅔. Clark, Register, p. 11.

[2] His name occurs in a list of members of that Hall of the year 1568. Clark, p. 29.

[3] Infra, pp. 139, 140, 183; Tanner, p. 538. The MS. of these and also of a
tract entitled ' Rabbinicæ quædam Observationes ex prædictis Commentariis ' is in
the British Museum, MS. Reg. 2. D. xxi.

[4] For this account of Neale see Wood, Ath. Oxon. I. 576–8 [I. 249 f.]; Tanner,
p. 538; Boase, Reg. Univ., p. 204; Pits, pp. 769, f.

[5] See below.

first printed by Nichols from Brit. Mus. MS. Harl. 7033[1].
The text of Nichols was carefully collated with the MS.
by Mr. Madan; and the results of this comparison appear
occasionally in the notes marked M. The other notes have
been reprinted with considerable abridgement from Nichols.
A few references enclosed in square brackets have been
added by myself. Of Richard Stephens, the compiler of
the second of these two pieces, I have been able to discover
no certain trace. There was a Corpus man of that name
who took his B.A. in 1568, and became Fellow of Corpus
in 1569[2].

Of Bishop Robinson the most complete Biography is in
Cooper's Athenæ Cantabrigienses[3], from which I borrow
the following facts:—Nicholas Robinson was born at Aber-
conwy, and educated at Queens' College, Cambridge. He
proceeded B.A. 1547–8, and soon after became Fellow of
his College. In 1551 he commenced M.A., was Bursar
of his College 1551–3, and Proctor of the University 1552.
In 1555 he subscribed the Roman Catholic articles, and
was ordained March 155⁶⁄₇. In 1557–8 he was Dean of his
College. About 1559 Archbishop Parker made him one of
his chaplains. In June 1562 he became Archdeacon of
Merioneth, and in that capacity sat in the Convocation
of 1562–3. He subscribed the thirty-nine articles. He was
at Cambridge during the Queen's visit in 1564, and has
written an account of the proceedings on that occasion[4].
He was created D.D. by special grace, April 1566, and in
the same year was elected Bishop of Bangor under a license
tested, Cambridge, July 30. His election was assented to
by the Queen, Sept. 15, and confirmed by the Archbishop
Oct. 5. On the 20th of the latter month he was consecrated
at Lambeth. A year later he reported to Cecil on the pre-

---

[1] The ' Brief Rehearsal' was not reprinted by Nichols in his second edition.

[2] Boase, p. 270.

[3] I. pp. 503-5.

[4] Commentarii Hexameri Rerum Cantabrigiæ actarum, &c. In Nichols
ed. 1, III. 27-134.

valence of superstitious customs among the Welsh. At the same time he sent his former patron, Archbishop Parker, a copy of a part of Eadmer's History, with a promise to send the remainder shortly. He also expressed his opinion that there were no faithful monuments of antiquity in Wales[1]. He sat in the Convocation of 1571 and renewed his Subscription to the articles. In May 1572, he with other prelates, on a complaint by the Cambridge proctors against the queen's new Statutes, determined that there was no great cause for reformation, and that the younger men were censurable for seeking an alteration by disordered means. We find him acting under several commissions royal and archiepiscopal during the remaining years of his life. He died Feb. 13, 158⅞, and was buried in Bangor Cathedral.

Besides the works already enumerated, he wrote: (1) Strylius, a comedy acted at Queens' College, 1553. (2) A Sermon on the character of Cain. MS. C. C. C. C. civ. p. 321. (3) Tractatus de Vestium usu in Sacris.

Elizabeth[2] arrived at Oxford from Woodstock on Saturday, Aug. 31, 1566, having been preceded by a few days by Leicester, Cecil and others. At Wolvercote the limits of the University Liberties, she was met by Leicester and the other University authorities, and Marbeck the late Public Orator, welcomed her in a Latin speech[3]. At the city boundaries she was met by the mayor and aldermen, who regaled her with an oration in English. At the North Gate (Bocardo) another speech awaited her from an under-

---

[1] This letter is in C. C. C. C. MS. civ., p. 503. Cp. ib., p. 499. It is interesting to find Bishop Robinson thus ministering to the antiquarian tastes of his former patron. He further showed his interest in the Antiquities of Wales by translating into Latin the Life of Gruffudd ap Cynan. This translation (probably the Bishop's autograph) is among the Hengwrt MSS., No. 155, though this fact is unknown to Cooper. He also made 'a large collection of Historical things relating to the Church and State of the Britains and Welsh.' This MS. was (according to Cooper) formerly in the library of Robert Vaughan of Hengwrt, but I have searched the Catalogue of the Hengwrt MSS. for it in vain.

[2] For this sketch of Elizabeth's visit compare, besides the tracts printed below, Wood, Hist. and Antiquities, ed. Gutch II. 154 ff.

[3] Printed below, pp. 235 ff.

graduate named Robert Deale of New College[1]. Thence passing on through the plaudits of the University to Carfax, she found the Professor of Greek, Mr. Lawrence, lying in wait for her with a Greek speech of a quarter of an hour. But the restiveness of the mules which bore the royal litter seems rather to have marred her Majesty's reply[2].

Arrived in Christ Church where she was to lodge[3], she had to endure another speech from Mr. Kingsmill the Public Orator[4], which Bereblock confesses was 'somewhat long[5].' At length after hearing a solemn Te Deum in the Cathedral she was allowed to retire. The next day, Sunday, the Queen wearied with her journey and the perpetual speech making did not come abroad, but Sermons were duly preached in the morning and afternoon[6], and in the evening a Latin play was performed in the Hall of Christ Church. On Monday the Disputations which were to have been held had to be put off because the Queen was still indisposed. Leicester, however, with the Spanish ambassador and other nobles attended some of the public lectures, and did some lionising in the morning. By the evening the Queen was sufficiently recovered to attend the performance of the first part of Palæmon and Arcyte, an English play by Mr. Richard Edwards, one of the Gentlemen of her Chapel[7]. The beginning of the evening was marred by an awkward accident whereby a scholar of St. Mary Hall, named Walker, the Corpus Cook, by name John Gilbert, and a townsman named Penny, lost their lives[8]. Apart from this the play seems to have gone off with great *éclat.*

---

[1] Clark, Register, p. 21.　　　　　　　　[2] Infra, p. 177.

[3] The Students turned out to make room for the Queen and her nobles. Infra, p. 177.

[4] Printed below, pp. 212 ff.　　　　　　　[5] Infra, p. 122.

[6] Wood says that the Queen was at the afternoon sermon; but in this he seems to contradict the other authorities.

[7] On him see Wood, Ath. Ox. I. 353-6 [I. 151, 152]; Boase, p. 208. The play has been several times printed. For the influence of these academical plays on the development of the English Drama, see Ward, History of English Dramatic Literature II, 148 ff., 364 ff.

[8] This mishap is mentioned by Harrison in his 'Chronologie' under 1565.

On Tuesday afternoon the deferred disputations took place in St. Mary's. And for four hours the Queen listened with exemplary patience to discussions on points of Natural and Moral Philosophy. In the course of the former the eternal problem of necessarianism was raised by Mr. Meyrick of New College, while among the latter the question was discussed whether princes should be appointed by election or hereditary succession. It is needless to say that the conclusion was in favour of the hereditary theory, though one of the partisans of the other view, Mr. Leeche of Merton, declared with simulated passion his readiness to die for his opinion, earning thereby the ironical applause of the Queen. It is interesting to find that among the disputants in Natural Philosophy was Edmund Campian of St. John's, who fifteen years later suffered martyrdom at Tyburn[1]. The next day, Wednesday, there were more disputations; this time on questions of the Civil Law. One of the points raised was whether in the event of the currency being altered between the time at which a debt was incurred and the date fixed for its repayment, payment ought to be made according to the old or the new Standard. It is said that the nobles listened to this discussion with great attention[2]. Indeed, for some of them the question, owing to Elizabeth's reform of the currency, may have had a very practical bearing. In the evening the second part of Palæmòn and Arcyte was performed with great success. The refusal of the Goddess to grant the heroine's prayer to be allowed to lead a virgin life, and the applause of the spectators when she was finally delivered in marriage to Palæmon[3], had probably reference to the Queen herself[4].

---

[1] This speech of Campian's is printed in 'Edmundi Campiani Orationes, Epistolæ,' &c., appended to the posthumous works of Robert Turner, Campian's pupil, and Professor at Ingoldstadt. (Ingolstadii, 1602.) The title of the speech is 'Oratio Magistri Edmundi Campiani Habita Oxonii in Comitiis Magistrorum coram Regina Angliæ Elizabetha in naturali philosophia respondentis, Anno 1566.'

[2] Infra, p. 136. It is interesting to find one of the disputants recommending the codification of the English Law. Ib., p. 182.

[3] Ib., pp. 138, 139.

[4] For another allusion to the same subject, cp. ib., p. 119.

On Thursday the Disputations were on Physick and Divinity. Under the latter head the question was discussed whether it is lawful to take arms against a bad prince. It is needless to say that the decision was in the negative. The proceedings were terminated by the Queen herself making a little Latin speech to the assembled audience, which caused great delight, and

'Such confusion . . .

As, after some oration fairly spoke
By a beloved prince, there doth appear
Among the buzzing pleased multitude;
Where every something, being blent together,
Turns to a wild of nothing, save of joy,
Express'd and not express'd [1].'

In the evening there was a performance of a Latin play named Progne written by one of the Canons of Christ Church, 'but it did not take half so well as the much admired play of Palæmon and Arcyte [2].' The next day, Friday, there was in the morning a Convocation, in which degrees were conferred upon the distinguished strangers who were present, and those of them who were Members of the University of Cambridge were incorporated. After which there was a Latin sermon in Christ Church; but the Queen seems not to have been present at either of these. At dinner-time the Vice-Chancellor and Proctors distributed to the Queen and the nobles and officers of her household divers 'pairs of gloves that were very fine, and very thankfully accepted.' After dinner the Queen set out for Rycot, Mr. Tobie Matthew making her a farewell oration in Christ Church. The city authorities took leave of her at the end of Magdalen Bridge. The University authorities accompanied her as far as Shotover, where their liberties ended. Here the oratorical talents of Marbeck and Deale were again called into requisition, and the Queen graciously took leave of her loyal hosts. 'Farewell the worthy University of Oxford;' she exclaimed as she rode away, 'farewell, my good subjects here; farewell my dear Scholars; and pray God prosper your

<hr>

[1] Merchant of Venice III. ii. 179 ff.   [2] Wood.

studies; farewell, farewell [1]!' She lamented greatly that she had not been able to visit any of the separate Colleges, and (less sincerely perhaps) that she had not heard any sermons[2].

She left behind her golden memories of her gracious courtesy and kindly bearing. And if some of the praise that was addressed to her[3] sounds to us somewhat fulsome and unreal, we must make allowance on the one hand for the difference of those times, and on the other hand we must admit that much of it was well and thoroughly deserved. After the years of Protestant misrule under Edward, and of Catholic misrule during Mary's despairing effort to restore the power of

'Rome
The slowly-fading mistress of the world,'

the accession of Elizabeth came like morning after night. Mr. Gardiner has truly said that with the exception of that of Edward I. there never was so fortunate an accession in English History. And when orators and poets enlarged upon the good peace which she gave to England, they were well within their right[4]. Compared with other countries the condition of England was, as they truly said, fortunate indeed. And she herself, on the occasion of a later visit to Oxford, declared that next to the salvation of her soul, her greatest aim had ever been to preserve England from foreign attack and internal strife[5]. And she succeeded, under God, beyond what any one would have dared to hope. Her policy may not have been a heroic one; her ecclesiastical system may not have been an ideal one; but by them she gave England peace ; and then as at other times peace was England's chiefest interest[6].

[1] Wood. [2] Infra, p. 150.

[3] Flattery of Leicester was also very much the order of the day. Cf. infra, pp. 180, 208, 235.

[4] Infra, pp. 178, 209, 214, 223, 225, 269. Another subject on which stress is deservedly laid is Elizabeth's restoration of the currency. Infra, pp. 209, 268.

[5] Infra, p. 272.

[6] We find frequent mention in our authorities of verses of greeting or farewell which were hung on the colleges and other public buildings during the Queen's visit. Infra, pp. 177-178, 185, 199, 204 ; Wood, pp. 159-163, 253. Some of these verses together with some of the speeches will be found in the Appendices to this part.

More than a quarter of a century later Elizabeth again visited Oxford, Sept. 1592. Of this visit but one account is here printed. This is the account of Mr. Philip Stringer, one of the two Cambridge gentlemen who attended Lord Burleigh, their Chancellor, on this occasion[1]. It is here reprinted from the first edition of Nichols. As to the author, I borrow the following facts from the notice of him in Cooper's Athenæ Cantabrigienses[2].

Philip Stringer, of Buckinghamshire, matriculated as a pensioner of St. John's College in June 1565, was admitted

They are printed from Nichols' first edition. The text of many of them is very corrupt in places; and as, with one exception, the MS. from which they are taken is not indicated, I have been unable to restore it. Where a correction was obvious I have made it; where it seemed probable I have suggested it in a note; but several passages are still quite unintelligible to me. The literary merit of most of the pieces is but slight. Some of them are tinged by extreme puritanism (e. g. p. 222), while one exhibits a curious attempt to combine the old and new learning by throwing a copy of Elegiac verses into a series of Syllogisms (p. 223). The text of Marbeck's speech (infra, pp. 235 ff.) was kindly collated with the MS. for me by Mr. E. J. L. Scott, of the MSS. Department, British Museum.

[1] The other being Mr. Henry Mowtlowe to whom Mr. Stringer wrote the following letter with reference to this matter. Nichols, u. s., p. 30.

'To the Right Worshipful Mr. Dr. Moutloe.

Sir, I do assure myself that you did take some notes of the manner of the entertainment of hir late Majestie at hir last being in the University of Oxford, and the sum and substance also of that which was then done or shewed by them; and may conceive that you have also set it downe in some order of writing for the use of the University here, if happily it should be required of us that were sent thither. Nevertheless, for that I know not how your leisure and late health hath suffered yow so to do, I have presumed somewhat hastily to put together such notes as I then took thereof, in such meane sort as here appeareth; very instantly intreating yow to run over it, and so to alter it, as yow shall finde cause, both for the matter and manner.

2. My desire was cheefly to set it down truly, according as it was done. Which if it have your allowance (my notes being somewhat worn out of my book of tables) I shall the better satisfy myself in the rest; whose manner is not to be over curiouse in the contenting of those that be curious. And so presuming upon your love and kindness (as ever I have done) I do for the present leave yow, with my true affectionate love recommended unto yourselfe; houlding still a purpose that I have longe had to se yow myselfe as soone as well I may, mine occasions and troublesome infirmities considered. This third of May, 1603.

Yours in all duty and true affection,

PHIL. STRINGER.

I will cause it to be written out somewhat more hansomely, after yow have perused and corrected it; and will so, either deliver it to Mr. Vicechancellor, or keep it in readiness for him.'   [2] Vol. II, p. 438.

a Scholar on the Lady Margaret's foundation Nov. 8 following, proceeded B.A. 1567–8, and on April 10, 1568, was admitted a Fellow on the Lady Margaret's foundation. He commenced M.A. 1571, was one of the opponents of the new Statutes of the University in May 1572, and was admitted senior bursar of his College, Jan. 21, 1576–7. In or before 1579 he became one of the Esquire-bedels of the University. In 1592 he resigned the office of Esquire-bedel, and in the same year he and Dr. Henry Mowtlowe were despatched by their University to Oxford to witness the Queen's reception. He was solicitor to the University, and a justice of the peace for the town of Cambridge. We find him in 1603 complaining of his troublesome infirmities. In 1605 he was again sent to Oxford in order to observe the proceedings in that University during the visit of the King, Queen, and Prince. He took with him from the attorney-general a book for the King's signature for endowing the divinity professorships with the personages of Somersham and Terrington. His widow, Agnes, died about the beginning of 1619.

He is author of:—

1. The account here printed.

2. Letter to Dr. Henry Mowtlowe touching the foregoing account, May 3, 1603, given above.

3. The Preparation at Oxford, in August 1605, against the coming thither of King James, &c. In Nichols's Prog. Jam. I. i. 530–559.

The proceedings on this second visit were so similar in their general character to those on the previous occasion, that it is unnecessary to describe them at length[1]. One or two points of interest may be noted. The Queen, remembering perhaps her experiences on the previous visit, only consented to hear the speech which awaited her at Godstow Bridge ' so that it were not too long.' This may, however, have been due to consideration for the orator and his audience, because

---

[1] Besides the account given below, that in Wood, History and Antiquities, II. pp. 248 ff., may be compared. The notes to Stringer are abridged from Nichols.

of 'the foulness of the weather[1].' On another occasion also she manifested some impatience[2]. On Monday, Sept. 25, the Lords of the Council dined with the Warden and Fellows of Merton in the College Hall. After dinner a disputation was held on the theme 'An Dissentiones Civium sint Reipublicæ utiles?' The Respondent was Mr. Henry Cuffe, the Professor of Greek. A few years later he put the question to a practical test with very bad results to himself at any rate, for he was hanged at Tyburn, March 30, 1601, for complicity in the rising of the Earl of Essex, to whom he was then Secretary. At the disputation held the next day in St. Mary's one of the questions for discussion was: 'Quod Aere magis mutantur Corpora humana quam Cibo et Potu.' 'And a merry Doctor of that (the Physick) Faculty, named Richard Ratcliff[3], lately Fellow of Merton, but now Principal of St. Alban's Hall, going about to prove the negative, shewed forth a big, large body, a great fat belly, a side waist, all, as he said, so changed with meat and drink, desiring to see any there so metamorphosed by the air[4].' However, the decision went against him. It is curious to think of this coarse buffoonery being enacted in church, in the presence of a maiden queen. A novel feature was introduced into the next day's entertainment, in the shape of 'a Lecture in Musick, with the practice thereof by instrument[5],' or, as we might say, 'with illustrations.' Finally, on the day of her departure the Queen assembled the University authorities in her presence chamber, and after 'schooling' the President of Corpus, Dr. John Rainolds, 'for his obstinate preciseness,' she made an oration to them in Latin[6]. The statement of Mr. Stringer[7], that he

---

[1] Infra, p. 250. [2] Ib. 252.

[3] It would appear from this therefore that Nichols is wrong (infra, p. 258, text and note) in identifying this disputant with Dr. Edward Ratcliff of Cambridge.

[4] Wood, u.s., p. 250. [5] Infra, p. 259.

[6] Printed below, pp. 271 ff. from Tanner MS. 461. Wood, u.s., p. 252, has printed it from the Register of Merton College. From what is said below, pp. 253, 254, it is quite clear that the speech of Sir H. Savile, also printed below, pp. 263 ff., was delivered on Sept. 23, as Nichols has it, and not on Sept. 28 as the Tanner MS. states. [7] Infra, p. 261.

was not present at this speech owing to his having to attend on his own Chancellor, Burleigh, elsewhere, throws doubt on the charming story that the Queen refused to go on with her speech until she had seen the Lord Treasurer accommodated with a chair, and then took up her discourse again as if there had been no interruption. But if the incident did not take place now, it may have taken place on some other occasion. As on her previous visit the Queen departed over Magdalen Bridge to Rycot ; the University authorities as before taking leave of her at Shotover, where the Junior Proctor made her 'a long tedious oration'[1]. But we must remember that it is a Cambridge man that speaks.

The last document in the volume has also to do with this visit of Queen Elizabeth in 1592. It is a reprint of the 'Apollinis et Musarum Eidyllia,' written by John Sanford, Chaplain of Magdalen, in honour of the Queen's visit, and especially in connection with a banquet given by the President and Fellows of Magdalen to the nobles and Privy Councillors of the Queen's retinue [2]. As a literary performance it is very much superior to any of the verses which have come down to us in connection with the Queen's former visit. After a dedication to the President, in elegiacs, and an introduction in hexameters, we have a series of complimentary odes in various

---

[1] Infra p. 261, Gutch, Collect. Curiosa, i. 190, 191, has given a list of the incomes of the different colleges according to which they were taxed for this entertainment of Queen Elizabeth.

	£		£
1. Christ Church	2000	10. Exon College	200
2. Magdalen College	1200	11. Oriel College	200
3. New College	1000	12. Trinity College	200
4. All Souls	500	13. Lincoln College	130
5. Corpus Christi College	500	14. University College	100
6. Merton College	400	15. Baliol College	100
7. St. John's College	400	16. Jesus College	70
8. Brazen Nose College	300	17. Wadham Coll. } at that time	100
9. Queen's College	260	18. Pembroke Coll. } not founded	100

From the Liber Computi of Magdalen for the year 1592 it appears that Magdalen paid £18 10s. It would seem therefore that the tax was about 1½ per cent.

[2] This banquet cost the college £25 18s. 2d. besides 3s. 4d. 'pro vasis figulinis' Liber Computi, u. s. (I owe these extracts from the Liber Computi to some MS. notes of the late General Rigaud.)

lyric metres, written with considerable facility and grace,
which are placed in the mouths of Apollo and the Muses.
Then comes a description of the dinner itself, and of the company present at it. Among them all the most personable
was Henry Wriothesly, Earl of Southampton, in whom some
have seen the 'only begetter' of Shakspere's Sonetts [1].

The author, John Sanford, according to Wood [2], was born
in Somersetshire, and entered Balliol as a commoner about
1581. Afterwards he became Chaplain of Magdalen, where
he formed the acquaintance of Mr. John Digby, afterwards
Sir John Digby, and Earl of Bristol. With him he travelled
much upon the continent, and went with him as his chaplain
to Spain when he went to negotiate the Spanish marriage in
1611. After his return Archbishop Abbot made him successively his Domestic Chaplain, Prebendary of Canterbury, and
Rector of Ivychurch, Kent. He died Sept. 1629, and was
buried in Canterbury Cathedral. Besides the present work
(which is not noticed by either Wood or Bloxam [3]) he wrote a
sermon entitled 'God's Arrow of Pestilence.' Oxford, 1604,
8vo.; and also several works on French, Latin, Italian, and
Spanish Grammar. The present tract is excessively rare.
Only two copies of it are known to exist; one in the British
Museum, the other in the Library of Lord Robartes at Lan-
hydrock near Bodmin. Dr. Bulley, late President of Magdalen,
had a transcript made from the former copy. And this transcript with General Rigaud's notes upon it, was kindly placed
at my disposal by the authorities of Magdalen College. The
transcript has been carefully collated by Mr. Madan; and
it is here reprinted page for page, with all the signatures
and catchwords of the original.

The accounts here printed show Oxford in a very ideal

[1] Infra, p. 294.
[2] Ath. Ox. II., 471, 472 [I. 540, 541.]
[3] Register of Magd. Coll. vol. II. p. 129. To the works mentioned in the text
Bloxam adds: Lines 'In Funebria nob. et præst. Equitis D. Henrici Unton,
1596,' in 'Acad. Oxon funebre officium in mortem Eliz. Reg.' Oxon. 1603, 4to.

light. Fitzherbert looking back upon his college days after long years of exile, sees in Oxford—

the Paradise
Earth never look'd to human eyes
Since Adam left his garden yet.

Hutten breaks off in his discourse when he comes to speak of Oxford in his own day. The accounts of Queen Elizabeth's visits show us Oxford merely in her holiday garb. There is, however, another account of Oxford and Cambridge under Elizabeth which is worthy of comparison in the third Chapter of the Second Book of Harrison's 'Description of Britaine and England [1].' Harrison graduated both at Oxford and Cambridge [2], and he says that he 'can not readilie tell unto whether of them I owe the most good will [3].' He contrasts the collegiate discipline of English universities with the system of foreign universities, where 'the students . . . dwell in common innes, and taverns, without all order and discipline;' and like Fitzherbert he quotes Erasmus' praise of the College system [4]. He laments, however, as others have lamented since, the tendency of endowments to get into the hands of those who do not need them, and for whom they were not intended ; so that the scholarships merely act as incentives to expensive living [5]. He laments, too, the tendency of men 'after forty yeeres of age . . . [to] give over their woonted diligence, & live like drone bees on the fat of colleges.' And he quotes a saying of Bishop Fox, the founder of Corpus, 'who thought it sacrilege for a man to tarrie anie longer at Oxford than he had a desire to profit [6].' Harrison would transfer all church patronage to the Universities, whereby 'the simoniacall practises of a number of patrons should be utterlie abolished [7].' Like Fitzherbert he comments on the greater

---

[1] Originally appended to the two editions of Holinshed's Chronicle, 1577 and 1587 ; reprinted by the New Shakspere Society, 1877. It is this reprint which is cited in the following remarks.

[2] P. 82. [3] P. 76. [4] Ib.

[5] P. 77. Stubbs, Display of Corruptions, I. ii. makes exactly the same complaint.

[6] Pp. 80, 81. [7] P. 82.

laxity of discipline in the halls as compared with the colleges[1]. He notes the common tendency of Oxford and Cambridge tradesmen to fleece the undergraduates, or, as he phrases it, to 'keepe them bare by extreame sale of their wares[2];' and the longing which there was in certain quarters for a confiscation of college property; in reference to which he quotes with approval the saying of the Duke of Somerset under Edward VI. 'When the lands of colleges be gone, it shall be hard to saie, whose staffe shall stand next the doore; for then I doubt not but the state of bishops, rich farmers, merchants, and the nobilitie, shall be assailed, by such as ... thinke that what so ever another man hath is more meet for them, ... than for the proper owner that hath sweat and laboured for it.' Hitherto these efforts had been 'without successe,' and Harrison trusts that 'so it shall continue for ever[3].'

The present volume owes very much to Mr. Madan for his kindness in collating with the originals, several of the pieces here printed; for the liberality with which he placed at the disposal of the editor many rare volumes belonging to his valuable collection of works relating to Oxford; and for the general supervision which he has exercised over the progress of the work. In all matters connected with the printing of the volume the editor desires to acknowledge the benefit derived from the willing co-operation and helpful advice of Mr. R. Wheeler, Assistant to the Controller of the Clarendon Press. The Index of this, as of some other volumes issued by the Society, is the work of Mr. George Parker.

CHARLES PLUMMER.

C. C. C. Oxon.,
March 19, 1887.

---

[1] P. 87.   [2] P. 73.

[3] Pp. 88, 89. For a good modern account of Oxford under Elizabeth see ch. viii. of the Warden of Merton's 'History of the University of Oxford.' (Epochs of Church History.)

I

FIERBERTUS

NICOLAI FIERBERTI,

OXONIENSIS

IN ANGLIA ACADEMIAE

DESCRIPTIO.

Ad perillustrem & Reuerendiss. D.

D. BERNARDINVM

PAVLINVM

S. D. N. CLEMENTIS VIII.

DATARIVM.

[*Arms of Cardinal Cesi omitted.*]

ROMÆ, Apud Guglielmum Facciottum. 1602.

SVPERIORVM PERMISSV.

ANTIQVI POETÆ

DE ANGLIA

EPIGRAMMA.

Anglia terra ferax, tibi pax secura quietem,
  Multiplicem luxum merx opulenta dedit.
Tu nimio nec stricta gelu, nec sydere feruens,
  Clementi cœlo, temperieque places.
Cum pareret natura parens, varioque fauore
  Diuideret dotes omnibus vna locis :
Seposuit potiora tibi, matremque professa,
  Insula sis felix, plenaque pacis, ait;
Quidquid amat luxus, quicquid desiderat vsus,
  Ex te proueniet, aut aliunde tibi.

BERNARDINO

PAVLINO

S. D. N. DATARIO.

NICOLAVS FIERBERTVS S.

*QVAM vellem equidem (Bernardine Amplissime) vt qualem
tu in me humanitatem, in populares meos charitatem, in egenos
omnes notos & alienos, beneuolentiæ singularis significationem
libenter soles ostendere ; talem*[1] *ego in te officii debiti, obser-
uantiæ summæ, gratique animi mei testimonium possem exhibere.
Esset hoc sanè cùm tuæ beneficentiæ debitum, tùm ad animi mei
consolationem apprimè accommodatum. Veruntamen, cùm eam
tibi facultatem Dei præpotentis bonitas, Pontificis optimi benignitas, & virtus tua inprimis probata & cognita concilianit, vt multa
multis, & benè velle, & bene facere valeas: mihi verò, & proprii
casus, & communis temporis calamitas potestatem omnem benè
merendi abstulit; quid tandem est reliquum ? solent debitores
inopes, at non improbi, astrictam suam fidem, quam præsenti
nequeunt pecunia, aut versura, aut venditione, aut alia aliqua
via liberare, & ego, à fortunæ bonis egentissimus nonne hoc
solo, qui mihi superest, ingenii industriæque meæ cuiusquemodi
fructu, tibi, vt possim, satisfaciam ? Iniquus certè in te, & in
me essem, ni id facerem : quandoquidem partus iste, qualiscunque demum à me editus, ità tibi debetur, vt sine iniuria alteri*

[1] *Sic.*

offerri nec possit, nec debeat. Nam nisi sæpè & seriò de Angliæ rebus academiisque exquirendo, tu mihi animum ad hunc conatum addidisses, hercle vix vnquam in tanta mei ingenii sterilitate fœtus iste extitisset. Qui quidem, quando nunc te non solùm authorem agnoscit suum, sed etiam fautorem defensoremque poscit, & veneratur; non eum, vti spero, tua humanitas reiiciet se offerentem, quem beneuolè adeò cupidèque perquesierit non adhuc existentem: Quinimò licet paruulum valdè & humilem ita amplectetur, fouebit, tuebitur; vt nostrorum vterque, ille videlicet de tanto autore, ego verò de tali patrono immortaliter, & perpetuò gaudeamus.   Vale.

OXONIENSIS

ACADEMIAE

DESCRIPTIO.

BRITANNIA est Insula omnium, quas antiqui nouerant, *Anglia breuiter describitur.* celeberrima & maxima. patet enim in circuitu ad mille octingenta & amplius millia passuum. Oceano vndique circumfuso ab Europæ continente non longo interuallo secernitur. Formam quodammodò triquetram intuentibus obiicit: nam in oblongæ scutulæ, vt cùm tacito dicamus; vel in ocreæ fortè rectiùs, si vniuersæ Insulæ situm picturamque intueamur; quasi similitudinem exiens, in tres, licet dispares, angulos desinere videtur. Horum vnus, qui ad Galliam, & orientem vergit solem, in Cantio finem habet. Alter, respiciens occidentem, extrema Cornuualliæ regione terminatur. Tertius, ad septemtrionem spectans, vsque ad vltimos Scotiæ fines extenditur. Atque hic quidem angulus latior, & productior, quique summæ potest ocreæ non malè assimilari, superiori parte sua Regnum Scoticum; hinc ad Orientem oceanumque Germanicum flumine Tueda, illinc ad Occidentem & Hiberniam versus, Esca & Kersop fluminibus, in medio verò asperis montibus diuisum; constituit. Alii duo anguli simul cum reliqua Insula, velut in tibiam pedemque crassiorem porrecti; maior fere duplo, multòque feracior Insulæ pars, ad Angliæ Regnum pertinent. Nam Angliæ *An. 80?.* nomen ab Egbrico Anglo-saxone, postquam maiorem Insulæ partem suæ potestati subiecisset, Britannia accepit. Mare genere omni piscium abundat; quòdque vndique portuosum ac nauigationi mercaturisque faciendis aptum, ideo fit, vt

Angli re nautica maxime delectentur, & excellant. Solum ipsum multis olim in locis vineis abundabat; nunc vite, nisi vmbræ & delectationis gratia, (rarò enim neglecta maturescit) penitus caret; olea itidem & similibus, quæ sunt regionibus calidis & magis tranquillis propria. Sed cuprum, ferrum, carbonem fossilem, pomum, fruges, lanam, plumbum seu nigrum illud, seu album, quod stannum appellatur, largè ministrat. Alit præfereà armentorum, & reliqui pecoris greges copiosissimos, præter mulum, lupum, bubalum. Cœli, etsi ventis imbribusque obnoxii, nulla tamen grauitas est. Fulmina, ac terræ motus rari. Aer quàm in Gallia temperatior, remissione tum frigoris, tum caloris. Hordeo decocto pro potu gens vtitur; Birram siue Ceruisiam vocant: vino tantùm ditiores; eoque ex Germania, Gallia, Hispania, Creta copiosè importato: Lacte, caseo, carne populariter victitant. carnem enim cuiuscunque generis nec sapore gratiore, nec maiori copia vspiam ferè reperies. Habitatur Anglia frequentissimè, coliturque passim vrbibus, pagis, villis pulcherrimis; eam inprimis ob causam, quòd Principes ipsi, & genere insignes viri partim veteri consuetudine, partim vitæ tum otiosæ fuga, tum liberæ delectatione capti, domicilia sua non intra ciuitatum septa, sed sparsim in amœnissimis quibusque locis collocant: in quibus bellè ædificatis non minùs laxè & commodè, quàm magnificè habitant. Etenim hospitales ipsi, atque in cultu, victuque sumptuosi; vt humanitate, sic etiam comitatus victusque splendore inter se contendunt, quòd præcipuam in hoc suæ domus familiæque gloriam repositam arbitrentur: qua propter & famulorum, quos sustentant, satis magnus est, pro cuiusuis conditione, numerus; & singulorum domus cùm pateant semper, & omnibus, in hospicii iure notum ab ignoto, veteri instituto, non distingunt. Venationibus autem quia summoperè capiuntur, ideo non tantùm canes omnis generis venaticos quamplurimos alunt; sed etiam plura habent Angli soli & publica, & priuata septis inclusa Ceruorum, Damarum, leporumque viuaria, quàm per reliquam Europam alii omnes. Libertas autem viuendi etiamsi ea in Anglia sit, vt in publica,

& quotidiana vitæ consuetudine non multò liberius viri inter
se, quàm cum mulieribus versentur, tamen aut ea est liberæ
consuetudinis vis, aut tantus in plerisque innatus vel famæ
pudor, vel pudicitiæ amor, vt fœminæ notitiam ante nuptias
habere in turpissimis reputetur. Ipsa verò gens vniuersè est
corporis habitudine ad formam ac dignitatem satis apta &
decora; animo excelso & alacri; pectore aperto fidoque,
ingenio sanè vehementi, & in quam partem sese dat constanti
ac peracri: Atque vt mente est in Deum religiosa, in homines
fideli, natura denique libera, humana, atque (si quis rectè
& commodè tractet) etiam perfacili, ita impatiens est iniuriæ,
nesciaque vim, aut scruitutem pati. quare sic Tacitus, qui *In vita*
multis ante nos sæculis hæc ipsa animaduerterit, Britanni *Agricolæ.*
iniuncta imperii munera impigre obeunt, si iniuriæ absint,
has ægrè tolerant, iam domiti vt pareant, nondum vt seruiant.

Diuiditur omnino Anglia in quinquaginta vnum comitatus, *Comitatus*
siue Prouincias. quorum medium locum tanquam vmbilicum *habere 51.*
obtinet comitatus Oxoniensis, eiusque caput Oxonia ciuitas,
quæ percelebri illi, totique Christiano orbi notissimæ Academiæ nomen indidit: de qua nunc mihi deliberatum est
ac constitutum, pauca aliqua hoc loco vt multorum desideriis
satisfaciam, in medium adducere.

Sunt enim in Anglia præcipui nominis Academiæ duæ, *Academiæ*
Oxonia, & Cantabrigia. Has inter vt locorum non magna, *in Angliæ*
sic morum studiorumque est parua distantia. Quamuis enim *duæ.*
Cantabrigiam Oxonia superet pulchritudine ædificiorum, Collegiorum multitudine, situs locique natura cùm iucunda ad
aspectum, tum ad vitam salutari; tamen scholasticorum
numero, & exercitationibus, victus vestitusque ratione, modo
denique discendi docendique tam propè videtur ad Oxoniam
Cantabrigia accedere, vt quàm pauca obstent, quò minùs
hæc conferri inter se vsquequaque possint; tam multa faciunt,
præclara in vtraque & singularia, vt cum aliis, quæ nunc
uspiam sunt, Academiis comparatæ, vel superiores omnibus,
vel nulli certe inferiores reperiantur. Quid enim? Originem
quæris? antiquissimæ sunt. Famam & splendorem nominis?

nobilissimæ sunt. disciplinam? præstantissima est. Fructus?
tanti tamque vberes sunt, semperque fuerunt; vt ausim dicere,
nec plures, nec magis memorabiles viros ex vlla alia Academia aliquando prodiisse. Ac ne quis fortè hoc à me temerè
& inconsultius dictum existimet, Oxoniensis Academiæ formam, ac studiorum modum primùm ponam ob oculos: deindè
præcipuos quosdam eius magistratus summatim comprehen-
dam: tertio loco ex innumerabilibus penè, qui ingenii, doctrinæ, zelique laude in ea floruerunt, paucos aliquot; sed
notissimos, in medio sistam: vt illi, qui hæc perangustè licet,
propalam tamen collocata intuebuntur; ipsi planè videant atque
cognoscant, orationem meam veritati, quam vanitati esse con-
iunctiorem. Verùm hæc pauca prius referre de harum Acad e-
miarum origine & antiquitate, non erit fortè omnibus ingratum.

*Beda lib.
pr. c. 2.
Lilius in
Chron.
Camdenus
in descrip.
Angliæ.*
     Sunt qui tradiderunt ortum nascentis Academiæ Oxoniensis
ad proximum post euictam Troiam seculum, & ad Mempricium
nescio quem regem, & authorem posse referri: Cantabrigiam
autem à Cantabro rege fuisse fundatam; qui annis ante Christum natum ccclxxv. ex Hispania expulsus, & humanissimè in
Britannia acceptus, illam, in clarum ac perpetuum grati animi,
nominisque sui monumentum, conuocatis ex Græcia literarum
professoribus, Musis ipsis consecrauit. Quæ quidem sententia
etsi vix credibilis quibusdam videatur, nostri tamen non est
eam aut refellere, aut confirmare. Atque vtcumque ea
quidem se habeat; hoc sanè, quod adiungunt, est valdè
probabile; insequentes ætates afflictas illas, & grauissimis &
continentibus Romanorum, Danorum, saxonumque bellis per-
turbatissimas, ita rem omnem literariam; pacis tantùm ociique
comitem; in Britannia euertisse, vt ex Academiis etiam istis
vel omnino, vel maxima ex parte eandem deturbauerit[1]. Ac
licet illa quidem denuò, in Cantabrigia verò sub Sigesberto
anno Domini 630, in Oxonia posteà sub Alfredo anno 886
Regibus, nonnihil recreata, & diuersis constructis collegiis
Ante quin- fuerit restituta: neutra tamen harum Academiarum ante
gentos an-
nos.   imperii Normannici tempora splendorem suum recuperare,

---

[1] ? *deturbauerint.* H.

& vera, tuta, tranquillaque pace frui potuit. Ab eo autem
tempore in iis tantoperè reuiuiscere literarum studia cæpe-
runt; tantusque ex omni parte ad eas semper, tanquam ad
virtutis & doctrinæ celeberima emporia, concursus factus est,
vt tempore Edouardi Primi (quod literis consignatum reliquit *An.* 1273.
Armachanus) triginta millia studiosorum Oxoniæ cense-
rentur. Qua propter vt explorati quid & certi de istarum
Academiarum origine statuere, valdè est difficile; ita omni
caret dubitatione, & ortu eas esse longè .antiquissimas, &
gloria florentissimas etiam extitisse. Etenim grauissimo *De bello*
Cæsaris testimonio testatum habemus, multò ante sua tem- *Gallico.*
pora præclaram Druidum disciplinam in Britannia repertam,
in Gallias fuisse translatam. Habemus etiam communi historicorum voce confirmatum, Carolum Magnum, quo tempore *An.* 790.
Academias Parisicnsem, Papiensemque constituerit, Anglis
præcipuè autoribus, doctoribusque fuisse vsum. Præterea
extare dicitur Honorii Primi Pontificis rescriptum, datum
Romæ anno 624 quo se literis operam Cantabrigiæ dedisse
fateatur, ægreque ferre, quod tunc à Paganis vexaretur: hocque
Honorii rescriptum Sergium Primum, & Eugenium Quartum
iterum comprobasse. Denique habet Alexander Necham, in
lib. 2. de Natura rerum, hæc verba, Iuxta vaticinium Merlini *Merlinus*
viguit ad vada boum, (idest, Oxoniam) sapientia suo tempore *vixit an.*
ad Hiberniæ partes transitura. Pro coronide ergò sint illa, *Domini*
460.
quæ in libro Procuratorum Oxoniensis historiæ initio habentur;
Contestantibus plerisque chronicis, multa loca per orbis climata
variis temporibus variarum scientiarum studiis floruisse leguntur: omnibus tamen inter latinos extantibus studiis Vniuersitas Oxoniensis fundatione prior, quadam scientiarum plura-
litate generalior, in veritatis catholicæ professione firmior,
& priuilegiorum multiplicitate præstantior inuenitur.

Vrbs autem Oxonia, Anglorum historicorum testimonio
Callena, ac Bellisita, ob situs amœnitatem antiquitùs deno-
minata, in meditullio ferè Angliæ, quadragesimo septimo
à Londino lapide, introrsùs posita est; eo solo, cæloque, vt,
si accessionis vndique facilitatem spectes, commodissimam;

si naturam amœnissimam; si aeris bonitatem saluberimam
dicas. Nam in æquabili & plano explicata loco, nisi quod
ab vna parte leuiter parùmque descendat, siluosis collibus hinc
inde cingitur, neque his longo interuallo disiunctis. Radices
enim horum extremas atque ipsam vrbem interfluunt fluuii
duo, Cheruellus ab ortu, ab occasu Isis. atque hic quidem,
postquam aquarum suarum diuortiis plures, easque amœnas
insulas effecerit cum Cheruello statim sub ipsa vrbe, quà
meridiem spectat, in vnum confluit: sicque consociatis aquis
non multa emetitur milliaria, ante quàm Tamam flumen
obuiam habens, cum eaque nomen perindè atque aquas com-
municans, Tamisim efficiat amnem; vix alteri Europæ flumini
secundum. Reliquis verò vrbis partibus, ex parte orientem,
sed maximè aquilonem spectantibus, planicies campestres
obiiciuntur, ea iucunditate vbertateque, vt abundè & facilè
omnia subministrent, quæ vel ad exercitationem corporis,
vsumque necessarium, vel ad honestam animorum voluptatem,
relaxationemque pertineant. Nam & aèr salubris, & solum
fertile, & piscosi fluuii, & colles siluis saltubusque septi,
denique planities pratis, aruis, pascuisque exculta, totam hanc
regionem ita exornant, bonisque omnibus cumulant; vt non
tantùm frugibus, carne, piscibusque, abundet; sed etiam cæte-
rorum omnium animantium, quæ ad cibum apta, aucupio ac
venatione capi solent, copiam suppeditet, & abundantiam.

Priuilegia. Habet Oxonia suas immunitates, & priuilegia antiqua &
amplissima à multorum Angliæ Regum indulgentia profecta,
& summorum Pontificum autoritate corroborata. Habet
Scholæ. scholas publicas multas ac varias, loco quidem commodissimo,
& à reliquis ædificiis muro, & lata via vnica distinctas ac
Gymna- seclusas. Habet augustissimum theologiæ destinatum gym-
sium
theologi- nasium, à bono illo Humfredo Glocestriæ Duce constructum
cum. ea magnificentia elegantiaque, vt opus verè regium, tantaque
Academia dignissimum meritò censeatur. Etenim ædificium
est peramplum, è saxo quadrato totum, diligenti Symmetria
magnoque artificio elaboratum intra & extrinsecùs, in altitudinem insignem, sed planam, exiens: circùm, circà turribus,

pinnis, varioque passim erecto lapideo opere pyramidato instructum & ornatum. Inferior eius pars theologicis prælectionibus, publicisque exercitationibus literariis assignatur: locus verò superior bibliothecæ publicæ erat constitutus, multique in ea conditi præclari, nec vulgares libri: quos in vnoquoque literarum, linguarumque genere ex Italia, aliisque locis perquisitos, Dux ille optimus magnis impensis coacceruauerat. pulcherrimum certè non solùm fundatoris gloriæ monumentum, sed æternum Academiæ ornamentum futurum; nisi hæreticorum quorundam mirifica improbitas ad extremum illius bibliothecæ exitium cum intolerabili iniuria exarsisset. Nam cùm impietatis illi, atque in scripturis deprauandis falsitatis suæ probè sibi conscii, nihil metuebant ac detestabantur magis, quàm publicas eiusmodi bibliothecas, in quibus *Hæretici vt* veterum omnium Patrum antiquissima illa & incorrupta volu- *veritatis, sic anti-* mina fideliter ac religiosè conseruantur, vtpote quæ ab homi- *quitatis inimici.* nibus consuli peruolutarique nequeant, quin mendaciorum suorum fraudes, & nouæ doctrinæ portenta grauissimis certissimisque testimoniis manifesto conuincant: non priùs sanè in Angliam, hancque Academiam inuaserunt, quàm sui furoris atque insaniæ impetum in nobilem istam bibliothecam intulerunt, &, nonnullis eius libris surreptis & compilatis, reliquos omnes vno incendio, & quasi communi elatos funere concremarunt.

Percensentur Oxoniæ Collegia sexdecim structuræ specie *Collegia 16.* magnifica, soliditate æterna. Nam qui primi eorum iecerunt fundamenta, non in eo solùm laborarunt, vt muros lapideos, quos vetustas conficit, suis collegiis excitarent, sed maiori studio præcauerunt, vt quibus locum esse in iis voluerunt, his necessaria omnia ad victum, cultum, studiorumque rationem essent parata. sic enim habebant persuasum, quando hæc omnia suppeterent, nunquam defuturos, qui suorum collegiorum dignitatem tuerentur, & disciplinam institutaque seruarent. Collegiorum nomina hæc sunt.

Primum autem (vt ab eorum, quæ extant, antiquissimo inchoemus) est illud quod appellant Vniuersitatis; ab Alfredo *Collegium* Rege, (quem literas Oxonia exulantes, longo interuallo in *Vniuersitatis.*

patriam reduxisse diximus) institutum, & à Gulielmo Du-
nelmensi Archiacono perfectum an. Christi nati. 893.

Baliolense.   Deinde Baliolense; cuius author Ioannes Baliolus Rex
Scotiæ an. 1273.

Merton-
ense.   Mertonense, à Mertone Episcopo Roffensi extructum. an.
1276.

Exoniense.   Exoniense, quod, à Stapledono, Episcopo Exoniensi, sub
anno Christi 1322 musis destinatum, posteà auxit Gulielmus
Piter Eques, Consiliique Regii Secretarius, beneficia ab eodem
à prima accepta adolescentia grata memoria prosequens.

Oriolense.   Oriolense, quod Adamum Brunum, Edouardo Regi 2. ab
eleemosynis ædificatorem, anno 1323. & Alanum Cardinalem
alumnum habuit.

Reginæ.   Collegium Reginæ, Philippa Regina vxor Edouardi Tertii
exædificauit, dotauitque. anno 1340.

Nouum.   Vuichamus Episcopus Vuintoniensis Collegium Nouum
quod dicitur, monumentum insigne ad sui nominis memoriam
sempiternam condidit. anno 1375.

Lincoln-
iense.   Lincolniense, per Richardum Flemming Episcopum Lincolniensem à fundamentis excitatum est an. 1430.

Animarum
omnium.   Chicheleius, Archiepiscopus Cantuariensis, Omnium Animarum memoriæ Collegium fundauit, consecrauitque an. 1437.

S. Mariæ
Magdal.   Sanctæ Mariæ Magdalenæ Collegium, opere magnificum,
& ad vitæ studiorumque commoditatem aptissimum, Guliel-
mum Vuainfletum Vuintoniensem Episcopum patronum veneratur. anno 1459.

Aenei
Nasi.   Gulielmus Smith, Lincolniensis Episcopus, Collegium vnum,
quod Aenei Nasi: Richardus etiam Foxius, Episcopus Vuin-
Corporis
Christi. toniensis, alterum, quod Corporis Christi nomine insigniuit,
fundarunt, optimaque disciplina institutisque formarunt. Illud
quidem, an. 1515. hoc verò, an. 1516.

Aedes
Christi.   Vuolseus Cardinalis Aedem Christi, amplissimum sanè
omniumque augustissimum Collegium, inchoauit an. 1539.
quod postea Henricus Rex Octauus magnis redditibus auxit,
locupletauitque anno 1547.

    Thomas Popus, & Thomas Vuitus Equestris ordinis viri,

ille Dunelmense, hic D. Bernardi olim Collegia, at ætatis
ac temporis vitio deformata ruinisque oppressa, nostra memoria
ædificiis instaurarunt, prouentibusque amplificarunt: atque vt
illud Sanctissimæ Trinitatis, sic hoc Beati Ioannis Baptistæ *S. Trinita-*
nominibus distinxerunt, illustraruntque an. 1556. *tis.*
    Illud omnium nouissimum Collegium est, cui Hugo Pricius *S. Ioann.*
Baptiste.
I. V. Doctor, dum senex admodum an. Christi 1572 : prima *Jesus.*
illius iecit fundamenta, Iesus saluatoris nomen, vt bonis sanè
auspiciis, sic casu quodam non infaceto imposuit. Nam vt
primum murorum frontem ad ipsius portæ altitudinem exci-
tasset, curauit lapide, qui portæ imminebat, hos versus incidi,

> *Struxit Hugo Pricius tibi clara Palatia Iesu,*
> *Vt doctor legum pectora docta daret.*

Quos cùm vir quidam non illepidi ingenii transiens forte
perlegisset, atque Pricii illius exactam iam ætatem, simul &
operis, vix dum inchoati, magnitudinem animo expendisset,
aliud statim tale distichon illi disticho opposuit ; quo præ-
properam senis in titulo præfigendo festinationem festiuè satis
redarguebat.

> *Nondum struxit Hugo, vix fundamenta locauit :*
> *Det Deus vt possis dicere, struxit Hugo.*

Vnumquodque igitur horum Collegiorum bibliothecis instructum, vectigalibusque munitum certum studentium numerum
alit honorificè ; eumque adeo copiosum, vt tria aut ampliùs
millia conficiant.

    Hos in tres ordines schola illa distinguit, magistros, Bacca- *Ordines*
laureos, Discipulos. Ordines istos confundi inter se piaculi *tres studen-*
tium.
instar habetur. Vnde fit, vt neque magistri temerè Bacca-
laureis admisceantur, neque Baccalaurei ad Discipulos se
dimittant ; multò minùs Discipuli omnium infimi audeant se
superioribus adæquare. His autem solis ne collegio quidem
exire, nisi adscito socio, permittitur. Atque hinc nascitur
cùm horum ordinum inter se harmonia quædam non iniu-
cunda, tum omnium erga Præfectos reuerentia summa. verùm
non tantùm gradus, sed etiam vestitus hos secernit. Nam vt
omnes pileo quadrato vtuntur, & illa, pacis otiique veste, toga

laxiori aut plana, aut crispulis in sinum contracta; sic togas illas distinctæ personarum conditiones peculiari distingunt nota, qua non solùm in scholis, & disputationibus, quæ proprium sibi vestium genus pro gradus cuiusque ratione postulant, sed alibi extra ostium limenque collegii internoscantur. Quin etiam horum collegiorum leges & instituta qui rectè nouerit, ac non modò ordinem in his disciplinamque, sed etiam studentium modestiam, taciturnitatem, obedientiam, summamque ad omnia præclara studia animorum contentionem alacritatemque diligentiùs perpenderit; ita horum omnium rationem *Erasm.* probabit, vt non poterit non laudare illius viri doctissimi sententiam, qui, tota eorum ratione perspecta & cognita, adeò motus est admiratione & amore, vt præclarum hoc iudicii sui testimonium literis consignatum reliquerit; Oxoniensis Academiæ collegia propiùs ad religiosorum monachorumque optimè ordinata cœnobia, quàm ad iuuenum & adolescentulorum in vnas ædes congregatorum conuentus accedere.

Aulæ octo. Sexdecim collegiis istis adduntur & alia octo, Aulas communiter nominant, diuitum nobiliumque plerumque filiis, qui propriis viuunt sumptibus, assignata: quamuis & reliqua etiam collegia ipsa, extra eos, quos nutriunt, alumnos, recipere possunt & solent magno numero adolescentes nobiles, & qui volunt insumere quod in proprios sumptus est opus; sed ea lege, vt suorum alumnorum præsidio periculoque viuant. Et sunt istæ, Aula Alba, Ceruina, Alborensis, Brodgates, Item Sanctorum Mariæ, (cui præerat olim Card. Alanus) Edmundi, Magdalenæ, denique Glocestrensis, quæ quondam fuerat Monachorum sancti Benedicti Collegium. Aulæ autem hæ singulæ à singulis ferè collegiis pendent, & ad earum exemplum se planè comparant: in eo solùm dissimiles, quòd hæ, quàm illa, legibus disciplinæ laxioribus paulò liberioribusque teneantur. Istud verò commune omnibus, quòd, quà intermissa ædificia, præalto muro cincta, portas suas vna eademque hora claudant semper & aperiant; Nam hyeme vesperi hora à meridie octaua, æstate nona, signo antè maximæ campanæ (vt ab omnibus longè latèque audiri possit) pulsu edito, occluduntur; nec ante horam post mediam noctem quintam reserantur. hoc interiecto interuallo, si quis scholasticorum extra sui collegii limen a Procuratore deprehendatur, vix vllam excusationem adeò legitimam poterit afferre, quæ eum ex carcere eximat, & Procuratoris manibus liberet.

Ad Academiam non accedunt, nisi qui in gymnasiis, scholisque publicis per omnes Angliæ prouincias, immò oppida fermè, disseminatis (inter quas habentur insigniores Vuintoniensis, Etonensis, Dunelmensis, Londinensis) grammaticæ, poeticæ, latinæque linguæ præcepta imbiberint. Admissi verò & in Discipulorum classem adscripti hoc modo exerceri *Exercita-*
tiones di-
solent. Consurgitur generatim in Collegiis omnibus primo *scipu-*
diluculo, idest, hora à media nocte quinta. mox congregati *lorum.*
in æde sacra statum tempus precationi dant, primam potissimamque diei partem Deo consecrantes: deinde reliquos diei labores in rem literariam seriò insumunt. Nam præter Regios & publicos omnis scientiæ, Græcæ etiam, & Hebraicæ linguæ professores, vnumquodque collegium suos habet priuatos Doctores; qui Aristotelis methodum vestigiaque persequentes, partim Logicam, cæterasque Philosophiæ partes exactè interpretantur, partim eloquentiæ rectèque dicendi præceptis tradendis, oratoriam loquendi vim & ornamenta adhibent, & absoluunt. Copulant namque cum scientia eloquentiam, vt quemadmodum eloquentiæ floribus scientiæ fructus præponderant; sic indiserta rationis barbaries orationis elegantia perpoliatur. Fuit enim illud prudens maiorum institutum, vt quas artes natura, ratio, vsusque communis coniunxerant, eas ipsi tractatione non disiungerent, sed in vtraque pariter iuuentutem exercerent: vt hoc modo, cùm via illis semper adesset, qua docte, prudenter, acutè cogitarent; tum ratio illis nunquam deesset, (quandocumque suum animum ad dicendum scribendumue applicuissent) qua excogitata sapienter proferre, ornatèque & copiosè eloqui possent.

Hoc modo biennium continuum intra priuatos collegiorum parietes exercitati adolescentes, tum primùm exeunt in arenam & puluerem, postquam in Academiæ spatiis suarum virium facto semel periculo ad publica certamina admittuntur, & Generalium Sophistarum nomine censentur.

Deindè verò cùm huic biennio aliud quoque biennium accesserit; iidemque perpetuò eisdem dicendi disputandique exercitationibus domi forisque, cum suis & alienis assuefacti, omnibus non vulgare specimen ingenii doctrinæque suæ dederint; Baccalaurei artium (consensu de more primùm à Magistris sui collegii, deinde à reliquis aliorum priuatim & suppliciter, præeunte Bidello, petito & obtento, Gratiam schola illa vocat) communi & honorifico omnium, ad id vnum in locum congregatorum, testimonio renunciantur.

Horum est, statis vicibus per sequentis quadragesimæ cursum quæstiones Logicas ac Philosophicas ponere, easque in scholis publicis contra quoscumque oppugnatores, nullo auxiliante, à superiori loco defendere. terribile hoc quidem theatrum est respondenti. Stat enim vnus contra vniuersos, nouus contra veteranos, discipulus contra magistros: qui tamen, nisi ita se gerat, vt fama sua non hæreat ad metas, non sibi modò, sed & collegio, vnde est, turpem inurit notam. cuius rei tanta solet haberi ratio, vt in quibusdam collegiis statuto firmatum reperiatur, eum, qui respondendo publicè collegii sui auctoritatem nomenque minuerit, confestim collegio esse expellendum. quod est summi inter eos supplicii genus.

Triennium in Baccalaureatu qui steterit laudabiliter, ac consueta certamina per interposita interualla obierit feliciter (incumbit enim illi priuatim sæpiùs declamare, ac moderante Magistro, theses ex vniuersa Philosophia desumptas bis singulis hebdomadis vel tueri, vel impugnare: publicè verò volumen aliquod Aristotelis. breuiter & cursim explanare: In Quodlibet, sic dicunt, disputationibus semel & iterum sui periculum facere: tandem in circulis Augustinianis, quos nominant, aliquot horarum disputationes pomeridianas ad D. Mariæ iterùm & tertiò habere) in huius exitu, solemni Actu, quo nihil habet terrarum orbis in eo genere aut ritu solemnius, aut ad speciem pulchrius, Magistri artium Laurea, doctrinæque insignibus decoratur.

In Comitiis enim (sic ad imitationem Romanam vocant) *Comitia.*
Magistri, & Doctores anniuersario ritu, ipsis Idibus Iulii,
fabricato ad hoc in D. Mariæ theatro magnifico & maximo,
creari solent. Huius spectaculi celebritas tanta est, vt ad id
quotannis visendum ex omnibus regni partibus eò confluant
summi, medii, infimi extra numerum. Per biduum autem
celebratur, habenturque in eo orationes plurimæ ornatu ora-
torio, & omni orationis flore expolitæ : concertationes variæ
multiplici eruditione scientiaque refertæ : quidquid est enim in
Philosophis, Medicis, Iurisconsultis, Theologis neruorum &
eloquentiæ, hic totum effertur atque expanditur. adeo vt ritè
suoque momento ponderans, tum actionis huiusce dignitatem,
tum conuentus frequentiam ; prætereà varietatem exercita-
tionum, subtilitatem doctrinæ, linguæque elegantiam: postremò
eorum, in quos laureola confertur meritum ac numerum, non
inuitè fortè fatebitur, verè tantam esse huiusce Actionis dignitatem, vt vix quidquam in hoc genere splendidius esse
possit, aut magnificentius. Emittit autem quotannis in lucem
hæc alma studiorum mater plus minus centum septuaginta
artium Baccalaureos, Magistros centum, Doctores theologiæ
quindecim, parem itidem Iurisprudentiæ, ac Medicinæ numerum. viros plerosque omnes non eo tantùm honore dignos, quo
augentur ; sed ad quos difficilima quæque in rep. munera
tutò deferantur. Sic enim hæc Academia suos cudit & effingit ;
sic eorum ingenia acuit & excitat ; sic, quod in animo latitat
neruorum ac roboris, elicit & perficit ; vt, qui non est plum-
beus, aut planè stipes, hunc non minùs vmbræ & scholæ
aptum, quàm soli & foro habilem dignumque præstet, probetque.
Neque hoc Angliæ Regibus obscurum vnquam fuit, qui ex
his semper eligere, pro sua prudentia, consueuere, non solùm
Pastores, quos Ecclesiis præficerent ; Legatosque, quos ad
exteros Principes de rebus maximis mitterent sed etiam
Consiliarios, quos asciscerent sibi, & Magistratus quos ad reip.
admouerent gubernacula.

Attigimus Academiæ situm, antiquitatem, collegia, studia :
nunc præcipuos eiusdem magistratus percurramus.

Magis-
tratus
Oxoniensis.
Procancel-
larius.

Magistratus publici, quique totius gubernationis pondus sustinent, multi sunt ac varii. Horum primus & summus est Procancellarius; Oxonienses nomen Commissarii ei indiderunt. Nam Cancellarius ipse vel ex Regio Senatu, qui autoritate apud omnes, vel ex præcipua nobilitate, qui gratia valet apud Principem, solet assumi; vt eo nomine honorem, priuilegia, maiestatem Academiæ tueri facilius ac protegere valeat. Procancellarius igitur præsens semper ex his doctoribus elegitur, qui collegiis præsunt; atque omnium colitur obseruantia singulari. Is enim ciuitati legem dicit, habetque potestatem animaduertendi in omnes non solum scholasticos, sed etiam ciues; quorum Prætor, qui anglicè Maior dicitur, quotannis ipso suæ creationis die (non enim vltra annum magistratus cius durat) ad cum accedens, fidem suam Academiæ, veteri instituto, astringit iureiurando; seseque ac suos in Procancellarii potestate futuros spondet. Visitat ergo Procancellarius (quoties ratio reip. id exigit) die noctuque non modò studiosorum cubicula, sed ciuium domos; & pari iure in cunctos delinquentes animaduertit. Congregationes, Conuocationesque cogit, in iisque præsidet. denique in summi honoris imperiique insigne sex Bidellos habet constitutos, qui eius, mandata exequantur; ipsumque in publicum producntem aperto capite antecedant, suasque clauas, fascesue præferant.

Procura-
tores.

Huic proximè accedunt Procuratores Academiæ duo: qui ex eorum numero, qui Magistrorum gradum adepti sunt, ad hoc munus assumpti, parem omninò locum, & indiuiduam obtinent potestatem. Hi Academicos in officio, oppidanos in obsequio continent. die præuident, ne quid contra ius fasque fiat: nocte obeunt plateas, & cincti milite petulantiam tenent intra ædes, & lineam. Errones & pellices lustris extrahunt, suppliciis vexant, ex vrbe emittunt. Ad hos spectat accedentes ad Academiam Principes viros, quosque nobilitas digni-

Commen-
dat.

tasque commendat, tecto conuiuioque accipere publico sumptu ac nomine: etiam in Principis aula Academiæ negotia tractare. vndè senatoribus, cæterisque dignitate præstantibus viris noti illi semper & gratiosi, nisi nullius cerebri sint, certissimum iaciunt futuri honoris sui fundamentum.

Sequitur flos populi delibatus, Academiæ Orator. Eius est, *Orator.* ordine suorum coronæ similitudine quasi circumuallati, aduentus legatorum, Illustriumque personarum publica oratione gratulari: literarum, quæ totius Academiæ nomine dari, recipique solent, curam habere præcipuam.

Adduntur his scholarum Magistri, qui disputationibus pub- *Magistri* licis in scholis moderantur, rixisque modum adhibent; denique *scholarum.* ne quid aut fiat turbulenter, aut dicatur procacius, curant diligenter.

Hos consequuntur alii duo, quibus Clericis fori nomina *Clerici fori.* imposuerunt; alter à Procancellario, alter à Procuratoribus huic muneri præpositus. Istorum oculus viris fæminisque nundinariis formidabilis est. rerum enim omnium, quæ pondere ac mensura veneunt, rationem poscunt; videntque ne quid Academia, in his præsertim, quæ ad victum pertinent, siue in officinis, siue in foro, capiat detrimenti. horum officium, quemadmodum & Procuratorum anno terminatur; aliorum verò, vt perpetua officia non sunt, ita neque certo termino circumscribuntur.

Restant, (vt fastidio parcens taceam reliquos) Bidelli, siue *Bidelli siue* Lictores sex, quorum tres aureas, alii tres argenteas ferunt *Clauarii* clauas. Omnes quidem ratione officii in Nobilium ordinem *sex.* singulari Regum Angliæ beneficio ascripti, illi tamen his dignitate priores. Horum munus est Baccalaureos, Magistrosque creandos educere, creatos reducere: quoties cogenda vniuersitas voce per Collegia antè pronunciare: denique vt exeuntem Procancellarium omnes; sic doctores singulos ecclesiam, scholasue adeuntes, singulos anteire.

Curiæ duæ sunt. minor, quæ Congregatio dicitur. In eam *Curiæ* mane omnes Iuniores, idest, illius anni Magistri, campanæ *duæ.* pulsu congregantur. hi namque, eò quòd Regendi onus illo *Congrega-* anno sibi præcipuè incumbit, Magistrorum Regentium nomen *tio.* inuenerunt. In ista Congregatione, præter leuiora quædam negotia, de purgandis vrbis plateis & similia (de quibus neglectis mulctam suo arbitrio Regentes indicunt) de conferendis honoribus præmiisque scholasticis potissimè tractatur. neque enim hæc leuiter, & in quoscunque petentes coniiciuntur. nam etiamsi quis omnibus à consuetudine scholæ requisitis exercitationibus fuerit perfunctus, legitimumque suorum studiorum tempus adimpleuerit, nisi tamen nonnullorum Magistrorum suffragationes habeat; quorum alii se scire, alii se credere religiosè affirment, eum esse dignum, in quem laureola scholæ meritò conferatur, sciat se frustrà petendo contendere, & operam famamque simul profundere.

Conuocatio.   Altera Curia est Maior, eique nomen Conuocatio. Etenim in hanc conueniunt Academiæ Doctores, & Magistri omnes, moniti campanæ sono, sed prænunciantibus Bidellis; qui in collegiorum atriis Conuocationem denunciant, his ipsis verbis ter repetitis, Ad Conuocationem omnes Doctores, Magistri Regentes, & non Regentes post pulsationem paruæ campanæ, hora &c. per fidem, per fidem. In hoc conuentu Procuratores in annos singulos solemnissima cærimonia, multisque ambagibus eliguntur: officia, dona, sacerdotia dispensantur: legationes, literæ audiuntur: postremò omnia maioris momenti negotia, Procancellario præsente ac præsidente, transiguntur.

Fœtus Oxoniensis.   Superest intueamur, si quos viros Anglicæ Academiæ mundo produxerint, hi tales tantique fuerint, vt nostram, quam initio posuimus, assertionem tueantur. certius quippe nullum est agri optimi argumentum, quàm frugum ex eo nascentium vbertas & præstantia. Ex hac igitur schola, postquam Christum colere & profiteri cæperat (vt, veteribus prætermissis sæculis, propiora tantùm nobis attingamus) clarissima & infinita christianæ philosophiæ lumina longa, eaque continuata serie prodierunt. quæ omnia in hunc locum congerere vt immensi laboris, multique tædii esset; sic paucula ex eis delibare, tum non inutilis, tum mihi, ad dicto fidem faciendam, necessarii penè laboris esse videtur. Itaque cùm Augustinus Monachus Romæ instructus, Roma missus, Euangelium Christi in inculto & derelicto Angliæ solo, idolorum vestigiis

Augustinus Monachus Anglorum Apostolus.

iterum conculcatis, ante mille annos inscuisset ; crebri adeò & abundantes in eo statim sunt nati præclarissimorum ingeniorum fructus; vt quàm altas radices Christi semen in eo sparsum egisset, repentè testatum orbi terrarum apparuerit. Vix enim ab Augustini in Angliam appulsu exierant quinquaginta anni ; cùm plurimi Angli fide, zelo, doctrina pleni, haud satis sibi putarint esse, Christum profiteri, nisi eundem etiam alios verbo, scripto, facto docerent. Dum igitur alii se domi ad docendum, scribendumque conferunt, alii ad Germanos, Gothos, Sueuos, Danos ea causa se transferunt, vt Christi nomen in illas gentes inferentes, vel eas, felici consilio, ad Christum amplectendum propellerent ; vel ab eis ipsimet insigni martyrio pro Christo afficerentur.

Angli fuerunt Bertuinus & Vuillebrordus; quorum ille Belgis ; hic cum duodecim sociis, Christi vestigiis insistens, Christi fidem Gallis annunciauit. *Prædicatores an. Christi* 690.

Anglus fuit Bonifacius, Moguntinus apud Germanos Archiepiscopus, qui post præclaram in predicatione Euangelii nauatam operam, & centum Germanorum millia ad fidem conuersa; vt planè testatur Gregorius Papa iii. in epist. quæ incipit, Doctor gentium ; à Frisonibus, dum in eorum salutem conuersionemque incumberet, cum sociis quinquaginta tribus interemptus est. 720.

Vuillebaldus & Burchardus Angli, Regiæque stirpis iuuenes fuere. Iste Herbipolensi, ille Eystensi in Germania Ecclesiis, post multos fidei causa exantlatos labores, à Bonifacio præpositi ; multa egregia virtutum, doctrinæ, piorumque sudorum exempla populis suis reliquerunt. 753.

Anglus sanctus Herbertus, qui Scotos à schysmate reuocauit.

Anglus Sygfredus Eboracensis Archiepiscopus, qui amplissima illa sede, soloque patrio relictis, vt Gothis, Succis, Danis Christianæ fidei sacramenta ministraret, eorum Apostolus vocari meruerit.

Ili cum multis aliis in fide propaganda laborarunt: Alii

non minorem operam in eiusdem fidei mysteriis enunciandis illustrandisque posuerunt.

Doctores. Nicolaus de Lyra totum corpus biblicum, vetus nouumque testamentum, commentariis dilucidauit.

Adamanni & Benedicti Abbatum leguntur praeter alia, illius de locis sanctis; huius de regularum concordia tractationes non contemnendae.

Beda venerabilis obiit an. 735. Ceolphedus, vel ea re clarus inprimis est, quòd suae disciplinae alumnum Bedam illum reliquerit; cuius doctrinae sanctitatisque praestantiam tantopere veneratus est christianus orbis, vt vni illi, dum adhuc viueret, venerabilis agnomen omnium consensus detulerit.

Platin. in vita Ioan. vi. Fratres habuit Beda strabonem & Haymonem viros doctissimos, quorum alter plurimas homilias eleganti sermone composuit; alter Genesim pulchrè commentatus est.

Alcuinus Bedae discipulus, Caroli Magni praeceptor fuit, tantaeque apud eundem authoritatis, vt, eo aliisque quibusdam Anglis impulsoribus, Academias, Parisiensem, Papiensemque instituerit. Hic bonarum omnium, ac praecipuè diuinarum artium, antistes multa post se opera praeclarè conscripta reliquit.

an. 1200. Stefanus Anglicus, gymnasii Parisiensis quondam Rector ac decus, perfectus fuit Philosophus, atque in Theologia ita versatus; vt, eo primùm docente & viam praemonstrante, sacrarum literarum sententia ab recondito illo & mystico sensu ad popularem rationem, moresque hominum confirmandos translata sit.

Haymo insignis theologus, Alexandri Quarti iussu Romanum breuiarium correxit, & in formam meliorem reduxit.

1240. Alexander Halensis, S. Bonauenturae magister, scholastico more primus theologiam tradidit: eam docendi viam aperiens, quam, à Scoto & D. Thoma postea tritam, doctissimi quique in scholis sunt amplexati. vir tanta innocentia & eruditione, vt à suae aetatis hominibus vitae fons, & Doctor irrefragabilis appellari meruerit.

1235. Robertus Episcopus Lincolniensis, vir latinae graecaeque

linguæ peritissimus, theologorum philosophorumque sui temporis antesignanus, foris spectabilis, domi præstantior, in
Pontificio munere obeundo industrius, & experientissimus.

Ricchardus de Media Villa diuinis humanisque literis ap- *1290.*
primè excultus; Pontificii iuris scientissimus; in paucis numerandus.

Gualterus Desseus, à Bonifacio Papa sæpè legatus, &
Ioannes Iacephalus, Concionatores celebres, summique theologi
sunt habiti.

Celebre nomen Baconum est: quorum Ioannes theologorum
suæ ætatis facile princeps, viginti septem libris testamentum
nouum illustrauit: alter, eius frater Rogerus in philosophia,
mathematicisque nemini cessit.

Vualdensis, vir abundanti doctrina: Morenus plurimo zelo
& scientia: nonnulli etiam alii contra Hussitas & Vuiclefitas,
illius sæculi hæresiarchas scripserunt ægregiè.

Occham, Scotus, sectarum Principes: Gallensis, arbor vitæ
nuncupatus: Sertorius, alias Fontenerius Cardinalis, & Rauennæ Præsul: Salisburiensis Adriani Quarti à secretis:
Bartholomeus, qui scripsit de proprietatibus rerum: Calculator:
Gilbertus Monachus: Ioannes de Sacro bosco: Versouius:
Burleus: Holcottus: Ioannes Canonicus: omnes scriptores
insignes, Anglicarum Academiarum, Oxoniæque inprimis, ciues
& alumni fuerunt.

Hic facere non possum, quin vos Oxonienses Cantabrigien- *Admonen*
sesque Academicos appellem; vestram scientiam obtester, con- *tur Aca*
demici.
tester conscientias. Num quisquam horum, quos recensui,
viros celeberimos planeque diuinos de hac, quam vos nunc
sequimini, secta aliquando somniauerit? nonne ad vnum omnes
illam ipsam religionem fidemque Romanam, quam traditam *Antiqui*
omnes Serio
ab Augustino acceperant, tamquam purissimam virginem pari *Catholici.*
studio à procorum impudentium iniuriis prohibuerint, intactamque conseruarint; atque alias omnes impugnarint, respuerint, detestati sint? Et vos talibus ingeniis, talium in re
tanta virorum repudiato consensu, neglecta doctrina, spreto
exemplo, ad quorundam tenebricosorum & opiniosissimorum

insomnia potiùs, quàm à ratione aliqua profecta iudicia, tanquam ad scopulum aliquod adhærebitis? Expergiscimini aliquando, mentisque vestræ cogitationes ad veri contemplationem excitate. Intuemini vestrorum collegiorum fundamenta, constitutiones, disciplinam: num aliud sonant, aliud sapiunt, aliud loquuntur, quàm pietatem priscam, mores antiquos, Romanam fidem? Ponite ante oculos, quoscunque antecedentia illa quindecim propè sæcula cum honore & laude viuos perinde ac mortuos celebrarunt; omnes Apostolicæ fidei, Petrique cathedræ addictos reperietis. Considerate cum animis vestris, quanta sit catholicæ veritatis potestas, quæ tot sæculis, tanta tyrannorum potentia, tanta insurgentium hæresum insolentia neque opprimi vnquam, neque supprimi potuit: immò ita semper caput extulit, vt eminuerit; ita vegeta ac viuida, Christo confirmante, permansit, vt innumerabiles, eosque omnium locorum ac temporum præstantissimos viros, suos amatores, defensores, adstipulatores assiduos acerrimosque inuenerit: neque solùm antiquos istos, quos vestrarum Academiarum flores & robora percurrimus, sed posteriores, & huius sæculi infinitos quamplurimos etiam adolescentulos, qui huius veritatis zelo pleni, patriis commoditatibus vestrisque relictis Academiis, in illa perquirenda alienas terras sunt peregrinati; inuentam autem sic amplexati sunt, sic secuti; vt, dum ei obsequendo Christo ac Petro seruiant, nulla incommoda periculaque defugiant; dum, eam profitendo patriæ prosint suorumque animulis, neque mortem metuant, neque vitæ suæ curam habere videantur. Hanc igitur veritatis lucem tam efficacem, tam illustrem, vos, in rebus aliis tam Lynceos, non videre, non ausim certè dicere: videre autem, & in eadem tamen ignoratione tenebrisque versari, incertum miserandum dicam magis, an erubescendum esse. Legistis interdum Polemonem Atheniensem, omnibus delitiis deditum adolescentem, cùm è conuiuio rediens domum, vnguentis oblitus, sertis redemitus, vino onustus, Xenocratis fortè domum intrauisset, eumque de modestia tunc temperantiaque disserentem audiuisset, adeò illius oratione fuisse commotum,

Vis veritatis.

Polemon Atheniensis.

Valer. Max. li. 7.

vt pudentem finem suæ impudentiæ in illo ipso vestigio im-
posuerit; atque corona abiecta, repressaque petulantia, ad frugem
bonum conuersus, ex perdito profusoque nepote maximus eua-
serit virtutis cultor atque magister. Et vos non à naturæ
sola, sed Gratiæ etiam lege informati; nec in gancis, sed in
scholis educati; neque vnum tantum magistrum, sed domesticos multos tum veteres, tum recentiores, Xenocrate maiores
melioresque audientes, qui suæ fidei doctrinæque firmitatem
non modò verbis & professione, sed vitæ & mortis exemplo
clarissimo corroborarunt; vestras aures talium virorum cæles-
tibus vocibus clausas esse patiemini? atque Lutherum nescio
quem, aut Caluinum, horumque similes; omnes ferè omnibus à
se inuicem dissidentes; toti christianæ antiquitati; suasque in
fidei causa & salutis sectas nouas, voluptarias, cænum merum
redolentes, maiorum religioni sacrosanctæ, seueræ, semperque
catholicæ, idest, terram cælo, luci tenebras, purissimis castissi-
misque animabus omnium scelerum colluuione inquinatissimas
anteponetis? Non potest profectò (nisi me valdè fallo) in plerisque vestrum vel ea imprudentia esse, vt huius rei magnitudinem
non animaduertatis, vel ea inconsiderantia, vt tantum vestrum
periculum planè negligatis. Sed quò vos longiùs procella hæc
patriæ, turbo ac tempestas temporis, à recta religionis semita
abreptos in periculosissima erratione constituerit; eò vos
impensiùs acriùsque exoptetis, vt pari vobis ac Polemoni gloriæ
possit cedere, Resipisse aliquando, testatumque omnibus facere,
non in nequitia habitasse vestros animos, sed ita peregrinatos
esse, vt vosmet tam diuturnæ peregrinationis quàm maximè
pœniteat. Quod quidem rectæ sanæque mentis desiderium vt
in vobis augeatur & expleatur, quemadmodum à Christo Iesu,
totius boni verique autore atque datore, peto precorque; ita &
eundem precatus sum assiduè, precaborque dum viuam, vt has
nobilissimas Academias, in tetris iam diu tenebris iacentes,
ad lucem aspiciendam tandem reuocet; in pristinæ pietatis
ac religionis suæ possessione collocet; catholicæ denique Eccle- *Sic liber*
siæ, cui prima militiæ suæ sacramenta dederint, & tam multa *Procurato-*
rum, à
sæcula fidelissimè meruerint, communioni restituat: ne quan- *nobis*
citatus.

tum claritatis atque splendoris in illa ipsa Ecclesia colenda, celebranda, illustranda antiquitùs apud omnes comparauerint; tantum sibi nunc ignominiæ & maculæ in eadem, sed frustrà tamen, oppugnanda contrahant, tum maiorum autoritatem, tum propriam partam dignitatem indignè & turpiter dedecorantes. Sed vereor, ne studio elatus, longiùs hæc conquerendo sim prouectus; pertexam igitur telam, quam exorsus sum, eamque paucissimis confectam dabo.

Antiquorum istorum chyliades vel prolixa oratione exequi nunquam possem. nam præter ante dictos, aliosque qui è D. Benedicti disciplina infiniti fluxerunt; triginta nobiles scriptores, & in his quatuor S. R. E. Card. ex D. Dominici schola prodiisse commemorat eius familiæ socius Seraphinus Razzius: neque certè minor fuerat Augustinianorum, Carmelitanorum, ac Franciscanorum numerus, & fama. Quid si recentiores, & nostri temporis Fisceros, Moros, Polos, Alanos, Bristolios, Campianos, reliquos vellem nominare? dies me deficeret; nec finem vllum oratio reperiret. ex hoc vno reliqua omnia cognosci possunt. Vnicum Oxoniæ collegium Nouum, nouissimis his quadraginta annis, ex suo sinu triginta duos viros præstantissimos emisisse; qui singuli vel docendo publicè, vel opere præclaro conscribendo fidem suam, catholicamque doctrinam verbo perindè, atque ipsa re, voluntarioque exilio tutati sunt. in his Sanderus, Hardingus, Dormanus, Staplitonus, Rarstaldus, Harpfeldus, Hidus, Poinetus, Odoucnus, Reginaldus, &, qui adhuc in viuis est, & multa scripsit, ampliusque viginti annos in iure profitendo regia Duaco stipendia meruit, Richardus Vuitus.

Hæc sunt quæ de Oxoniensi, & etiam Cantabrigiensi, (sorores enim sunt, sibique persimiles) Academiis, aut ab aliis accipere, aut ipsemet, qui adolescens admodum Oxoniam reliqui, diuque iam ab ea ac longè absum, memoria retinere potui. nequaquam profectò paria earum amplitudini; pro meis tamen viribus, atque in eas studio merita ac debita. Quæ qui euoluet, idem vellem de iis cogitet, quod eos, qui Platonis libros lectitabant, de Socrate suspicatos esse tradit Cicero:

Li. 3. de Oratore.

Maius nimirùm quiddam animo expendat, quàm quantum à me tenuiter, ac tam paucis conprehendi potuit. Sic enim breuitatem, facultatisque inopiam excusabit meam; neque tamen de earum dignitate, minus quid, quàm æquum est, sibi cogitatione formabit, atque concipiet.

NOTES ON FIERBERTUS.

P. 11. *in libro Procuratorum*] Printed in Anstey, Munimenta Academica, pp. 377 ff.

P. 12. *Habet Scholas publicas*] A drawing of these 'Scholae publicae' is given here by Hearne from the original MS. of Nele's Verses on the University of Oxford. [v. inf. pp. 151 ff.] From Hentzner's Itinerarium (cited by Hearne, ad loc.) we learn that the following mottoes were placed on the Schools when they were re-built by Queen Mary:—

'Maria etiam Regina publicas scholas belle à fundamentis ædificavit his additis inscriptionibus:

Septem Artes liberales.

1. *Grammatica ;* — *Literas disce.*
2. *Dialectica ;* — *Imposturas fuge.*
3. *Rhetorica ;* — *Persuadet mores.*
4. *Arithmetica ;* — *Numeris omnia constant.*
5. *Musica ;* — *Ne tibi dissideas.*
6. *Geometria ;* — *Cura quæ domi sunt.*
7. *Astronomia ;* — *Altiora te ne quæsieris.*

Sequuntur virtutes Scholasticæ.

1. *Patientia ;* — *Patientia vincit ferendo.*
2. *Humilitas ;* — *Modestia amicabilis.*
3. *Fortitudo ;* — *Fortis est qui omnem fortunam devincit.*
4. *Spes ;* — *Spe vivimus omnes, sed omnis fiducia sine* DEO *vana est.*
5. *Cautio ;* — *Cautus vincit omnia.*'

P. 14. *Vuolseus Cardinalis*] 'Quin & ipse Wolseus primum posuit lapidem, ut è Registro Caroli Boothe penes Joannem episcopum Eliensem liquet ; ubi hæc habentur:

'Hic textus-insculpitur in prima petra jacti fundamenti collegii Cardinalis Oxon.

'Reverendissimus in Christo Pater ac Dominus, Dominus Thomas Wulcy, miseratione Divina, titulo Sanctæ Cæciliæ sacrosanctæ Romanæ ecclesiæ Presbyter Cardinalis, Eboracensis Archiepiscopus, Angliæ Primas, & Apostolicæ sedis Legatus, Episcopus Dunelmensis, exemptique Monasterii Sancti Albani perpetuus Commendatarius, Cancellarius Angliæ, & dictæ sedis Apostolicæ ad vitam suam etiam de latere Legatus, hanc petram posuit in Honorem Sanctæ & Individuæ

Trinitatis gloriosissimæque Virginis Mariæ Sanctæ Frideswydæ, & omnium Sanctorum vicesimo die Martii anno Domini millessimo quingentesimo vicesimo quinto.'—[H.]

P. 16. *Alborensis*] 'Forte *Albonensis*, vel *Albanensis*. Vulgo enim vocatur "Albon Hall," vel "Alban Hall." Nec absurde. Nomen etenim duxit à Roberto de Sancto Albano, cive Oxoniensi regnante Joanne. Me tamen non fugit in aliis etiam antiquitatis infimæ monumentis *Aulam Alborensem*, vel *Alburnensem*, sive potius *Ealdburnensem* appellari. "Alburn" vel "Ealdburn" idem valet quod "Old Brook" sive *vetus fons*. Adeo ut Aula (si ista scriptura fidem aliquam mereatur) à fonte quodam antiquo & paullo insignioris notæ hîc loci scaturiente nomen suum traxerit.'—[H.]

P. 25. *quorum Joannes*] 'Pro *Joannes* legend. *Robertus*.'—[H.]

II

ANTIQUITIES OF OXFORD

THE

ANTIQUITIES OF OXFORD

A DISSERTATION

BY

LEONARD HUTTEN

Sir,

Your two Questions, the one concerning the Antiquity of Oxford, the other concerning the proofe of that Antiquity by some old Records, Monuments, Buildings or signes of Buildings, *&c.* did, att the first, trouble me very much. For by the Antiquity of Oxford, though I knew well you meant and intended the Antiquity of the University, yet I saw I could make noe just accompt thereof, except I first could find out the Antiquity of the Citty, noe more then it were possible to find out a Jewell, before a man could know where to find the ² <u>scale</u> and place wherein it lay. Soe then this your first Question is indeed become two, the first concerning the place, the second concerning the quality and employment of the place.

The Question of the place is easily answeared out of our Chronicles. For they report, that the first building of this Citty was in the tyme of the auntient Brittaines Dominions and Government, and that the founder thereof was the Brittaine King Mempricius, who reigned about the yeare of the world. 1009. hee beeing the fift King after Brutus. Pag. 2. After which Mempricius, saith John Rossus Warwicens. *nihil boni commemoratur, nisi quod probum filium & heredem generavit, nomine Ebraneum, & unam nobilem urbem condidit, quam à nomine suo Caer-Mempric nominavit.* Noe other good is remembred, then that hee was Father to a vertuous Sonne and heire called Ebran, and builded a noble Citty, which after his owne name hee called Caer-Mempric. John

---

¹ The number of Pages answering the MS. is placed in the Margin.   ² Sic.

Stow doth ascribe this honor, not to Mempric himselfe, but to Ebran his sonne, which Ebran began his Raigne in the yeare before Christ. 989. And further then the limitts of our Chronicles wee cannot speake.

2. The second Question touching the qualitie of the place, (*vizt.*) when the Universitie began, is a matter of greater difficultie, both because it is odious, as employing a Comparison with that of Cambridge, and because I find noe man speaking particularly to that point, but in generalitie onely and att large, as Samuel [1] Leukner, in his English Booke of Universities, saith, that the Citty of Oxford was consecrated to the Muses, even att the first tyme of the Brittons, and Cambden, *prudens Antiquitas (ut in annalibus nostris legitur) hanc urbem etiam Britannico seculo Musis consecravit*: prudent Antiquitie consecrated this Citty to the Muses even in the first age of the Brittaines. For the particuler, in what King's Raigne the Muses entred, seemeth unto mee like that old dispute among the Athenians, *sub quo Rege olea in arce nata*, in what King's tyme the Olive Tree first grew in the Tower att Athens; which as it stood undetermined for a long tyme, with this onely necessary Illation, that, therefore, the Tower or Castle att Athens was before the Olive, soe I graunt, as I said before, that certainely the Citty or Towne of Oxford was before the University; And yet as the Olive is said to have sprung upp in the daies of Cecrops [2] Diphues, the first King of Athens, soe I saie againe, that our Universitie, most probably, had her beeing and begining not long after the Citty. And this maie bee a waie to reconcile John Stow with other Chronologers. Other Chronologers attribute the Building of this Citty to Mempricius the Father, concerning, perhapps, the Edifice and the Walls. And John Stowe, peradventure, may meane that which was built by Ebran his Sonne concerning the planting the University therein. If this should onely be said, without further proofe, who could contradict it? For both it giveth a sufficient space

Pag. 3.

Pag. 4.

---

[1] *Leukner* MS.   [2] *Diphues* MS.

betweene the Citty and University, and it well agreeth with the first tyme of the Brittaines, as Leukner speaketh, and with *seculo* [1] *Britanico*, as M[r]. Cambden, which both were not much above a hundred yeares from the first entry of the Brittaines.

And yet the *seculum* [2] *Britanicum* of Mr. Cambden, giveth 3. us leave to extend it further, even to the tyme of Vortigerus, who is said to have repaired it beeing defaced, and to have recalled the Schollars beeing driven thence by the warrs of the Saxons. This repayring, noe doubt, extended as farr as Pag. 5. the harme the Saxons had wrought in their warrs. They both destroyed the building, and dispearsed the studies of learning. Tis very likely, therefore, that Vortiger's repaire restored the one and other, according to that [3] dislike of Daniell Rogers, which thus writeth concerning Oxford:

Non ingrata suis, queis crevit regibus olim;
Menpricio sese Vortigeroque refert.

But leaveing these things to them that are skilfull, I will remitt you to that most learned and industrious worke of M[r]. Bryan Twyne, who hath fully and plentifully examined this wholl matter in his three Bookes that hee writeth, *De Antiquit. Acad. Oxoniensis.* I will here onely remember, out of him, three famous things, that have happened concerning this busines.

The first shall bee that renowned translation of the two 1. Schooles, Greeke lade and Leech lade, from their first plantation to this place of Oxford, then knowne or called by the name Pag. 6. of *Bellesitum, propter montium, pratorum, & nemorum adjacentium amœnitatem*, for the pleasantnes of Hills, Meadowes, and Woods thereunto adjoyning. This Translation what yeare it fell out I cannot tell. Some conceive, that it was about the yeare of our Lord. 440. about which tyme the noble and renowned Clerke S[t]. German, Bis. of Altesiodore, was sent out of France, First with Lapus Bishopp of Trecassa, and

---

[1] Sic.   [2] Sic.   [3] [Sic; leg. *dislike.*]

afterwards with Severus to allay the heate and rage of the Pelagian Herisey, which a litle before that time newly began to trouble the Church. Some think, that it was long after that, in the tyme Theodorus the Græcian, who taught att Greek lade, and was after that made Archbishopp of Canterbury about the yeare of our Lord. 668. But for the Translation it selfe, I beleeve such a thing to have beene, beeing induced thereunto, not onely by our [1] *Historiola Oxoniensis* in the Proctors Booke, but by Johannes Rossius alsoe *in libro de Regibus*, who thus testifyeth: [2] *(idem & Chronica docent.) ipsi magnæ literaturæ viri à Græcia cum ipso eorum Rege Bruto novi advenæ locum pro eorum habitatione congruum eligebant, cui & nomen ab ipsis Græcis Greekelade appellatum est. A quo quidem loco non multum* [3] *distantes situ medici qui erant inter eos periti, locum iis appropriarunt congruum & situ salubrem, qui usque hodie ab ipsis medicis Leechlade appellatur:* as Chronicles teach, men of Great Learning comeing out of Greece as new guests with their King Brutus, chose a place meete for their habitation, which of them is called by the name of Greekelade; from which place not farr distant those which amongst them were skilfull in Phisick, appropriated to themselves alsoe another place, wholsome in [4] Cituation, which deriveing it's name from these Phisitians, is even att this daie called Leechlade. Here, you see, mention is made of two Schooles, whereas the History in the Proctors Booke nameth but one. Unto this of Rossius Leland alsoe doth accord concerning both these Schooles, saying: *veteres Britannos. 2. scholas habuisse, tam eloquentia quam omni literatura florentes, quarum quidem una Greekelade à Græcæ linguæ professione dicta est, altera vero Latslade à linguæ professione: verum nunc corrupte Greeke lade & Leech lade nomen:* that the old Brittons had two Schooles, flourishing aswell in Eloquence as in all other Learning,

Speed page 208.
Bed. lib. 1. cap. 17.
Bed. lib. 1. cap. 21.

Pag. 7.

Pag. 8.

Leland apud Balæum in vita Alfredi Magni.

---

[1] This I have printed exactly in p. 123. of the ninth Vol. of Leland's *Itin.* [v. s. p. 31.]

[2] *Et, ut cronicæ docent, ipsi* &c. in Ed. nostra Rossi.

[3] *Distante* Ed. nostra Rossi.   [4] Sic.

whereof one was called Greeke lade of the profession of the
Greeke Tongue, the other Lastlade of the Lattin Tongue :
now they are corruptly called Greeke lade and Leech lade.
Hereunto wee maie add two other Testimonies, the one of
M[r]. Cambden in these words : *Musas à Græcolada (quæ jam
tenue in Comitatu Wiltoniæ oppidulum) huc, tanquam in
felicius [1]plantarium, viri prudentes transtulerunt.* The other
of [2] A.M. There were in old time two Schooles, the one for Pag. 9.
Greeke att the Towne of Greeke lade, which after was called
Kicklade, the other for Lattin, which place was called Lattin- 130. pag.
lade, afterward Lethlade, neare to Oxford.

The second thing to bee observed is the dispersion of the 2.
Schollers, which happened by the interdict of Pope Gregory
the First. For a dispersion must needs inferr a reunion, or
recollection of those which were dispersed. It seemes, that
it had beene related to the foresaid Pope, that this place had
beene generally infected with the Pelagian Herisie, then
lately sprung upp; which interdict was executed with soe
much severity, that all the Schollars abandoned the Towne,
and betooke themselves to severall Monasteries, some to
Glocester, some to Abington, some to Ramsey, and most
of all to Malmesbury and other places, where they might
best be fitted and entertained. This dispersion continued Pag. 10.
long, almost till such tymes as the Danes came in and
destroyed, as other Townes and Citties, soe this alsoe.

The third thing I would observe [3] is that, famous shall 3.
I saic or infamous? discention, that fell out betweene the
old Schollers of this place, and those new ones which King
Alfred, when hee first repayred and restored this Universitie,
did bring hither.

The Story is this : When King Alfred with his forces had
valiantly repressed the Danish fury, and caused Gutrum
their King, and manie of his Nobles to become Christians,
Alfred himselfe beeing [4] Gutrum's Godfather att the font,

---

[1] *Plantatium* MS. [2] See the Appendix to this Work, num. I.
[3] *In that* MS. [4] *Grutums* MS.

and Christening him by the name of Athelstane, hee gave
to the said Athelstane, and to them that were baptized with

Pag. 11. him, the Kingdome of East Anglia, containeing Northfolke
and Suffolke and parte of Cambridgshire, for their habitation.
The rest that would not be baptized, [1] he caused to take their
Shipps and returne to their owne home. This thing (beeing
thus for a tyme quietted and settled by King Alfred's valour)
a blessed Calme of peace happilie ensued, and gave the King
occasion to exercise his wisdome and pietie alsoe for repayring of Churches, and building of Monasteries, and restoring of good letters in every part of his dominion ; in which
last care his thought was not a litle busied, how hee might
best cure the double sore and malady of Oxford, intending
by some present remedy to releeve it. For the better effecting whereof, hee called to his Court Neotus, a certaine Abbott
in Cornewell, esteemed a man of great Religion and Learning,

Pag. 12. by whose direction hee sent for divers other learned men out
of other places, as Grimbaldus out of France, Asserius Mene-
vensis out of Wales, Werefridus out of Winchester, Johannes
Scotus out of Scotland, and certaine others, as maie better
appeare by these words of the Register of the new Abby of
Winchester, which this King had, a litle before, builded. It
speaketh thus : *Anno secundo adventus* [2]*Grimbaldi* &c. About
the second yeare of the comeing of Grimbaldus into England,
the Universitie of Oxford was begunne, where, by King
Alfred's appointment, Neotus the Abbott Doctor of Devinitie,
and Grimbaldus the most sweete and eloquent professor of
the same were made Regents in that facultie ; Asserius the
Monke, a most learned man, was ordained Regent M^r. of

Pag. 13. Grammer and Rhetorique ; John, another Monke of the
same Monastery of S^t. David's, was appointed to read Logick,
Musique and Arithmetique ; John the Monke and Colleague
of Saint Grimbald, a man of a sharp witt, and every way
well learned, was ordeyned to teach Geometry and Astronomy ; and all this in the presence of King Alfred, who,

[1] *Deest he* in MS.   [2] *Grimbaldiæ* MS.

beeing formerly advised soe by Neotus, did not onely repaire the old Studies there, but alsoe builded three new Colledges, one for Grammer, which hee called *Aula parva Universitatis*; another for Phelosophy, which he called *Aula major Univer-sitatis*; and the third for Devinitie, which hee called *_Aula magna Universitatis_; ordaineing alsoe, besides the foresaid Schooles, dyvers others, and franchising the same with manie great liberties. After which immeadiately this Contention arose, which Asserius, one of the forenamed Professors, de-livereth in these words: *Exorta* [1] *est pessima* &c. There fell out a most unhappie and foule discention in Oxford betwixt Grimbald and those learned men, which hee brought with him, on the one side, and those auntient Schollars on the other side, which hee found there before his commeing, who refused fully to receive att his comeing such lawes, manners and formes of reading, as had bin instituted by the same Grimbaldus. For the space of three yeares togeather, there was noe outward shew of dissention betweene them, but yet it was as plaine as the light, that there was a secrett malice among them, which afterward did breake out in great extre-mity; of which Contention the most victorious King Alfred beeing certifyed, by the Message and Complaint of Grim-baldus, came himselfe in person unto Oxford, that hee might pacify this matter, and bring it to a peaceable and quiett end, who there himselfe tooke exceeding great paines to heare the Causes and Quarrells on either side. The cheife point of this Controversie consisted herein, *vizt.* Those auntient Schollers constantly avouched, that, before such tyme as Grimbaldus came to Oxford, Learning did there flourish in every place, though there were fewer Schollars in those daies, then there had beene in former tyme, by reason that the most part of them had beene driven thence by the Tyranny and Crueltie of the Pagans. And further, they did alsoe prove, by the undoubted testimony of the auntient

* Called this daie Universitie Colledge.

Pag. 14.

Pag. 15.

---

[1] See what I have said about the Gennineness of this Passage, in p. 177. *&c.* of Sir John Spelman's *Life of Ælfred the Great.*

Annalls, that the Orders and Ordinances of that Place had beene established and confirmed by divers godly and learned men, as of S[t]. Gildas, [1]Melkicius, Ninnicius, Kentigernus, and divers others, who all haveing beene auntient Students governed all things in happy Peace and Concord, and that St. German alsoe did exceedingly approve of those Orders and Lawes, and continued here for the space of halfe a yeare, att what tyme hee himselfe, then Bishopp of Antisiodore, and with him Lupus the Bishopp of Trecassa in France, both of them beeing by a Counsell there holden sent hither to that purpose, made their Journey through Britany to preach against the Pelagian Herisie.

The King heard both parties most attentively, [2]with wonderfull humility exhorting them againe and againe, with manie Religious admonitions, to preserve mutuall Conjunction and Concord amongst themselves, and soe departed, with the perswasion and hope, that all of either side would obey his Counsell and Advise, and embrace his Ordinances. But Grimbaldus, taking these things with a discontented mind, went presently unto the New Monastery of Winchester, which King Alfred had then lately founded, and after tooke order that his Tombe, which hee had provided of purpose to laie his bones in, in the Vault [3]which was made under the Chancell of St. Peeter's Church in Oxford (which Church Grimbaldus himselfe had builded from the foundation, of Stone curiously cutt and carved) should be brought after him to Winchester. Thus farr Asserius, out of which narration I make these three Observations.

1. First, concerning the tyme of the comeing of Germanus into England, which beeing well considered, will add much unto the Antiquitie of this University (for his comeing

---

[1] L. *Melkinus, Nennius.*   [2] *And with* MS.

[3] This Vault is a fine one, and is still to be seen under the Chancell of St. Peter's Church in the East Oxford. I have printed an exact Draught and Platform of it (as I have also a Draught of St. Peter's Church it self, and of the very old Font that lately stood in the Church) in p. xxviii, xxix of my Preface to Leland's *Collectanea,* since which the Entrance on the East side into the Vault hath been stopt up.

hither was about the yeare 450.) and the restauration thereof by King Alfred in the yeare 880.

Secondly, I doe observe, that this deed of Alfred was not 2. a new Foundation of the University, but a Restauration of the old.

Thirdly, that this restitution was the Conclusion and finall 3. abrogating of that interdict, which Pope Gregory the Greate Pag. 18. had given out against the Schollers of this place. And this shall suffice mee to have spoken thus much concerning your first Question of the Antiquitie of Oxford.

Now to your second, *vizt.* how this Antiquity maie be proved by some old Records, Monuments &c. And herein I meane to follow this method. First, to declare these old Reliques and *rudera* of such Religious houses as have beene heretofore in this Universitie, and now, with their memorie, are utterly exstinguished and decayed.

Of this sort I find there have beene these ensueing houses, *vizt.*

> The Church of St. Frideswide.
> The Castle of St. George's.
> The Abby of South Osney.
> The Colledge of St. Marie's.
> Glocester, ⎫
> Durham, ⎬ Colledges.
> Canterbury, ⎭
> North Osney, alias Rewley.
> St. Barnard's Colledge.

Pag. 19.

All these houses belonged unto Nunns, Munkes Seculer or Reguler of divers sorts, as shall more fully appeare in the severall treatises of each of them.

Besides these, there were fower houses of Mendicant Fryers, containeing alsoe their sundry Orders, which were these:

First, the Black Fryers Prædicants of the Order of St. 1. Dominick.

Secondly, the Black Fryers Eremites of the Order of 2. St. Augustine.

3. Thirdly, the Gray Friers, comonly called *fratres Minores*, of the Order of St. Francis.

4. Fowerthly, the White Friers, comonly called Carmelites.

But before wee come to the perticuler handling of these severall houses, and the divers qualities thereof, it will not be amisse to sett downe some *Prolegomena* necessary for the understanding of the Universitie.

1. The first is, that, besides the houses before mentioned, which were all Religious, and belonging unto Monasticall habitt, there were alsoe laie habitations for Schollars, and those more auntient then these, not consisting of sumptuous and stately buildings (for they had not beene till King Alfred's time) but in low and humble houses, comonly called Halls and Inns, and were, for the most parte, private mens houses of the Towne. Of these there were manie, as may appeare by M^r. Bryan Twyne his Booke written of this Argument, and by divers such titles and appellations applyed to sundry places, though, att this time, they bee not used to such purpose.

Pag. 20.

Secondly, it will not be amisse to declare, what is meant

2. by [1] such gencrall appellations of Secular and Regular Cannons, Monkes and Fryers, and how they began to multiplie and increase in this Kingdome. Alsoe of Fryers, their severall Orders and Differences, soe much as belongeth to our purpose.

Pag. 21.

First, therefore, concerning the differences betweene Cannons or Preists Secular and Regular, wee must understand, that in this kingdome, before the tyme of Dunstan, first a Monke and Abbott of Glassenbury, then Bishopp of London, and lastly made Archbishopp of Canterbury, the Bishopps [2] Seas and Cathedrall Churches were replenished with noe Monkes, but with Preists and Cannons, called then Clarkes or men of the Clergie. [3] After this, when Monkes came in,

---

¹ Sic.   ² Sic.   ³ Sic.

which professed a greater strictnes in life and habitt, then these Clarkes did, these different titles of Secular and Regular, were first [1] invented for the old Preists and Clerkes, who because they lived more free from Monkish Rules and observances, and were then commonly, or att least lawfully marryed, and in their life and habitt came nearer to the Secular sort of other Christians, were therefore called Secular Preists Pag. 22. and Cannons; Secular, because they had Commerce, and were *implicati rebus secularibus*: Preists and Cannons, because they followed noe personall rule, but onely the auntient received Cannon and Rule of the Church, in preaching the Word and administration of the Sacraments.

The other sort, which lived after a more severer Order and Holynesse, taking upon them the rules and perticuler devotions of some will worshipp invented by them, and professed Chastity, that is, liveing from wives, (for soe was Chastity in those blind dayes defined,) as if holy matrimony were noe Chastity, according as [2] Paphnutius did well define it in the first Councell of Nice, were called Monkes Regular: Monkes, because they professed a solitary Life, beeing alone without either Comerce with the people or with wives; Regular, Pag. 23. because they addicted themselves to the spetiall Rules and Orders of their severall Patrons, some of St. Augustine, some of St. Benidict, some of St. Ambrose, St. Jerom, or the like.

These differences and distractions beeing thus raysed in the Church, gave occasion to the Regulars, upon anie advantage offered, to remove the Seculars out of their severall Churches and Possessions, and to intrude themselves into their places. And they were thereunto espetially encouraged by the manie and seveare decrees of divers Popes against Preists Marriages, by the naturall and inbredd malignity of the Laity against the Clergie, (according to the saying, *Laici Clericis oppido infensi.*) and by the particuler [3] patrionage of

---

[1] F. *invented. For the old Preists and Clerkes, because* &c.
[2] *Paphuntius* MS.   [3] Sic.

Dunstan the Archbishopp of Canterbury, Oswaldus the Archbishopp of Yorke and Bishopp of Worcester, and Ethelwardus Bishopp of Winchester, Examples whereof wee have in the Raigne of King Edwyn, about the yeare. 955. that where Secular Preists and Cannons had beene placed by the devises of Dunstan, and Regulars putt in their places, there (Dunstan beeing then by the said King Edwyn banished into Flaunders, and living in the Monastery of St. Amandus) the said King did soe vex all Orders of the Monkes so intruded, that in Malmesbury, Glassenbury, and other places more hee thrust out the Monkes, and placed Secular Preists and Cannons in their steed ; the like whereof was alsoe practized in the Priory of St. Friswide, as, when wee come to speake thereof, more plainely shall appeare.

Touching the first entrance, encrease and multiplication of Monkes in this Land, I find, that, about the tyme of King Edmund the Brother of Ethelstone, and Father of the forenamed Edwyn, which was in the yeare. 940. when hardnes and strictnes of life, joyned with superstition, had now gotten veneration, and was counted for great holynes, men, either to wyn publike fame among themselves, or merritt with God, gave themselves to follow this strictnes of Life, thinking thereby, that the more strange the Conversation was, and further from the common trade of vulgar people, the more perfect it was before God and Men.   There was att that time, and before that, a Monastery in France, named Floriacke, after the Order and Rule of Benidict, from the which Monasterie did spring a great part of our English Monkes, who beeing there professed, and returning into England, did bring more men dayly to their profession, and soe, partly for the strangenes of their rule, partly for outward holynes of their strict Life, partly for the opinion of holynes that many had of them, were in great admiration, not onely with the rude sorte, but with Kings and Princes who founded their houses, maintained their rules, and enlarged them with possessions.   All this is testified by Guil. Malmesburiensis in

Pag. 24.

Pag. 25.

Pag. 26.

these words, (*lib. 3. de Gestis pontif.*) *per id [1] tempus Anglis* ^{temporis}
*consuetudo fuit, ut, si qui boni afflati essent desiderio, in
Beatissimi Benidicti Monasterio Cœnobialem susciperent habi-
tum, à quo Religionis hujusce manavit exordium.* That is, It
was a comon custome att that tyme amongst English men,
that, if anie man were moved with a desire of that which
was good, hee went to the Monasterie of blessed St. Benidict Pag. 27.
in France, and there received the habitt of a Monke, whereupon the first Originall of this Religion tooke begining, and
soe increased and multiplied, that many houses of that Order
were erected in this land.

Wee are further to understand, that, as the Regular Monkes
did, by professing of a more seveare life and holines, disgrace,
and, in the end, utterly thrust out the Preists and Cannons
Secular, soe alsoe the Orders and manifold diversities of
Religious and holy Fryers did much ecclips the Cannons
and Preists Regular, as Diogenes sometymes did *fastum
Platonis altero fastu conculcare,* trample under foot the Pride
of Plato with another Pride. For these holy Religious persons seeing, that the Austeritie and Opinion of Holynes
prevailed more with men, then Holynes it selfe, tooke upon
them a more plausible and likeing [2] visible vizard of [3] Holynes, Pag. 28.
then the Regulars by their outward shew and formall habitt
had gotten all the Churches and Church livings of the
Seculars ; these, by a more profound and deepe stratagem,
did not soe openly repugne, as cuningly undermine the
Regulars. These left unto the Monkes their Churches, Tithes,
Livings, Possessions and Oblations, unto them belonging (farr
more liberally then the Monkes had donne unto the Seculars,)
and, under pretence of greater Holynes and Perfection then
the Monkes, contented themselves with such benevolences
and voluntarie Contributions onelie, as the good affecctions
and holy devotions of God's people should conferr upon them,
offering themselves to performe all Preistly functions of house-

---

[1] Sic.   [2] Sic. Sed *visible* forsan delend.
[3] F. *Holynes then the Regulars.   And whereas the Regulars, by* &c.

ling and aueyling, (as they then cald it,) that is, of hearing Confessions and giveing Absolutions, of saying Prayers, and ministring the Sacraments, and all other Ecclesiasticall duties and observances, and further of obliging and devoting themselves to the proper attendances and dayly walkes of their Parishes and Circuits, without anie other Reward, then what their confined masters and dames should, of their owne motion and free hart, bestow upon them, assuring the multitude, that, as the Monkes profession was Chastity and Abstinencie from Marriage, soe theirs [1] was poverty in abstayning from the desire of riches and worldly goods, and to doe onely for Conscience sake, without all hope of reward with men, other then to be maintained with food and rayment, liveing according to the Rules of Evangelicall Counsells and heavenly perfection, which they falsly fayned unto themselves to bee farr more meritorious, then those devine præcepts of the Law, which enjoyne us to love God with all our soules, with all our hart, and with all our strength, and our neighbour as our selves.

The last observation is, that these Religious excluded noe Sex, but entertained aswell women as men, yet soe, as they were alwaies enjoyned to live a part, Males of all orders in their severall Churches and Societies, and Nunns in their severall Cloysters, to have noe Comerce nor Familiarity with each other.

To discourse of the severall Orders of these Religious persons, would bee a matter of greater difficulty, and more labor then I am willing to undertake. My purpose, therefore, is, to lymitt my speech within the compasse of this Citty and University, and to treate onely of such Religious persons, as, in former tyme, have beene here, and are not now, though they had buildings, large possessions, and firme setling for manie yeares in this place. Haveing laid, for a ground and foundation, these few observations, I come now to the per-

---

[1] *Was poverty in abstaineing from marriage, soe theirs was poverty in abstayning &c.* MS.

ticuler discourse of these severall houses before specified;
and first of the most auntient Church of St. Friswide, which
I find to bee farr before all other buildings of note in this
University. This Church of St. Frideswide was founded and
builded (as some saie) by St. Friswide her selfe, which Friswide was daughter unto Didacus, alias Didanus, called in the
Register of that Foundation *Regulus Oxenfordiæ*, Prince and
Cheife Ruler of Oxenford, and Safrida his wife, about the
yeare of our Lord. 700. And it was dedicated to the honor
of the holy and undevided Trinitie, without anie more title Pag. 32.
and addition. Others say, that it was builded by Didanus
the Father of Fridiswide, which I rather beleeve, and that
shee, with her Parents consent, tooke upon her a Monasticall
vaile or habitt, (as the Register speaketh,) and by her
example provoaked twelve other Virgins, borne of noble
Parentage, to doe the like. Of these shee herselfe became
the first Prioresse or Abbesse, and they and shee soe continued all the daies of her life. Shee was, in those daies,
reputed for a Saint, as in other respects, soe, espetially,
because shee had vowed herselfe to God in perpetuall Virginitie.

And here wee must observe, that this Church, since the
first foundation, hath undergone manie changes and varieties
in the estate thereof. For hitherto it doth appeare by the
Booke of St. Frideswide, that it was a Nunnery, and that
it continued soe noe longer, then till the dispertion and death Pag. 33.
of Frideswide and her Fellowes. Afterward it came to bee
a Priory of men, and those of divers ages and qualities, as
in the processe of this Story shall appeare; but, first, wee
will alleadge, what wee have to saie concerning the Nunnery.
This holy Virgin St. Friswide was not onely accompted
a Saint by reason of her vow, but alsoe, by occasion of a
certaine Miracle that shee performed upon Algarus, Prince
or Earle of Leicester, whom shee, because hee sought to
take her awaie by violence, against her vow and will, struck
with blindnes, but, att his earnest entreaty, restored him by

her prayers to his sight againe. Yet the Earle, for all this, did still continue to constraine her, against her resolved purpose, soe as shee was constrayned to fly into Wiltshire, to some unknowne and hidden place, where shee remained either till his or her owne death. The Virgins her fellowes, in the meane season, betooke themselves to their severall Parents, and were matched to honourable Houses of the Saxon Nobility. And this was the first Fortune and Change of this Foundation. Besides this, there [1] were three other Changes alsoe in this Foundation, before it was surrendered into the hands of King Henry the Eight, and after that two other before this Foundation, which now standeth, was established.

The three first, to avoid confusion, I will devide into three severall tymes or ages; and because the Inhabiters thereof in these tymes doe all call themselves Monkes of the Order of St. Augustin, some Secular and some Regular, it will not bee amisse, before wee proceed further in this discourse, to examine and enquire, whether St. Augustine were Author of anie such Monasticall Orders or Religions? And, for my owne parte, I must needs confesse, that I find noething, either in St. Augustine's owne workes, or in Possidonius the writer of his life, that soundeth any thing materially to this purpose. Yet I will not denie, that there be three things in Possidonius, that may seeme unto men, that fancy that opinion, to give some Colour for this Monkish conceite. The first maie bee his sojurning for a tyme in the Farme of one Viricundus, a Cittizen of Millan, with Alpius and other of his followers, after hee had forsaken the Heresie of the Maniches, and became a Christian.

The second maie be his abiding and remaineing in his owne house and possessions in Affrick, for the space of three yeares, following privately, with some others, the Study of the holly Scriptures, and frequenting holy Exercise, after the death of Monaca his mother, and before hee was called to the Bishopprick of Hippo.

------

[1] *Was* MS.

about
Bishopp
Stone.
Pag. 34.

Pag. 35.

Pag. 36.

The third, his building of a Monasterie neare his Cathedrall Church, and conversing and takeing his diett with Clerks and learned men [1]then. To these I answere, that the two first of these belong onely to his private Study and Conference with his frinds concerning Religion, and Studdy of the holy Scriptures, and beare noe other interpretation. The 3^d. mentioneth, indeed, his building of a Monasterie; but building of a Monastery, or Colledge, is noe Instituting of a Religious order, and conversing with Clarkes and learned men, and takeing his diett with them, is noething different from the Pag. 37. Use and Customes of our Cathedrall Churches of old erection, as it was att the first in the Church of Sarum, and divers others, where, after the manner of the Church of Antioch, they had a comon diett togeather with the Bishopp, a publike Reader alsoe, and moderator of Divinitie, disputations once a moncth or oftner, as the Clergie there, and in the neighbour Parishes could best agree. The Fryers, which are called likewise after the name of S[t]. Augustine, claime him alsoe for their first Patron and Founder; and, to make proofe hereof, they doe alleadge his Booke intituled, *Ad Fratres in Eremo degentes:* but this carrieth noe better credit, then the former. For that Booke, or rule of his *Ad Fratres in Eremo,* is censured by divers learned men to be spurious or misbegotten. And Erasmus by name is bould Pag. 38. to censure it with these peremptory words: *Nihil habet Augustini,* it hath noething of S[t]. Augustine in it, neither Phrayse, nor Composition, nor anie thing els worth the name or credit of soe judicious and learned a man. But, sparing to speake further of these matters, I referr the inquisitive reader, desirous to know the truth, unto Polidorus Virgilius *de inventoribus. lib.* 7. *cap.* 3. and unto Sabellicus, *Æunead.* 7. *lib.* 9. But all this onely breifely by the waie.

To returne, therefore, where wee left: After the glorious death of S[t]. Friswide, and the dispearsing of her Nunns, a good space of tyme comeing betweene, (as the Register

---

[1] F. *there.*

of the Foundation speaketh,) the Cannons Secular were brought in, which were noe other then such as are in our Church att this daie : onely these were called Cannons of that Rule of Christ, which hee calleth *onus leve*, in living after the prescript of the Gospell, or of that Cannon whereof the Apostle speaketh, when hee prayeth, that peace and mercy and the Israell of God may fall upon them, as manie as walke according to this Rule, which is to become a new Creature in Jesus Christ. And they were called Secular for their Conversation, and applying themselves unto the Lay people, as wee said before. And this I call the first age of those three, which before I mentioned, comprehending that time, wherein the Cannons Secular did onely injoy it without anie interruption, which was till the yeare of our Lord. 1060. There fell out in this age a most remarkeable and strange accident, sufficient to have ended both the persons and the place, but because it pleased God to continue it to the fore-named period, wee will reckon this rather an interruption, then a finall ending thereof. The Accident was this. King Ethelred (who was the third sonne of King Ethelwolfe, King Alfred's brother, and immediate predecessor in the King-dome) had, by his valour, brought the Danes to a desperate Condition, and saw, that, with a litle more following of them, hee might drive them utterly out of the Land. By the advise, therefore, of his Counsell, hee adjudged the Danes generally to death. They that were neare this place, fledd into this Church, as into a Sanctuary, for Reliefe and for succour of their lives. The King beeing hereof advised, sent a Comaundement to his Captaines and Governors here, that the Church and the other Buildings about it should be sett ˙ on fire, that they that were within might be consumed with the flame. This was donne according to the King's Comaund-ment, who, not long after, repayred the Church againe, and restoring it to it's former beauty, planted therein the Seculars againe, who continued there quietly untill the tyme of Edward the Confessor. And with him I begin the second

Pag. 39.

Pag. 40.

Pag. 41.

age of these [1]Augustinian Cannons, which [2]containeth that space of tyme, wherein the Seculars and Regulars by their mutuall contentions expelled each other for the space well nigh of. 60. yeares. This alteration, which I call the second age, tooke occasion upon a certaine Vow made by Edward the Confessor, that hee would undergoe a pilgrimage to the Holy Land, which hee never performed. Pope Nicholas, therefore, understanding soe much, would not dispence with him for the said Vow, when hee came to the Crowne, except hee first expelled the Seculars out of this Church, and placed the Regulars in their steed. The cause why the Seculars were expelled was, because they were married. This was donne by the King in recompence of his Vow, and the Pag. 42. Regulars according to the Pope his pleasure enjoyed it. But they held it not long. For by King Harold, sonne of Earle Godwin, and immeadiately Successor to King Edward, it was restored againe unto the Seculars, which afterward proved the cause of his death. It was not long after this, but that, with the advice of the Regulars, it was almost utterly forsaken, and relinquished, in the troublesome warr betweene King Herald and William the Conqueror, a very few persons onely remaineing in it, 'till, att the length, it was given by William the Conqueror to the Abbott and Monkes of St. Mary the Virgin in Abbington, for a Cell or Grange, as they best pleased to use it. But the Abbott and Monkes of Abbington, perceiveing it to bee very ruinous, and that the Charges of repayring it would rather bee a burthen, then the Church Pag. 43. an honor to them, gave it to Roger the Bishopp of Salisbury their Ordinary, (for Abington is scited in Barkshire, which is under his Jurisdiction,) haveing first obtained leave of King Henry the first soe to doe. Whereupon the Bishopp understanding, that the King had already (as much as in him lay) given it[3] to *Guimundas his Chaplaine, a man very Religious *Guimundus. and excellently learned, gave presently the disposition thereof to the King, and the King to Guimundus. Soe that it was

---

[1] *Augustian* MS.   [2] *Containe* MS.   [3] Sic.

now utterly taken from the Seculars, and given to the Regulars, 'till it was finally surrendred into the hands of King Henery the Eight, and this I reckon to the third age.

Now if you bee disposed to take a little recreation by the waie, and to heare what meanes, policies and devises Guimundus used to obtaine his purpose, and [1] alsoe to admonish the King, how ill hee did bestow his Bishopwricks and Ecclesiasticall promotions, the Booke of Friswide telleth us this ensueing tale : *In die Rogationum* &c. Upon Rogation Sundaie the King beeing att Masse, and Guimundus performeing the devine Service, when hee came to that percell of the Prophett, where it is said, *It did not raigne upon the Earth for the space of three Yeares and six Monethes*, read it on this fashion, *It did not raine upon the Earth for the space of one, one, one Yeares and six Monethes*, &c. which the King observing, and all the Clarkes marvailing and languishing att it, when Masse was ended, the King reproved him for it, and asked what hee meant to read on that fashion? Guimundus smilingly answeared, because you (my leige) [2] are wont to bestow your Bishopwricks, and other Ecclesiasticall dignities to them that read soe. And, therefore, bee it knowne unto you, henceforth I will serve noe other Master, but Christ my King, who knoweth aswell to confirme Temporall benifitts, as Eternall upon his servants. The King hereatt abashed, gave unto him the Church of Frideswide in Oxford, which belonged to his Chappell, togeather with all thereunto pertaineing; who immeadiately thrusting out the Seculars, brought in Regulars into their places, and makeing himselfe their Prior, governed them the space of nineteene yeares. In their possession it remained, untill the tyme of Cardinall Woolsey, about the space of 380. yeares. This Priorie or Monastery then, haveing sustained soe manie changes of new Masters and Inhabitants, after it had continued from the first to the last, sometime in prosperity, sometyme in adversitie, for the Terme of. 822. yeares, was,

Pag. 44.
withall

Pag. 45.

Pag. 46.

---

[1] Sic.   [2] *Art* MS.

by the then Prior thereof John Bourton and the Covent, surrendered into the hands of King Henery the Eight, att the request and instance of Thomas Wolsey, Cardinall and Archbishopp of Yorke, the yeare of our Lord. 1522.

And now because wee are handling of such Foundations, as have beene heretofore and are not now, though these two next ensueing erections are noe auntienter then King Henry the Eight, and by that meanes farr inferior in tyme to divers others, that wee shall mention heareafter, I can referr them yet Pag. 47. to noe other place better then unto this, haveing both of them beene planted successively the one after the other in this same scite, place, and circuite, that old Friswide's was, though much altered, changed and enlarged. First wee will speake of Cardinall Woolsie's Foundation.

Cardinall Wolsie's Colledge.

THE Priory of St. Frideswide beeing surrendred, as aforesaid, and from the King conveyed over to the Cardinall, hee made noe long delaie, but in the yeare. 1525. on the 15th. [1] daie of July, and the 17th. yeare of the King's Raigne, began the foundation of his Colledge, which hee stiled by the name and title of *Thomas Wolsey Cardinall of Yorke his Colledge in the Universitie of Oxford.*

This hee builded to the praise, glory and honor of the holie and undevided Trinitie, the most holy Virgin Mary, the blessed Virgin St. Friswide, and All Saints.

To the Erection of this Colledge, hee first provided how hee might be able to mainetaine it, and, for that purpose, Pag. 48. obtained of Pope Clement the 7th. in the yeare 1524. a Bull, whereby license was given him, to suppresse and extinguish certaine Monasteries of smaller value, to the number of. 22. (Master Speed saith 40.) by the revenue whereof hee might enrich his Colledge, [2] *ex omni sui parte insigne,* as the Bull

---

[1] The Foundation Stone was laid by the Cardinal himself, March 20th. 1525. the Inscription on which I have published in p. 127 of the IXth Vol. of Leland's *Itin.* and in p. 137 of the VIth Vol. of Leland's *Collectanea.* [v. s. p. 31.]

[2] *Ex omni sui plenisique* MS.

speaketh. Hee secondly prepared the place, and, to make roome for it att home, pulled downe. 3. Pillars, or Arches, of the West end of the old Church, the wholl West side of the Cloyster, and soe much of the North and South sides, as were answearable to the length of the Church; which donne, hee laid the Foundation of the Kitching, Hall and other Lodgings, as now you see them. Hee alsoe pulled downe the Parish Church of St. Michaell's in the South, which stood where was the lodging of Doctor Weston, with a litle Church yard thereunto adjoyning, and certaine houses a long the Streete of that side, for the West side of his Quadrangle, 'till you come almost to St. Edward's Lane. This Colledge the Cardinall ordeined to be a perpetuall Nurcery of Learning of the facultics of Divinitie, the Cannon and Civill Law, of Humanity alsoe and Phisick, and for a perpetuall observance of God's worshipp in and of the number of one Deane and. 60. Cannons Seculars, more or lesse, augmenting and [1] diminishing, according to the abilities and exigences of this Foundation. Of this number. 60. here were placed att the first, a Deane. and 18. Cannons Secular, which were these following. The first Deane hee appointed was John Hygdon, Doctor of Divinitie, who before had beene President of Magdalen Colledge. The 18. Cannons were these:

An old Hall called Peck-water's Inn.

Pag. 49.

Pag. 50.

1. Mr. Thomas Cannar.
2. Mr. John Brysett.
3. Mr. William Battenson.
4. Mr. Edward [2]Lighton.
5. Mr. Richard Barker.
6. Mr. Andrew Stockton.
7. Mr. Richard Champian.
8. Mr. John Tucker.
9. Mr. John Peirson.
10. Mr. John Crayford.
11. Mr. Richard Langrege.

---

[1] *Diminishing according to the abilities and exigences of this Foundation of this number. 60. here placed att the first, Deane. 18. Cannons &c. MS.*

[2] L. *Leighton.*

12. Mr. Walter [1] Butler.
13. Mr. Thomas Baggard.
14. Mr. Thomas Baggarre.
15. Mr. Thomas Reynolds.
16. Mr. Edward Bete.
17. Mr. Thomas Newton.
18. Mr. William Weston.

Unto these hee added afterward more. For, of sett purpose, hee made certaine pauses and delaies, that hee might make choise of the sharpest and quickest witts, among whom William Tindall, that translated the Bible into the English Tongue, was one, and Taverner, the worthy Musitian, was the Organist. Hee placed alsoe, att severall tymes, as manie Pag. 51. more as made upp. 30. before hee died. For, all the time of his life, hee kept, perpetually in himselfe, power to manage the lands of his Colledge, not makeing anie setled Corporation, nor stating them with anie dotation in the tyme of his prosperity, but intending, towards his death, to dispose firmely and strongly in law all things to their use. This Colledge continued from the yeare of our Lord. 1525. unto the yeare. 1530. *vizt.* for the space of 5. yeares. For when the Cardinall, by the Law of Præmunire, fell into the King's danger, his Colledge alsoe fell with him, as beeing loose, and not by Law setled and established.

King Henery the Eight's Colledge in Oxford.

IT pleased the King, within a litle space after, namely the yeare. 1532. the 18th. daie of July, and of his Raigne the 24th. to found in the same scite, ground and circuite, the Circuite Pag. 52. beeing by Canterbury Colledge and Pickwater's Inne, augmented and compassed about with a faire Stone wall, from the North end of Oriell Colledge Stable, to the East end of Pickwater's Inn, and from the West end thereof, to the West end of Edward Lane by the Gatehouse. This Colledge hee erected to the praise and honor of the Holy and Un-

---

[1] L. *Bucklar* vel *Buckler.*

devided Trinitie, the most blessed Virgin St. Mary and St. Frideswide. Herein hee ordained one Deane. 12. Cannons Secular to make a full Chapter, and Body Corporate. Their names were these:

John Higdon, that was Deane of the former Foundation, who died within 5. Monethes after this Erection. And after him John Oliver, Doctor of the Civill Law, who continued unto the surrender thereof into the King's hand againe.

Pag. 53.   The Cannons were these:

1. John Roper, Doctor of Divinitie, which was the first reader of Divinitie Lecture, instituted by Lady Margarett.

2. John Cottesford, Doctor of Divinitie, and Rector of Lincolne Colledge.

3. Richard Crooke, Doctor of Divinitie.

4. Richard Current, Doctor of Divinitie.

5. William Tresham, Doctor of Divinitie.

6. Robert Carter, Batcheler of Divinitie.

7. John [1] Harding, Batcheler of Divinity.

8. Thomas Canner, Batcheler of Divinity, first Cannon of Wolsey's foundation.

9. Edward [2] Lighton, Batchelor of Divinity, the fourth in the Cardinall's foundation.

10. Henry Williams, Batchelor of Divinity.

11. John Robins, Batchelor of Divinity, and a good Mathematician.

12. Robert Wakefeild, Batchelor of Divinitie.

Pag. 54.   This Foundation endured from the yeare of our Lord. 1532. to the yeare. 1545. the sixth daie of September, and the 37th. yeare of Henry the 8th. his Raigne, that is, for the space of 13. yeares, and somewhat more, att what tyme it was surrendred by John Oliver the Deane, and the rest of the Cannons, into the disposition of King Henry the Founder, who, not long after, erected, in the same place, this now and present Foundation, which hee called by the name of *the Cathedrall Church of Christ in Oxford of King Henery the*

---

[1] *Hastyngs* Woodio.   [2] L. *Leighton.*

8th. *his Foundation,* as shall more largely appeare, when wee come to speake of Churches and Colledges, now in our age flourishing and standing.

The Castle of St. George's in Oxford.

HAVEING delivered all such Antiquities, as wee find in the Scite of St. Frideswide, now called Christ Church, wee addresse our selves to the next house in Antiquitie, which is the Castle of St. George in Oxford. This Castle[1] was builded in the yeare of Christ's Incarnation. 1071. beeing the first yeare of William the First, comonly called the Conqueror, by Robert Doily the First, that came into England with the Conqueror, and, in recompence of his Valour, and great paines taken in the Warrs, had great lands and possessions given him in this Shire. For hee had two Barronies given him, the one called the Baronie of Doily, the other the Baronie of Walewrick. This last named the said Robert the First gave to Roger Ivery his sworne Brother. For when they came out of Normandy, these two confederated themselves by Oath and mutuall Amitie, which they Religiously observed to their dying daies. Within three yeares after, *vizt.* 1074. the Church, or Chappell of St. George in the Castle was founded, and soe both it and the Castle were consecrated by the brotherly Consent and Agreement of these two brothers. They placed in it certaine Cannons Secular of the Order of St. Augustin, and endowed it with Lands, Tythes and Revenues out of their severall Baronies, and not long after they gave unto it, the Parish Church of St. Mary Magdalen in the Suburbs of Oxford thereunto adjoyning, with three Hides of Land in Walton Farme, as maie be seene[2] in the Charter of Robert Doily and Roger Ivory in Oseney Booke, pag. 9. Now it must bee also remembred, against wee come to speake of Osney Abbey,

Pag. 55.

Pag. 56.

Pag. 57.

---

[1] I have printed a Draught of the Remains of this Castle, both as they are now, and as they were many years agoe, in the Appendix to my Preface to my Ed. of Guilielmus Neubrigensis.

[2] Deest *in* in MS.

that this Robert the First had alsoe a naturall brother, by the same father and mother, whose name was Nigellus, and that hee was married, and begatt a sonne, whose name was Robert Doily the Second, and became Robert the First's heire, as shall be farther shewed when wee speake of Osney.

The Church of St. George was governed by the Cannons Secular, till the Monasterie of South Osney was erected, which was the wholl space of. 55. yeares. For it was soe much auntienter then Osney, and after a sort gave Robert the Second [1] sonne occasion to build it, that hee might not be judged lesse devoted to the Church then his Uncle. Lastly, it fell alsoe to the Monkes of Osneye's lott. For they beeing instructed by a familiar Example of the Regulars in Frideswide, learned quickley to be as ambitious as they, and to over topp all them whom they might by one way or other undermine. This Castle was builded att the West end of the Citty, *magnis aggestis molibus*, as Mr. Cambden speaketh, with digging deepe Trenches to make the River runn about it, and raysing high great Hills, with lofty Towers and Walls to overlooke the Towne and Countrie round about. This kind of Fortification was then thought very strong, and gave [2] Matildis, or Mawd, the Empresse, beeing then a widow and daughter to King Henry the first, and by that meanes [3] theire to the Kingdome, occasion to enclose herselfe therein, their to expect the aid of her frinds, to make head and resistance against Steven Earle of Bloys, who (before shee could come out of [4] Jermany with Henry her sonne) had taken upon him the Crowne, and heareing of her beeing in this place, with a strong Army came against her, and beseiged her soe strait, from Michaelmas to Christmas, that shee had much adoe to be provided of Victualls and to escape takeing prisoner.

During this Seige, two things, very remarkable, fell out. The one was the building of a new Church. For while, by

Pag. 58.

Pag. 59.

---

[1] F. *Some occasion.*   [2] *Matildus* MS.
[3] Sic, pro *the heire.*   [4] Sic.

the long continuance of this Seige, the Parishioners of that
Suburbs, which wee now call by the name of Saint Thomas,
could not have accesse unto this Church of St. George, which
then was their Parish Church, the Church of St. Nicholas,
otherwise St. Thomas, upon this occasion was builded, and
soe became their Parish Church. The second was the Empresse her escape, [1] who, in the dead of the night, in a tyme
of Frost and Snow, when all places were bedewed with the Pag. 60.
one, and covered with the other, by a woman like Stratagem,
cast over her owne bodie, and five other of her servants, white
sheets, and, by the stillnes of their goeing, and whitenes of
their apparrell, through a posterne doore, deceived the watch-
fullnes of the Enimie, (who did feircely urge, and undoubtedly promisse to himselfe, either her yeilding, or the utter
overthrow of the Castle,) and comeing to the River side,
passed over the Ice, and went on their Journey (a laborious
and hard Journey indeed, but yet safe and free from danger)
towards the Earle of Wallingford, where, beeing first mett
by some Companies by the way, they were willingly and
joyfully received.

There was in this Castle, towards the latter tyme, a Col- Pag. 61.
ledge, or an intendment of a Colledge, of Students, as maie
appeare by certaine Statutes, made for the Goverment thereof,
which I have seene in a Manuscript that Mr. Allen of Gloster
Hall lent unto mee. These Statutes call this Colledge by
the title of St. George, as the Castle Church before was
called, and the Government thereof given to the Cannons
Regular of Osney, (into whose possession all was by this
tyme come.) It seemeth, that alwaies one of those Cannons
was the Warden hereof. For in that Statute, which containeth the office of the *Pauperculus*, (whom I take to be the
Sexton or Bellringer) which is the last of all the Statutes,
it is thus sett downe: *The Sexton shall upon Christmas Eve
demaund of the Sacrist, or him that keepes the Wax lights in
Osney, a Torch which hee shall carry the Christmas Hollydaies,*

[1] *Whom* MS.

Pag. 62. *and as often as need shall bee betweene that and the Epiphanie, when that it shall please him to lodge there. And it is to be noted, that all the Schollars throughout the wholl yeare, as often as the Warden shall lodge in the Castle, as soone as supper is ended, shall in the Court expect their Master, 'till hee bee ready to goe home, and shall bring him to the Hamlett, and there sing an Hymne by his appointment,'till such tyme as hee was come to Osney, and they returned againe unto the Castle.* What tyme this Colledge began, and how long it continued, doth not appeare by anie date. But the Castle, and the Church (though dayly diminished, soe as, att the last, they were but three) continued 'till the fatall period of all Religious places.

Pag. 63. There was alsoe another intendment of a Colledge in this Castle by Henry the 5th. who beeing brought upp att Oxford in [1] Queene's Colledge [2], under the tuition of his Uncle Henry Beuford, Chancellor then of this University, and afterward Cardinall of Winchester, purposed to found a magnificent Colledge (as M[r]. Speed [3] saith) for Devines and Students of the seaven liberall Sciences, the plott and ordination of which Foundation hee had already drawne, and resolved to endowe it with all his Lands in England belonging to Priors Allien, but his untimely death prevented both that, and manie other noble workes.

The Monasterie of South Osney.

THE Monastery of St. Mary the Virgin of Osney was founded in the yeare of the Lord. 1129. by Robert Doily the Second, the sonne of Nigellus, as wee said before. This

---

[1] And not (as John Stowe [Annals, p. 342. Ed. fol.] mistakes) in New-Colledge.

[2] John Ross, or Rowse, assures us (p. 207. *de regib. Angliæ*) that his Chamber was over the great Gate of the Colledge, just opposite to Edmund-Hall Gate. Both the Gate and Chamber are still (June 28. 1720.) remaining, and are much noted by curious Persons that come to Oxford. A Draught of them may be seen in p. 134 of Thomas Neale's *Collegiorum Scholarumque Publicarum Academiæ Oxoniensis Topographica Delineatio,* that I printed at the end of Mr. Dodwell's *Dissertatio de Parma Equestri Woodwardiana;* and I have got a more modern Draught of the same among my MSS. Papers.

[3] And John Ross had noted the same long before, in his Book *de Regib. Angliæ,* p. 208.

Robert flourished in the tyme of Henery the First *Beuclarke*, on whom hee attended in his Chamber, as M^r. Cambden speaketh, or was the Constable of his house, as the Booke Pag. 64. of the Monastery of Oseney. This Monasterie hee builded *in mediamni*, as M^r. Cambden saith, in a percell of ground compassed about with Rivers, and makeing it an Island, under the view of the Castle, by the perswation of Lady Edith his wife, the daughter of a certaine great Man called [1] Fornus, which had beene formerly the Le͞mon of Henery the First. Shee beeing admonished by a certaine Augurie, taken of the Chattering of Pies, moved her husband to the building of a Monastery in the foresaid place. And here wee maie observe, that Cannons Secular were more auntient in this University then the Regular by many yeares. The Title whereby this Monastery was dedicated was this, *To the honour and praise of Christ and the blessed Virgin St. Mary of Oseney*, and by the Founder ordeyned for Can- Pag. 65. nons Regular of the Order of St. Augustin. For this age began to be a wonderfull admirer of this Order. When it had flourished for the space of. 410. yeares, *vizt.* from the yeare of our Lord. 1129. which was the 30th. yeare of the Raigne of Henry the First, untill the yeare of our Lord. 1539. which was the 31th. yeare of the Raigne of Henry the Eight, it was surrendered into the King's power by Robert King, then Abbott Commendatory of this Church, and titular Bishopp *Roannensis*, or *Roueniensis*, (imagined to have beene in the Province of Athens) and the Covent of Monkes there. And this is the third house of this sort of Monkes.

And here I think it fitt, before wee part from hence, to tell you of another Erection upon this surrender founded Pag. 66. in this place, which I therefore doe, for causes which shall be hereafter specified.

[1] *Tornus* MS.

THIS Church then of Oseney, without anie alteration of
the Fabrick, (but of the persons onely, and their qualitie)
was, within short tyme, from a Monastery turned into a
Cathedrall Church, adorned with an Episcopall Chaire, the
Sheire and Countie of Oxford called a Diocesse, the Towne
and Universitie honored with the stile and title of a Citty,
and subordinated to the Bishopp, the old Rights and Customes of the Universitie alway reserved intire and wholl to
the Chancellor and other Officers thereof. The Archdeacon
alsoe of Oxford, which was before incorporated in the Church
of Lincolne, was from thence translated, and by a new
Insition planted and united into the body of this Church.
Of this Erection I may [1] lawfully speake the lesse, because
the doore must not be bigger then the house; yet something
I may speake, both because it outlived the other Abbies and
Religious places for a space, and the handling thereof will
give great light to that wee shall say of Ch. Ch. when wee
come thither, and, lastly, because it was one of those Erections, which have beene heretofore and are not now, though
not Monkes and Regular persons, yet Secular and restrayned
from marriage and secular affaires, by noe force of Monasticall rule, but onely by the Pope's plenitude of power and
supremacie of Authoritie which hee then usurped. The continuance of it was not long, not much above three yeares.
The Foundation was large and ample, of one Bishopp with
his Revenues and proportion allotted severally to himselfe,
of one Deane and six Prebendaries Preists Secular for his
Chapter, of [2] Chaplings, Singing men, Choristers and an
Organist for Devine service, of Servants and Officers for
attendance in every severall Charge and Office. When King
Henery the Eight's Colledge, in the Scite of Frideswide,
had flourished for the space of 13. yeares, and this for the

Pag. 67.

Pag. 68.

---

[1] *Lawfull* MS.   [2] Sic.

space of three, it was againe, by Doctor Cox the Deane that then was, and the Chapter, surrendered and yeilded upp Pag. 69. into the King's disposition, who presently caused the Church and Cloyster, and manie of the buildings to bee utterly subverted and removed, the Bishoppwrick and Cathedrall Church to be translated to his owne Colledge att Frideswide, then already surrendered and prepared to give them Roome and Entertainement. I read, that the Church was both surrendered and translated. I doe not read that the Bishoppwrick was surrendered, but translated onely. For the Bishopp, that had formerly beene of Oseney, was the same person which removed unto Frideswide, and the same endowment, that had beene first made att Osney (for ought that I could ever learne to the contrary) went with him alsoe unto Frideswide. The Endowment of the Church was, indeed, much altered and changed. The first Bishopp was Robert King, Pag. 70. who had beene Abbott Commendatorie of Osney, and tituler Bishop *Roanensis* or *Roueniensis*, supposed to have beene in the Province of Athens. The first Deane was John London, Doctor of Law and Warden of New Colledge in Oxford, and Cannon of Windsor, who remained here about the space of. 15. Monethes. The second Deane was Richard Cox, who continued untill the Dissolution of this House, and Translation of the Deane and Chapter unto Frideswide. The Prebendaries were. 6. *vizt.* these :

   1. Alexander Belsyre, Mr. of Arts.

   2. Tho. Day, Batchelor of Law.

   3. William Haynes, Doctor of Divinity, and [1] Provist of Oriell Colledge.

   4. Richard Beeseley, Doctor of Divinity.

   5. John Dyer, Mr. of Arts.

   6. Gervase Lynch, Mr. of Arts.

This Church endured for the space of two yeares, eight Pag. 71. monethes, and 20. daies, beeing surrendered into the King's hands was utterly destroyed and abolished, the persons for

---

[1] Sic.

the most part translated over unto Ch. Ch. as wee shall declare hereafter.

The Colledge of St. Mary of Black Augustinian Monkes Regular.

THE fowerth house of this Order of Black [1] Augustinian Monkes Regular, was St. Mary Colledge, scited betweene the North end of the Corne Markett and Bocardo on the West side of the Streete within a perticuler lane leading thereunto, of the North side of the Inn called the Starr, which of this Colledge is called St. Mary Lane. It was builded by Thomas Houlden, Esquire, and Elizabeth his wife, about the yeare. 1448. It consisted of one Prior and certaine Students Novices, beeing subordinated to the Monasterie of Osney, and trayned upp there in good Arts, 'till they might be fitt to be admitted into the greater Abby. Their habitt differed somewhat from the older Monkes, to signifie that they were but young beginners. In testimonie whereof there is yet to this daie standing a faire Hill, to what uses imployed I doe not know.

And thus haveing declared all the Houses of that [2] Order of the Benedictin Monkes.

The Monkes of the order of St. Benidict.

THE Order of the Benidictine Monkes tooke their begining from Benidictus the first Patron and Founder in Campaine, a Countrey of Italy, *Anno Domini.* 528. It is reported of him, that hee kept himselfe unknowne, for the space of three yeares, in a certaine wildernes or desert place. 40. Miles distant from Rome. After that hee builded the Monastery of Cabinum, neare unto Capua, into the which hee received all such Monkes of divers Orders, as hee had found scattered in sundry places, and induced them, as well as hee could, to follow his rule, but much against their wills. Out of this Schoole proceeded infinite Sects and Divisions of Monkes.

---

[1] *Augustian* MS.   [2] F. *Order, I come to the Order of &c.*

For beeing manie and divers, every man retained his old name, or invented unto himselfe a new, yet generally they were all called Benedictines, because they had subjected themselves to his imitation and rule. How they agreed afterwards, I doe not read; but it seemeth, as these old Reluctants decayed and died, the diligence of Benidict, by Pag. 74. continuall urging and following them with his best Counsell and Advise in his life tyme, and by his directions after his death, prevailed by litle and litle, to the closing upp of this scarre. For this Order increased mightily, and in processe of time, by reason of the Monasterie of Floriack in France, [1] propigated his Branches farr and wide in this Kingdome, (as I said before.) For almost all the greatest Abbies of this Land, as Canterbury, Durham, Glacenbury, Yorke, gave nourishment to these plants.

There were three severall Houses of this Order in the University, which were Glocester Colledge or Hall, Durham Colledge, and Canterbury Colledge, all, as I suppose, erected for Novices, for their severall and greater Abbies, as I will declare in their particuler courses. Pag. 75.

Glocester Colledge, or Glocester Hall.

ABOUT the yeare. 1281. a certaine Noble man, called John Gifford, provided a certaine place att Oxford without the walles, and gave possessions sufficient for the sustentation of 13. Monkes, which hee chose out of the Monasterie of Glocester, beeing desirous, that his soule and the soule of Maud de Longespæ his wife, should bee perpetually prayed for by these Religious men professed of the Order of St. Benidict.

This first institution manie other Abbies alsoe of the Benidictine Order did immitate, as it should seeme, which, upon their owne perticuler charges, nourished one or two Monkes out of their severall Monasteries in that place, which, afterwards, when they came to their owne perticuler Churches, should professe good Letters. That this was soe, it maie

---

[1] Sic.

 appeare, partly by those diverse Fashions and Names of buildings, which are yet extant in that Hall, some beeing called Glocester Lodgings, some Westminster Lodgings, some Winchcombe Lodgings, &c. Concerning the first Founder and what hee did, this House had the nature of a Colledge. For hee endowed it with Lands and Possessions, as wee said concerning the other Editions, it referred the nature of an Hall. For the severall Monasteries either allowed some rate and proportion to the Colledge, or defraid, of their owne charge, the expences of their Novices. The most part of the buildings there stand yet. The Chappell onely, and some few other buildings, sustained the fortune of Demolition, when the great Storme of King Henery the 8th. fell upon all Religious places, the Execution whereof upon this House hee staied, because hee intended, as alsoe afterwards hee performed, to allott this House for the ordinarie habitation and dwelling house of the Bishopp of Oxford, which, never-theles, in that long Vacation, that fell out betweene the tyme that Doctor Current and Doctor Underhill were Bishopps, was alienated from that use, and sold to Sir Thomas White, Knight, the Founder of St. John Baptist Colledge, and was by him ordained an Hall for the use and Commoditie of his Colledge.

Canterbury Colledge.

THE same use there was of Canterbury Colledge, and to that end and purpose it was builded by Adam Islipp Arch-bishop of Canterbury, in the Raigne of King Edward the third, *Anno Domini* 1353. for the supplie and service of that famous Monasterie of Ch. Ch. in Canterbury, in the which Church Langfranck, one of his Predecessors, had placed Benidictine Monkes, and from the number of. 30. had ad-vanced them to. 40. Adam Islipp, therefore, beeing borne within three Miles of Oxford, thought it would be a glorious thing, that soe great and ample Foundation should have in it manie men of eminent Note, to justifie the number. To maintaine a few in some Hall or Colledge would not be sufficient. Therefore hee builded this wholl [1] Colledge to be a Schoole and Nurcery thereunto, and endowed it, as with other things, soe with the Impropriations of Pagham and Magfeild in the Countie of Kent. There were in it one Mr. and 13. Monkes, or thereabout (as I suppose.) It stood 'till the generall Suppression of all Monasteries, and then suffered, though not destruction of the Walls and Edifices, yet dissolution of Lands and Society, and standing yet, in a manner wholl, is a part and member of Ch. Ch. att this daie.

Durham Colledge. Pag. 79.

DURHAM Colledge alsoe, both for occasion of building, and immitation of use and service, was erected within few yeares after this, *vizt.* in the tyme of the said King Edward the third, about the yeare. 1370. by Thomas Hatfeild, Bishopp of Durham and Keeper of the King's Great Seale, for the use of the eight Monkes of Durham and 7. Clarkes, by the Prior of Durham and by his direction and arbitrament to be placed there. This Colledge was planted upon an auntient Foundation, *super* [2]* *Canditch, extra* [3] *muros in territorio ubi* Candito. *Monachi studentes* [4] *inhabitabant antea per multos annos,* upon the Towne Ditch, called Canditch, in a place where Monkes had formerly studied and inhabited for manie yeares. In this place Richard Bury, Bishopp of Durham, called [5] *Philobiblos* for his love to Learning, the immeadiate predecessor of Thomas Hatfeild, had formerly builded an Hall, or House, Pag. 80. and indued it with revenues needfull for his Schollars, and had alsoe provided, in a goodly Library, great store of Bookes, for the use of the wholl University, as the said as Jo. Stow Bishop himselfe writeth in his Booke entituled, *Philobiblos,* p. 241. and appointed the Masters of that his Hall to assigne. 5. Schollars for keeping of the said Library.

The generall Fortune of all Monasteries brought a period

---

[1] See my *Apparatus* to Thomas Sprott's *Chronicle*, p. lxv.
[2] Sic.   [3] *Mures* MS.   [4] *Inhabitant* MS.   [5] *Philobilos* MS.

to this Colledge alsoe, yet soe as Sir Thomas Pope, Knight, beeing an Actor in the Tragedy, and haveing a purpose to erect a Colledge, kept the Walls and Buildings safe, and repairing the wants and ruines that were, endowed it with Lands, and by a new Title called it Trinity Colledge.

And thus from the Houses of the Benedictine Order, I come to this of the [1] Cistertian.

The Order of the [2] Cistertian Monkes, and their Houses in the University.

Pag. 81.
THE Order of the [3] Cistertian Monkes tooke their Birth and Originall from the many declinations and corruptions of Manners, that the Benidictine Order had fallen into. For when, in the yeare 1098. a certaine Abbott, called *Robertus Abbas Molinensis*, perceived the Benidictine Order to be extreamely decayed, and falne from the integritie of their first institution, hee did his best endeavour to reduce them to the right course againe, and to that purpose retired him-selfe, with some followers and frinds of his, into Burgundy, to a certaine Wildernes or Solitary place, called *Cistertium*, and there labouring to bring them to their old nature (which they had falne from, hee failed of) did, undoubtedly, adorne them with this new name of [4] Cistertians. These were re-puted the renued and the reformed Benidictines, and, upon that imputation, were esteemed much holier, and, conse-
Pag. 82.
quently, obtained greater priviledges of the Pope and second Lateran Councell, then anie other order, [5] *utpote ferventissimi ad devotionem*, as beeing most earnest men in their devotion. Of this refined and sublimed order, there were in this Towne two perticuler Houses, the first the Abby of North Osney, comonly called Rewley, and the other Barnard Colledge, as presently and breifely you shall understand.

---

[1] *Cistertion* MS.   [2] *Cisterian* MS.   [3] *Cisterian* MS.
[4] *Cisterians* MS.   [5] *Ut potem* MS.

The Abby of North Osney, otherwise called Rewley.

IN the yeare of our Lord. 1281. [1] Edmund, Earle of Cornewall, founded a Monastrey of the [2] Cistertian Order in Oxford, and brought from Thame Monkes of that Fraternitie, whom hee there placed, and, att his first donation, gave unto them the Manner of [3] Erdington, causing Robert Barnehill, then Bishopp of Bath and Wells, and the King's Chancellor, to dedicate the place of this Abbey, which hee did the third Ides of December, in the forenamed yeare, and the same daie laid the Foundation, and called the Church by the name of North Osney. Pag. 83.

This place afterwards (I know not upon what occasion [4]) was better knowne by the name of Rewley, then North Osney, though well enough by both. The number of the Monkes alsoe, I can better deliver by unwritten tradition, then by any written verity that I have scene, that is to saie, by 21. Elme Trees, standing in two Rankes on each side of the way from the outward gate to the dwelling house, and of one Tree planted att the upper end, which, they saie, representeth the Abbatt and his Covent, Capittularly assembled. This house alsoe susteyned the common Calamitie of Henery the Eight his displeasure, and is now a percell of the possession of Ch. Ch. but hath noething of the old Edifices remaineing, save onely a convenient dwelling, with a small portion of ground wherein it standeth. This was, and is the tradition of the people, but the truth is, there were but [5] 12. Cannons, and their [6] Abbotts.

Barnard Colledge. Pag. 84.

THIS Colledge, alsoe, was of the same Order of Cistertians, but, peradventure, called Barnardines, which I doe the rather suppose, because that I find, that St. Bernard, borne in

---

[1] *Edward* MS.   [2] *Cisterian* MS.   [3] Now called *Yarnton.*

[4] Which, however, may be learned from Leland's *Itin.* Vol. II. p. 71.

[5] In p. 71. of the IId. Vol. of Leland's *Itin.* it is noted, that here were an Abbat and fifteen Monkes. As for the Elme Trees here mentioned, there are severall old men now living in Oxford that remember them standing.

[6] Sic.

Burgundy of noble Parentage, did immitate the example and zeale of Robert aforenamed. And as hee, by [1] this endeavour to reforme that Order, had caused them of the Benedictines to be called after the place Cistertians, soe that St. Barnard likewise, by his second and greater endeavour to bring it yet more neare *ad primævum sui nitorem*, caused them of Cistertians to be called, after his private person, Bernardines. For in the yeare. 1113. beeing then about 22. yeares of age, with more then thirty Associates and Companions, hee betooke himselfe into the Wildernes of *Cistertium*, for the same end and purpose, att what tyme one Stephen was Abbott there. Soe that though wee have here three names, Benidictines, Cistertians and Bernardines, yet

Pag. 85.   are wee but one onely Order of Benedictines, revised and sett out in two newer and later Editions. The first whereof gave unto them their life and beeing, the second immunities and priviledges, the third honor and high reputation of holines and puritie of their profession, by reason of [2] the Eminencie and Excellencie, both in vertue and learning, of that Holy man who was their last Reformer. This Foundation was erected by Henry Chichely, Archbishopp of Canterbury, in the daies of King Henery the Sixt (before hee began his other Colledge of All-Soules) *Anno Domini.* 1438. This building, likewise, haveing three sides, after the common Suppression, fully standing, was by King Henery the Eight given unto Ch. Ch. and of the Deane and Cannons there Sir Thomas White, Knight and Alderman of London, did, in the Raigne of Queene Mary, purchase it, and the Grove,

Pag. 86.   upon such occasion, as wee shall relate, when wee come to speake of St. John Baptist Colledge.

Of those severall Fraternities of Friers Mendicants, as have beene heretofore in this Universitie.

HAVEING spoken of these Orders of Monkes, which, under the pretence of Holynes, wonn favour in the World to [3] dispose

---

[1] F. *his.*   [2] Their MS.   [3] [Sic. ? *depose,* or *displace.*]

the Seculars, wee now come to holier men in shew then they were, which though they could not displace the Monkes from their Roomes and Possessions, yet they did disgrace and abate the opinion and estimation of that holynes, which they had assumed, as much, (if not more) then they had donne unto the Secular Preists and Cannons before them.

Although the Orders of Friars Mendicant, or Beging Friers, grew to be almost infinite, and a burden of idle vagrant people, not to be endured in this Realme, yet I doe not ^{Pag. 87.} find, that this Universitie gave entertainement to anie other, then those fower Orders, which were tolerated by the Great Counsell of Lions about the yeare of our Lord. 1273. or 4. holden under Pope Gregory the. 10. which Councell I, therefore, call Great, because there were in it Bishopps. 500. Abbatts. 60. Prelatts. 1000. besides all the principall heads of the Mendicant Friers. In this Councell two things were ordained; First, that noe order of Begging Friers should be allowed, but these 4. onely, *vizt.* the Dominican or Black Preaching Friers, the Mynors of the Order of St. Frances, the Fryers Eremites of the Order of St. Augustin, and the White Friers Carmelites. Of each of these severall Orders there was one House of Fraternity in this Universitie.

The Black Preaching Friers of the Order of St. Dominick. ^{Pag. 88.}

THE Friers of St. Dominick's Order began in the daies of King[1] John and Pope Innocent the third, *Anno Domini* 1205. They had a faier Colledge and Church here in Oxford, in that place which is to this daie called *the Black Friers*, haveing Grand poole on the East side, the Gray Friers on the West, the River of Thames on the South, the Water of Trilmilbo, and the Brewers lane on the North. There House was builded by Isabell Bulbeck, Countesse of Oxford, who was buried there *Anno Domini*. 1245. The mother of this Dominick beeing great with him, dreamed, that shee had in

---

[1] *John John and* MS.

her wombe a wolfe, which had a burning Torch in his mouth. This dreame they of his Order doe greatly advance, and expound to the glory and credit of their Founder. Their profession standeth upon three principall points, which are thus described: *Charitatem habentes, humilitatem servantes, & paupertatem voluntariam possidentes.*

First, to shew that they be men haveing Charitie, keepeing humilitie, and possessing wilfull poverty, their habit and cloathing [1] black, Gowne, Coate, and Cassocke, and Stockings all of the same collour. This Fraternitie was wont much to glory and tryumph of two famous persons buried in their Church: the one Isabell Bulbeck their Founder, of whom wee spake before; the other [2] *Peirse Gaveston, the great Favorite of King Edward the 2ᵈ. who, in his flight to Wallingford Castle, beeing taken by Guy Earle of Warwick, from Dathington, *alias* Dadington, and from thence carried to his Castle in Warwick and there beheaded, was first interred in the Church of this Fraternitie for a time, and from thence afterwards, by the King himselfe, and manie of his Bishopps and Clergie, was [3] from thence solemnely translated to King's Langly in Hartfordshire, and with all Ceremonies, Pomps and Signes of honor, as in a more honorable place, againe buried.

Peirs. [margin note]

Pag. 89. [margin note]

Pag. 90. [margin note]

The Franciscan or Gray Friers, otherwise called Minors or Minorites.

ABOUT the same time that the Dominicans came hither, the Franciscans alsoe arrived, who were called Franciscans of their Patron, Grey Friers of the collour of their habitt, *minores & minimi* of their pretended humilitie. Their Patron *Franciscus* was an Italian of *Assisium*, who died *Anno Domini.* 1227. His Order was confirmed by Pope Honorius the 3ᵈ. *Anno Domini.* 1224. They of this Order have a fable, that Christ and his Saints did stigmatize him with 5. wounds, and thence blasphemously called him, *Typicall Christ.* Though

---

[1] F. *are* vel *is black.*   [2] Sic.   [3] Delenda forsan.

they bee all under one Rule and Clothing, which is a Gowne Pag. 91.
of Grey, and that very course, noe stockings to their leggs,
but a latchett to their shooes, and a hempden coard for their
girdle, yet they are divided into manie sorts and differences.
Some goe on treen-shoes or pattens, some barefoote, some
Observants Regular, some Minors or Minorites; yet they all
follow the Testament of St. Frances, and are alwaies opposite
unto the Dominicans or Black preaching Friers, espetially in
two things. First, concerning Senioritie, which of them should
bee the auntienter. Though this question bee decided very
well by Antonius, (*vizt.*) *quantum ad quandam concessionem
simplicem habitus & modi vivendi quasi permissionem, prius
fuisse institutum Minorum per Innocentium.* 3. In respect
of a certaine simple Graunt both of their habit and manner
of liveing, by waie as it were of permission, the Institution of Pag. 92.
the Friers Minors was first allowed by Innocentius the. 3ᵈ.
but in respect of solemne approbation by Apostolicall Bulls,
authentically written and sealed, the Order of the Dominicans (though confirmed by Honorius the. 3ᵈ. the Successor of
Innocentius) had the priority; yet they remaine not satisfied
with this decision, but continue in their former strife and
contention still. The other point, wherein they differed, was
concerning the conception of the Virgin Mary. For the
Franciscans held, that shee was conceived without originall
sinne.

The Dominicans held the contrary, that shee was conceived
in originall sinne. And Pope Sixtus the 4ᵗʰ. decided the
matter on the Franciscans side, by putting them to silence
upon paine of Excommunication, and besides added a Fes-
tivall daie unto the Calender, which hee called the Concep- Pag. 93.
tion of our Ladie, in remembrance shee was borne without
Originall sinne, which is celebrated upon the 8ᵗʰ. daie of
December. For their House in Oxford, I find noe spetiall
Founder, but onely certaine percells of ground, for the scitua-
tion of their House, given to them by divers speciall persons,
as namely by one Thomas de Walonges, and some others:

and by King Henry the. 3ᵈ. of whom it is recorded in the
Tower of London, that in December. 22. *Anno Domini.* 1244.
and in the 29ᵗʰ. yeare of his Raigne, hee did, by his Letters
[1] Patens, give them leave, (*vizt.* the Franciscan Friers) to
enclose a place in Oxford from Water gate under the Walls
of the Cittie, to another gate there in the Wall Westward,
for their habitation in Saint Ebb's Parish: which place, hee
saith, hee purchased of one Henery the sonne of Symeon,
a Jew as is probable. Hereby it doth appeare, that their
habitation was in the backside of Saint Ebb's Church Westward, the Entry whereinto was att Little-gate *alias* Water
gate. They had their faire and convenient Lodgings, and
alsoe a decent Church. The Roome was farther enlarged
with the West end of that Ile, wherein the Colledge of the
Dominican Preaching Friers stood, with a litle Bridge to
passe over [2] Trilmilbo Streame to it. This percell of Ground
they used as a Walke or Grove for their Recreation. They
were all honored with two great Prerogatives, *vizt.* the bookes
of that most learned and worthy Prelate Robert Grosthead
Bishop of Lincolne, who, while hee lived, gave them to this
Fraternitie. *Anno Domini.* 1253. *Anno* 38°. of King Henery
the. 3ᵈ. his Raigne; the other, of the body of that most
learned Clarke Roger Bacon, an English man, borne in the
Countie of Dorsetshire, and most deservedly created Doctor
of Divinitie in France, who was buried in their Church, as
Johannes Rossius testifieth.

Pag. 94.

Pag. 95.

The Augustin Friers Eremites.

THERE be manie Relations concerning the [3] Order and
Author of this Order. If you will beleave themselves, they
come immeadiately from St. Augustin, that great Bishopp of
Hippo; but wee have partly heretofore shewed this to be
otherwise, and Sabellicus in his. 7. *Ennedde, lib.* 9. Vola-
teranus, Polidorus Virgilius, and diverse others do more fully

---

¹ Sic.   ² *Trilmalbo* MS.   ³ Sic, cum lineola in MS.

refute it. That storie that I think best of them to bee allowed of, is this, (*vizt.*) that Innocentius the 4th. considering that there were divers Eremites wandring abroad in desarts and solitary places, which were not all of one Order and Name, and that they might be profitable for the advancement of his Roman Sea, hee had a purpose to reduce them all into one Companie, and soe ordered that they should all live Pag. 96. under one Prior generall, and all compose themselves to the Rule of St. Augustin, and should all use one habit and forme of Apparrell, one office, and the same institutions, and, that this Order might prosper more effectually, hee appointed one of his Cardinalls to be the Provost and cheife Provisor of this Order. But while hee was busy hereabout, hee died and could not bring his purpose to effect. They invented, there-fore, that St. Augustin, beeing desirous to have an Order of his name, to flourish here upon Earth, appeared to Alexander the 4th. Successor to this said Innocentius, in a Vision, wherein hee presented himselfe, *grandem quidem capite, sed membris exilem*, that is, with a great head, the rest of his parts and members very small; by which Vision the Pope was admonished to perfect the project, which Innocentius had intended. For all the Friers Ermites, though they were Pag. 97. called formerly by divers names, hee brought into one Com-panie, and comaunded that they should stile themselves by noe other title, but this, *vizt. Fratres ordinis Erimitarum Sti. Augustini*: Brethren Eremites of the Order of St. Augustin.

In this Universitie in the Raigne of Henery [1] the 3^d. prin-cipally by his guift and authority, they were planted in that place, which of them was called the Augustin Friers, and where now Waddam Colledge standeth, as it maie appeare out of this Deed, extracted out of a Manuscript of Mr. Denham's of Borstoll in these words: *Notum sit vestris reverentiis*, &c. Bee it knowne unto your Worshipps, that the most excellent King Henry the 3^d. for his soules health,

---

[1] *The 8th.* MS.

Pag. 98.

and att the request of John Handlow of Borstoll, Knight, purchased certaine percells of Land of divers persons in the Suburbs of Oxford, which lieth over against the posterne of the Citty, which is called Smith gate; which percell of Ground the said King, upon the instance of the said Knight, gave to the said Friers Eremites of St. Augustine, and to their Successors for ever, to the end that they might build there a Church, and other Houses of necessarie use, for the Commodity of the said Brethren. And, therefore, principally the King, and after him the honorable Knight John Handlow were, almost, reputed Founders of this Fraternitie. These Augustine Friers were great Disputers, and, by their diligence att home in their owne house, brought manie of the University to come and heare their Disputations, whereupon grew those Disputations which wee call the Augustins, and were

Pag. 99.

there first begunn, and by the Authority of the University enjoyned to bee performed by all Graduats before they should be created Masters. There the Bachelors disputed first in the old Logick, secondly in the new, and thirdly in Philosophie. These Disputations afterwards, by reason of a plague that happened in the Augustines, were translated to St. Marie's, where they continued ever since.

The habit of this Order is black. Of the same colour is their Cowle from the Head to the Shoulders; under that a litle white Coate, with a white List. Their Girdle is of Leather, button'd with a Button of Oxhorne. This apparrell was enjoyned them by Alexander the 4th. and therefore came not from St. Augustine, as maie appeare by this old ensueing Distick :

Mendici fratres induti vestibus atris :
Augustinus ego nomen habere nego.

Pag. 100.

'I Augustine beare noe name of that rude pack
Of begging Fryers, which cloathed are in black.'

The Carmelite Friers, commonly called the White Friers.

THESE Friers tooke their name of White from their Habit, which, att the first Institution, was of divers colours, white

and edged about with red, such (as they say) Elias the
Prophett was wont to weare; which (as I understand) was
that kind of habit, that Albertus the Patriark of Constantinople, *Anno Domini.* 1204. gave them, *vizt. Cappam superiorem ex serico*, &c. their uppermost Capp or Cowle of silke,
adorned with certaine long white stricks peckled grey, which
they alsoe thought to have beene after the fashion of Elias.
But afterward Honorius the 4th. Pope, changed that Habit, as
not fitting for Religious men, and, instead of their various Pag. 101.
collours, enjoyned them to weare white onely, soe as their
Apparrell might be sutable and agreeable to virginitie, and
thereupon caused them to be called the Brothers of the
Virgin Mary, which [1] title liked themselves soe well, that
they procured of Pope Urbane the. 6. [2] three yeares pardon
for all such as would soe call them. But certaine merry
fellowes (seeing [3] their vanitie, and knowing how litle they
were a kin to Mary the blessed Virgin) called them Brothers
of Mary Egiptiall the Harlott, whereat the Pope himselfe Lambert
was [4] so sorely offended, that hee plainely pronounced them pag. 208.
Heritickes for their labour.   in Neue-
                                                               den.

They were alsoe called Carmelites, from the Mount Carmell
in Palestina, according to that verse in Baptista Mantuan one
of that order:

Mons Carmelus ubi gentis cunabula nostræ.

And in that Mount neare unto the Well of Elias the Prophett, Pag. 102.
whom they imitated to betoken their holines. And because
there was, neare unto the Well of Elias, a litle Chappell of
our Lady, they built thereby their first Monasterie. Upon
which occasion they were alsoe called the Monkes Carmelites
of the Virgin Mary, as Polidor Virgill testifyeth. They came
into England *Anno Domini.* 1240. in the Raigne of King
Henery the third, and had their first Harbor at Newenden
in Kent. They were placed in Oxford in the tyme of
Edward the second, *Anno Domini*, 1313. in that Palace,

---

[1] *Litle* MS.   [2] Deest *three* in MS.
[3] *The vanitie* MS.   [4] Deest *so* in MS.

which King Henry the first had builded, and called by the name of Beamonts, which King Edward gave unto them upon this occasion. In the seventh yeare of his Raigne hee fought a sore Batle in Scotland, neare Strivelin, not farr from [1]*Buanack borne, where manic of his Nobles were overthrowne. But hee himselfe with his Bishopps and Hugh Spencer escaping by Flight, vowed to God, that hee would build unto the poore Carmelite Friers an House, in the which hee would place. 24. Brethren, to be Students in Divinity, which hee afterward did in Oxford, by converting the forenamed Beamounts from a King's Palace, [2]into an habitation for Friers Carmelites. This Order procured themselves admiration and opinion above all the Mendicants or Begging Friers, and continued untill the great Destruction, when they suffered the common Calamitie of all other Orders.

** Baunack.*

Pag. 103.

*Stow. p.
217, col. 1.
Cambd.
Brit. pag.
269.*

The Beaumonts.

By this last Narration of the Carmelites, it doth appeare, that the King alsoe himselfe had a Palace, or Habitation, in Oxford called *the Beamounts*, which was scituated betweene Glocester Hall, and the opposite parte of St. Giles Parish, whereof part was standing, untill such time as St. John Baptist Colledge translated the Stone and Timber for the building of their Library, in the yeare of the Raigne of Queene Elizabeth   and of our Lord[3].

Pag. 104.

Thus have wee performed the first parte of our Project, and declared all such Houses and Foundations, as have beene heretofore and are not now in this Universitie, I meane are not now in those Titles and Endowments, as they then were, though since, by the benevolence of worthy Founders, they are standing and continuing, yet under other Names : 6. of the same. 13. *vizt.* Ch. Ch. Canterbury Colledge, St. John Baptist, Trinitie Colledge, Glocester Hall and Watham Col-

---

[1] Sic.   [2] *Into an into an habitation* MS.

[3] Supple 1596. qui quidem fuit partim 38, partim 39. Reginæ Elizabethæ.

ledge, as hath beene heretofore alreadie touched, and shall bee hereafter more fully declared, when wee come to our third part, which concerneth the Colledges standing and flourishing now. In the meane season wee will proceed unto our second Part, and, by a cursorie view or perambulation, Pag. 105. wee'll deliver what wee find worthy of observation, spetially belonging unto Antiquitie, in every small Streete and Suburbs of this Citty. And first, to begin our entrance into the Citty, wee'll compose our selves, as comeing from Abingdon, and beeing arrived att the Gate of [1] Balywood, which is next to Oxford, because that Gate is the outmost Bounds of our Limitts and Jurisdiction Southward, wee will take a view of the next adjacent Villages on both sides, and posting on our waie towards Oxford, wee will observe such things as in each of them shall bee worth observation.

The first that occurreth to our eies from this place, is an House upon the left hand called [2] Childswell in the ascent of an Hill where old traditions saie was sometymes a Religious Chappell neare unto a Well, which Well, by the Holynes of the Chaplaines successively serving there, had a vertue to make Women that were barren to bring forth Children, and Pag. 106. soe gave name to that Place. Now leaveing Hincksey on the left Hand, cast your Eie downeward over the Water, and you shall see a Towne, on the opposite side, called Ifley, knowne espetially by that title, that the Parsonage thereof is the peculiar Corps of the Archdeaconry of Oxford. And now beeing come to the descent of the Hill, and entered into the [3] Causy, it will not bee amisse to know upon what ground wee goe. For it is not naturall Ground, but forc'd and made Ground, and called (as wee said before) a Cawsie, haveing in it above 40. Arches of Stone, I will not saie first founded, but very well repaired and restored by the charge of Doctor John

---

[1] Vulgo, *Bagley-wood.*

[2] See what I have said about this Place in p. 134 of the Vth. Vol. of Leland's *Itinerary.* There is also a hint about it in p. 188 of the VI. Vol. of Leland's *Collectanea.*

[3] *Causy it, it will* MS.

Claymond the first President of C.C.C. according to that which [1] <u>Sheprene</u> speaketh of him writing his life:

Egrederis portam, quæ recta vergit ad Austrum :
Clamondi[2] munis compita strata vides.

Betweene the foresaid Towne of Ifely and [3] Kennington, the River is very broad and shallow, and maketh that famous Ford, which giveth name unto the Citty, which, as the Historie of Oxford saith, *à quodam vado vicino populus Saxonicus nominavit Oxenford, & ad locum Studii prælegit* : The Saxons from a certaine Ford neare unto the Towne named Oxenford, and appointed it for a Place of Study. If any man require auntienter names; it was called Caer Mempric, Caer Vortigerne, [4] Rydychen, Bellesitum, Caer [5] Bosta, &c. in the Brittaine time, as Johannes Rossius testifieth. Passing along the Cawsy, wee see noething, on either hand, saveing onely spatious Meadowes, devided by the severall Streames of the River, which runn under the forenamed Arches, and when wee [6] come somewhat neare the Towne, two severall Farmes, the one on the left Hand belonging unto Brasennose, the other on the right belonging unto University Colledge, and betweene both a litle House, called the Archdeacon of Barksheire his Court; and, lastly, att the Entrance into the Towne, that Tower which standeth upon the Bridge, like a Pharos or Watch Tower, is [7] commonly called by the name of Frier Bacon's Study, not that it was soe indeed, neither can I learne anic other reason of that name ascribed thereunto, then what is delivered by old Tradition, *vizt.* that that beeing a remote place, and farr enough from Companie, Fryer *Bacon (knowne to bee a great Astronomer) did, perhapps, sometymes [8] use, in the night season, to ascend thither to take

[1] Sic, cum lincola. Lege, *Sheprcve.*

[2] F. *nummis.* [The MS. of Shepreve has *Claymondi nummis.*]

[3] *Kennington* MS.

[4] *Rydychen* MS. Vide Joan. Rossum de Regib. Angl. à nobis editum, p. 21.

[5] Vel potius *Bossa.* Vide J. Rossum, loc. cit.

[6] *Came* MS.

[7] *Common called* MS.

[8] *Use to, in the night season, to ascend* MS.

the Altitude and Distance of the Starrs. This maie bee the more likely, because hee was a Franciscan Frier, and his Pag. 109. Chamber not farr of, from whence commeing over the great Bridge wee passe by Houses on each side, 'till wee come to a litle Bridge, which is the limitt, distinguishing Oxfordsheire from Barksheire, haveing a small Streame running under it into the water of Trilmilbo, whose Course before of old was not to fall into Isis, as now it doth, but into [1] Charuell through the midst of Ch. Ch. Meadow, which though it be now one, yet, in former tymes, was two, the farther part, next unto Isis, belonging unto the Citty of Oxford, and called the Towne Meade, and the higher parte, next to Friswide's, belonging now to Ch. Ch. and of old called Friswide's Meade, but, in the daies of King Edward the. 6th. the Deane and Chapter, haveing then an annuall Markett, or Fare, usually kept about St. Friswide's daie in the Quadrangle, and on that Foundation did exchange it with the Towne, for their parte of the foresaid Meadow, and daming upp the old Channell Pag. 110. that ran into [2] Charwell, [3] continuated the two Meadowes into one. In memory whereof, there are yet, att this daie, certaine Meere Stones sett [4] in a Meadow, according to the course of the Streame, [5] beeing yet to be perceived is to this daie called by the name of Sherelake. From this litle Bridge wee come into the Suburbs of Oxford, commonly called Grampoole, not that it is soe now, but that it was soe heretofore, before the Ground was drayned, by the division of Trilmilbo Streame into. 2. the new Course running behind the [6] Houses of this Streete on the West side, and parting them from the Preach-ing Friers, 'till it come to the forementioned Bridge, and the old Streame houlding his Course by Ch. Ch. Saw Pitt, and behind the Houses of the East side of the same Streete, and soe meeting with his Fellow runn both togeather into Isis over the old Streame. There is one other Bridge, before wee Pag. 111.

---

[1] *Charnell* MS.

[2] *Carnwell* MS.

[3] Sic.

[4] Sic. F. *in the Meadow.*

[5] Sic. F. *which being.*

[6] *House* MS.

come into the Citty, which runneth by the Bishopp of Oxford
his House, from whence wee come from the South gate of
the Citty, the Cardinall's building lying on the East side of
the Streete, and the Almes House on the West, where it is
to bee observed, that, betweene those 2. Corners of each side,
there stood, within these few yeares, an old auntient Gate of
Stone, which though now wanting, and cleane taken away,
yet is therefore to be remembred, because it was the South
Gate of the Citty, continuing on the Wall onwards, and there
on a faier Stone were quartered the Armes of England and
France in one Scutchion, the Armes of England beeing graven
in the former and upper place, and those of France in the
nether, contrarie to all that I, heretofore, have seene, which
seemeth to mee worthy to be remembred for that it gave
honor and precedencie to our Nation, and was a Monument
not elce where to be found.   Proceeding, therefore, from this
Gate onwards to Borcado (omitting to speake of the [1] *Lands
and Buildings of both sides) wee find on the waie, on the
right Hand, in the Fish Markett, first the two Towne Halls,
the upper and the lower, auntient both and serving, att the
Quarter Sessions, for the meeting of the Justices of the
[2] Countrey, and ordinarie Affaires of the Citty.   From hence
wee goe upp to Carefax, or Quarvex (soe called, because
quatuor in ventos ibi se via fundit cunti) upon the highest
part whereof standeth a faier Conduit, the late and worthy
worke of Mr. Otho Nicholson, a Gent. of London, who, for
the publike good both of the Universitie and Citty, builded
the same, every Colledge from thence haveing a Cock to their
Kitchins, and the wholl Towne recourse thereunto for their
Water.   On the left hand, under the East end of St. Martin's
Church, yee see that Seate, which is called Pennelesse Bench,
builded by the Cittie, aswell for their solace and prospect
every waie, as for the conveniencie of the Market Women in
the tyme of Raine; and soe leaveing the Innes and Tenements on both sides, wee come to the Corne Markett, which

Pag. 112.

* Lanes.

Pag. 113.

---

[1] Sic.   [2] F. *County*.

Fabrick Doctor Claymond, the first President of C. C. C. (of
whom wee spake before) builded att his owne charge, and
covered it with Lead,

Vt possit[1] circum saccus habere locum.

Hence wee passe on to the North Gate called Bocardo,
famous, as for Antiquity, soe for imprisonment of Thomas
Cranmer, Archbishopp of Canterbury, Doctor Ridley Bishopp
of London, and old Father Latimer sometimes Bishopp of
Worcester, in the daies of Queene Mary, all of them burnt
in the Towne Ditch, over against Baliell Colledge, and not Pag. 114.
farr from this Prison. And here wee will make staie from
proceeding further, 'till wee goe back againe, and take a view
of those severall Lanes and Streets, which, on the West
side, open themselves towards the West Gate of the Cittie.
[2] Comeing, therefore, out of Grandpoole, the first Lane Westward is that which is called Brewers Streete, and hath
noething memorable in it, but onely that it leadeth towards
the Preaching Friers over the Streame on the left, and to the
Grey Friers directly goeing on, hard by Litle-gate, of both
which wee have alreadie spoken. From hence wee passe
backwards againe to the Almes House (sometyme called the
Tenement of   ) right over against Ch. Ch. Pag. 115.
great Gate, where wee see, on our right hand, the Church of
St. Aldate, *alias* Eldad, a Saint not commonly knowne, but
worthy to be remembred in this place, both for the Antiquitie
of the Church, and the worth of him, to whose Name it is
dedicated. The Church is as auntient as the Saxons tyme, and
Aldate, or Eldad, whose Name it beareth, was, in those daies,
Bishopp of Gloucester, of whom this ensueing Storie is related.

Att what time Aurelius Ambrosius, King of the Brittaines, Speed 269.
had opposed himselfe in a great Battaile against Hengist at col. 1.
Massebell, beyond Humber in Yorkshire (for Horsa, the
Brother and Companion of Hengist, had formerly beene

---

[1] *Sircum* MS. [Shepreve's MS. has *siccum.*]

[2] *Comeing therefore out of Grandpoole the first Lane Westward of the Cittie
Comeing therefore out of Grandpoole the first Lane Westward* &c. MS.

Stow pag. 52.

Speed pag. 207. Pag. 116.

slayne att Alford in Kent by Catagerne, Brother to Vortimer, immeadiate Predecessor unto Aurelius, in which Combate Catagerne himselfe died alsoe) and in that feight had taken him Prisoner, the King and his Nobles assembled themselves in Gloucester, to consult what was to bee donne with their Prisoner. Among other of the Nobilitie, there were, att that tyme, of the Cittie of Glocester three noble and renowned Personages, Edell the Earle, Eldad the Bishopp, and Eldo the Maior or cheife Governor there att that time, all of them present att the Consultation; and when the greater parte of the Companie seemed to favour the life of Hengist, Eldad the Bishopp spake to this purpose, that his life was, by noe meanes, to be spared, both because hee had broken his faith and promisse unto the Brittaines, (for beeing sent for to aid them, hee sett himselfe, and all his Forces to their utter Destruction :) and his Daughter Rowena, beeing now growen potent in the Land, did many exceeding

Pag. 117.

ill Offices unto the State, esptially in beeing the cause of Vortimer's death. And, therefore, there was noe more mercy to be shewed towards him, then God comaunded to be shewed unto Agag, the King of the Amalekites, whom when Saul spared, Samuell the Prophett tooke and hewed in peeces, before the wholl Companie of the Israelites. This did hee desire to bee executed and performed upon Hengist, and if there were noe man found willing to doe the Execution, hee would, in that point, follow Samuell, and become the Exe-cutioner himselfe. This was spoken with such Gravitie and Courage, that hee moved all the Companie to be of his opinion, and, by the common sentence of all that were present, the Prisoner was committed unto Eldo the Maior, and hee leading him out of the Cittie, to the place of Execution, there

Pag. 118.

putt him to death. This was the Saint in whose name the Church was dedicated. In this Church there is a Chappell of newer building then it selfe, but the Founder or Builder thereof I doe not find. It is peculier and propper to Broad-gates. where they daily meete for the celebration of Divine

Service. There is in this Chappell a Tomb of Alabaster, under which is entombed the bodie of John Noble Doctor of the Civill Law, and in his time Principall of Broadgates, and Officiall to the Archdeacon of Berkshire.

On the left hand standeth the old and auntient Hall Broadgates, now weary of it's former name, and stiled by the title of Pembroke Colledge by King James, not long before his death. From thence proceeding further, there is another Hall called Beefe Hall, not inhabited with anie Schollars, but become the Tenement of some private person. This Lane Pag. 119. alsoe leadeth downe to Litle-gate, and both the forenamed Friers on the left hand, and to St. Ebb's Church Corner on the right, where standing wee see backwards towards Ch. Ch. Penny Farthing Streete, on the left hand the West gate of the Citty, leading downe to St. Thomas Parish, and before us, on both sides, the Litle Baylie, and St. Peter's Church in the Great Bayly. This St. Ebba, of whom the Church is named, was daughter to Etheldred, 7th. King of Northumber- Vide land, and Acta the daughter of King Ella. Shee was reputed Cambd. 606. for a Saint, and, for that cause, bare the Dedication of this Ebba cla- ruit an. sal. Church. Shee was alsoe Abbesse of Coddingham Abby, and 630. had under her Government and Education Ethelrid, or Audrid, daughter of Anna, King of the East Angles, which alsoe was canonized for a Saint, and building the Abby of Ely, became the first Abbesse of that Church. This memorable thing is Pag. 120. related of Ebba, that, to avoid the lust and fury of the Danes (who spared noe Religious persons, or places where they came) cutt of her owne Nose and upper Lipp, as alsoe did all the Nunnes under her charge, least the baite of their Beauties should prove the bane of their Honors and Honestie.

From thence goeing onward to St. Peter's, wee goe through the Litle Baylie to the Great Baylie, wherein that Church standeth, of which Saint wee need speake [1] noething, because hee is sufficiently knowne by the Scripture. In this place alsoe wee have another [2] quadrapartite waie, where, on the

---

[1] *Noething of because* MS.   [2] Sic.

left hand, wee may diserne the entrance into the Castle of St. George. And a litle beyond that, the West gate of the Cittie, which before wee have discryed. From St. Ebb's Church directly before us looking towards Bocardo, wee see on our right hand those poore Tenements, called the Seaven deadly Sinns, and the Back sides of St. Marie's Colledge, and those Houses which are in the Corne Markett; on the left, the Hall called New Inn, with poore Tenements and Gardens till you come to Bocardo; on our right hand the Shambles or Bucherrow in the midst of the Streete, from whence wee maie easily diserne the corner of St. Martin's Church, and the Conduit of Carefax whereof wee spake before. There is then noe difficultie here, but onely why these two Streets are called the Baylies, and what kind of Saint, St. Martin was. Of the first I can give you noe other answeare, but conjecture, that as in London the Old and Litle Bailies were soe called, because there were kept the Sessions Court of the Chamberlane of London, soe, peradventure, here, in former tymes, some like Courts might have beene held. Concerning St. Martin, what kind of St. hee was, I answeare, hee was Bishopp of Towers in France, and died about the yeare. 397. Hee had, in his younger yeares, beene a Souldier, in his midle age did manie great and wonderfull workes, and haveing lived Bishopp. 36. yeares, died in the. 81. yeare of his age. And here wee end our Survey of the West part of the Cittie within the Walls. And now wee will take a view of the Westerne and Northerne Suburbs, and after that returne to the Easterne parts within the Walls, and Suburbs alsoe without the Walls of this Cittie.

In the Westerne Suburbs, therefore, of this Cittie wee find litle more worthie observation, then those Places whereof wee have alreadie spoken, I meane the Castle of St. George, the Abby of South Osney, the Abby of [1] North Osney, the Parish Church of St. Nicholas, and Glocester Hall. The onely thing here to be enquired is, what Saints St. George

Pag. 121.

Pag. 122.

Pag. 123.

[1] *West Osney* MS.

and St. Nicholas [1]were.   And, first, for St. George, hee was
a Military and a Martiall St. and *in sortitione Gentium*, when
all Countries cast lotts what peculiar Saint every one should
have to it selfe, it fell out, that as St. Dennis happened to the
French, St. James to the Spaniard, St. Patrick to the Irish
people, St. David to the Welch, St. Andrew to the Scotts,
St. Anthony to the Italian, St. Marke to the Venetian, soe
St. George happened to the English : but *quo jure*, and how
wee maie deduce our title and claime to him, I leave that to
men more skilfull and studious of those things.   All that
I can saie is, that hee delivered a King's Daughter from a
Dragon neare to the Citty of Lysia, when shee was ready Pag. 124.
to be devoured, as *Petrus de* [2]*Natalibus* reporteth in his
Legend, and that hee suffered Martirdome att Militena under
Decianus the President in the persecution of Dioclesian, and
that the Calender doth assigne unto him the 23th. of Aprill.
Now whether his Historie, as alsoe that of St. Sebastian, and
Christopher, and others, maie be allegorized, and made Tipes
and Emblemes of Religion, St. George (as Mr. Spencer
maketh him) of Husbandry, St. Christopher of a Ferryman,
St. [3]Sebastian of Imperiall State, *&c*.   I will not busie my
selfe to enquire, onely hee grew famous here in England,
principallie and espetiallie att such tyme as King Edward
the. 3. instituted the most noble Order of the Garter, and
dedicated that most beautifull Chappell att Windsor in his
name.   [4]Secondly, for St. Nicholas, hee was an Ecclesiasticall Pag. 125.
Saint, and Bishopp of Mira in Licia.   The most famous thing
that I read of him is, his liberalitie towards a certaine noble
Cittizen, falne to decay.   Hee being come to that want and
miserie, that hee [5]intends to prostitute his. 3. Daughters,
Nicholas hearing of it, to prevent the mischeife, went privily
in the night, and conveyed a bagg of Gold into his House,
wherewith the Cittizen married his eldest Daughter.   The
like hee did the second night, and therewith his second

---

[1] *Was* MS.   [2] *Natilibus* MS.   [3] *Sabastian* MS.
          [4] *Second* MS.   [5] Sic.

Daughter was bestowed in Marriage. The third tyme doeing the like, the Citizen, beeing desirous to know his Benefactor, of purpose watched to see if hee could find him, and following him fell at his feete, and thanked him, whom hee raised from the ground, and charged him never to reveale what was donne, nor who hee was. This Saint after hee had lived prosperously and religiously manie yeares, [1] hee *Anno Domini.*

Pag. 126. 342. and was buried in his owne Citty. This was the Saint that gave name to this Church, although both the Church and the Parish to this daie are more usually called by the name of St. Thomas then St. Nicholas, the reason whereof (as I have heard of auntient men) is, that att what tyme King Stephen besciged the Castle, the Parishioners were invited by the Monkes of Osney to their Church, alleadging, that the middle Isle of that Church was called St. Thomas Ile, and was, indeed, a Parish Church, and, therefore, they might there lawfully celebrate Divine Service, which they did, while their own Church was building, the custome whereof hath soe beene confirmed ever since from the Fathers to their Children, that they will willingly acknowledge noe other name. If this onely thing had beene but remembred and alleadged att the generall Destruction of Monasteries, Osney Abby might have beene preserved standing unto this daie. From hence wee

Pag. 127. maie see on our left hand a litle Village called *Hincksey Laurentii,* from whence Mr. Nicholson deduced the Springs of his Conduit, which now serves both the Universitie and the Cittie. On the right hand you may discerne another litle Village, called [2] Binsey, and [3] att the furthest end of the Cawsy a third, called Botley, which is the utmost limitt of the Universitie's Jurisdiction.

Returning backward to the High Bridge, wee see on our left hand Glocester Hall, and the ruines of the Beamonts *alias*

---

[1] F. *died* vel *hee died anno* &c.

[2] I have published a Draught of the small, but ancient Church or Chapell of Binsey, in p. 779 of my Ed. of Guilielmus Neubrigensis.

[3] *Att furthest* MS.

Carmelite Friers, whereof wee spake before. [1] Then passing
onwards, wee come to the Parish Church of Mary Magdalen,
which appeareth to be more auntient then the Castle, because
it is said in the Ledger Booke of Osney Abby, that Robert
Doily the Elder, and Roger Ivie his sworne Brother, gave
this Church, *cum tribus hidis terræ in Walton, & [2]*patris* * Pratis.
& decimis eidem Ecclesiæ pertinentibus, to the Church of
St. George in the Castle and to the Cannons Seculer serving
God. Thence goeing upp the Streete, wee discover, on the Pag. 128.
right hand, Barnard Colledge, now called St. John's, as wee
said before, and directly before us, att the furthest end of the
Streete, the Parish Church of St. Giles, which alsoe is exceeding auntient, as haveing, sometymes, beene the principall
Church for the Universitie, as Rossius speaketh in these
words: *Ecclesia Sti. Egidii, tum sub nomine alterius Sti.
dedicata, erat locus creationis Graduatorum, sicut hodie est
Ecclesia Sanctæ Mariæ*: this Church of St. Giles, then dedicated in the name of some other Saint, was the Place where
the Graduates were created, as St. Marie's is now. This
Giles was an holy man, borne att Athens in Greece of
Princely Progeny, and haveing donne manie good deeds
among the impotent People there, gave all that ever hee
had unto the poore, and, desiring to see other Countries,
came by Shipp unto that part of France, where [3] Rhodanus
falleth into the Sea. After conference had with Veredemius,
a Religious Hermit, hee betooke himselfe into the Wildernes Pag. 129.
of Septimania, intending to lead a retired and solitarie life,
where wanting necessaries, the story saith, that hee was fedd
by an Hind for manie daies, and with his holy prayers
defended that his Nurse from the fury of Doggs and Hunters
that chased her, which Miracle beeing knowne unto the King,
hee much honored the Man, and builded him a Monasterie,
and made him Abbott thereof. Hee flourished in the tyme
of Charles the Emperor, about the yeare. 700. and his daie

---

[1] *The passing* MS.   [2] Sic, cum *pratis* in margine.
[3] *Rhodamus* MS.

is Registred to be the first of September. His Church, in what Towne soever it is, is, commonly, placed att the uttermost end thereof, because hee shunned the fame of Men, and did his best and greatest workes upon lame and diseased Persons. Hence, according to our former use, wee must passe to the furthest limitt of our Universitie Northward, which extendeth it selfe beyond Wolvercott, even unto the Crosse standing upon Godstow Bridge, att the very doore of that Monasterie: and beeing now soe neare, it will not be amisse to enter in, and take some litle view thereof.

Pag. 130.

This Monastery [1] of Godstow was builded by the Lady Ida, a rich Widow of the worthiest blood of this Land. Shee, after the death of her Husband Sir William Lanceline, had a desire to come to [2] *Binslye neare Oxford, wher shee had a Vision to build an Abby for Nunns there, where from hence shee discerned a light Fier to appeare. This Fier appeared in that Place, which is Godstow now. There shee builded a Nunnery for herselfe and. 24. Ladies. Shee became the first Abbesse herselfe, in the tyme of Henry the first, King of England. Shee had 2. daughters, Himme the eldest, who was Prioresse of the House, and Anis her second daughter, the second Prioresse. The Church was dedicated, in the fowerth yeare of King Stephen, by Alexander Bishopp of Lincolne, *Anno Domini.* 1138. the King and Queene beeing present. King John in his tyme repayred it, and encreased it with a yearely Revenue, to that end and purpose, that those holy Nunns should pray for the soules of Henry the second his Father, and Rosamunda his Concubine, for such were Mens perswasions then. This Rosamunda was buried there, with this ryming Epitaph:

** Binsey.*

Pag. 131.

[1]. See what I have said about the Nunnery of Godstow in p. 74 of the II. Vol. of Leland's *Itinerary*, and in a Discourse, that I have printed in p. 730 of my Ed. of Guilielmus Neubrigensis, entit. *A Discourse about fair Rosamund and the Nunnery of Godstowe, with occasional Notes about Binsey: written in the year* 1718. In which Discourse is, likewise, inserted, *A Prospect of the Ruines of Godstowe, taken in the year* 1718.

[2] Sic.

Hic jacet in tumba Rosa mundi, non Rosa munda:
Non redolet, sed olet, quæ redolere solet.

Cambd.
p. 266.

' Within this Tombe lies Rosamond the faire,
  Rose of the World: but now an uncleane Rose:
  Shee yeilded once a sweete and pleasant Ayre;
  Yet now (alas!) offensive to the Nose.'

And now returne wee back againe to the North gate, from whence, on the left hand, wee first descry Balioll, and Trinitie Colledge, sometymes called Durham Colledge, as wee said before. On the right hand wee see the Cittie Wall, and some [1] Tokens of that Ditch, wherein the Bishopps were burned. The Ditch is called [2] Candich, because the reflex of the Water against the Wall seemes to resemble a certaine kind of shineing whitenes to the eies of the Beholders. This Suburb is long, and reacheth from Bocardo unto Holywell Parish. There is noething in it greatly worthy to be remembred for Antiquitie, but onely on the right hand that old round Building of Stone att Smithgate, which is said sometimes to have beene a Synagogue of the Jewes, inhabiting in or about the Citty. This is the common received opinion; but I have understood since, that it was a private Oratory, built by a certaine Ladie, and dedicated by the name of St. Margarett's [3] Chappell. And unto this place the Ditch is altogeather damn'd upp with Rubbish and small Cottages builded thereon, and on the left hand the Augustine Friers, where now Wadham Colledge standeth, haveing yet left behind them a memorie of the Augustine Disputations, begunn first there, and, upon occasion of a Plague, removed to St. Marie's, as wee said before. Nothing else is to be seene in this Streete, but onely the opposite Walles, enclosing Wadham Colledge Grove on the one side, and the Groves of Trinitie Colledge and St. John's on the other. The rest of the Ditch hath yet Water standing in it under the Towne Wall, enclos-

Pag. 132.

Pag. 133.

---

[1] *Token* MS.

[2] See what I have said about *Candida Fossa*, or *Canditch*, in § 17 of my Preface to *A Collection of curious Discourses, written by eminent Antiquaries upon several Heads in our English Antiquities.*

[3] It is commonly called *The Virgin Chapel.* See § 6 of my *Occasional Remarks* at the end of *Roper's Life of Sir Thomas More.*

ing on the one side New Colledge, and on the other Tenements leading to Holywell Church, which Church is consecrated by the name of St. Crosse, and is a Chappell[1] of Ease,
as is alsoe the Church of Woolvercott, unto the Parish of
St. Peter's in the East. For though the wholl Suburbs beare
the name of Holiwell, from a certaine Well att the East end
thereof, yet the Church is dedicated to the Holy Crosse.
Now you must understand, that in our Calender there are
two daies devoted unto this[2] *Holy-wood, the first called the
invention of the Crosse, and celebrated the 5. Nones — or 3.
daie of May, the 2. called the Exaltation of the Crosse, kept
holly the. 18. [3]Callends, or 14. daie of September. Now
because I know not which of these two daies is intended
to this Church, you shall take a breife History of them both.
For the Crosse is reputed one and the same, though the
Attributes of inventing and exalting be divers.

First, for the Invention, or finding out of the Crosse, was
the labour of Helena the Empresse, an English Woman, and
-Mother to Constantine the Great. Shee, upon an holy zeale,
made a Journey from Constantinople to Hierusalem, to seeke
out this holy Tree, and haveing digged out of the rubble
in Mount Calvery, neare unto the place where Christ was
Crucified, tooke it out of the dust, and caused it to be cutt
in two equall Parts; the one whereof shee carried with her
into Constantinople, the other shee inclosed in a Silver Case,
and placed it in the Church of the Holy Sepulcher, which her
selfe had builded there.

The Exaltation[4] of the Crosse was performed by Heraclius
the Emperor, upon this occasion. [5]Cosidore, the King of
Percia, a Pagan added unto his Kingdome the greatest parte
of the Nations in the East, and, among the rest, comeing to

Pag. 134.

* Holy-
rood.

Pag. 135.

---

[1] See what I have said about the Churches or Chapells of Holywell and Wolvercote, in p. 80, &c. of the IId. Vol. of Leland's *Itinerary*.

[2] Sic.

[3] I., *Callends of October*, or 14, &c.

[4] *Of the the Crosse* MS.

[5] Sic.

Jerusalem, carried away that part of the Crosse, which Helena
had left there, and using it as an instrument to deifie himselfe,
and to make him to be honored as a God, hee placed it in
his Royall Tower. Att that time the most noble King ^{Pag. 136.}
Heraclius was Emperor of Constantinople. Hee hearing,
that the young Cosdroe, Sonne of the Peircian King, was
come with a mighty Army against him, as farr as the River
[1] Danaw, went out with his Forces to give him Battaile.
When both Armies were mett, it was agreed by both the
Comaunders, Heraclius and Cosdroe the younger, that they
two should, in single Combate, save the shedding of more
blood, upon the condition, that the Emperor, without anie
further losse to the Conquered parte, should obtaine the
Commaund of and over both the Armies. Heraclius, therefore, comending his Cause to God, fought with Cosdroe on
the Bridge, in sight of both Armies, and kild him, whereupon
the wholl Armie of Cosdroe yeilded, not onely their obedience
to the Emperor, but (as beeing toucht with God's holy Spiritt) ^{Pag. 137.}
to the Christian Faith, and received Baptisme. Old Cosdroe,
knowing noething of this matter, had by the Emperor this
Offer made unto him, that, for asmuch as hee had some waie
honored the Crosse, if hee would yeild to become a Christian,
and bee baptized, and, withall, give pledges to the Emperor,
hee should enjoy both Life and Kingdome of his guift. This
if hee refused, hee should expect suddaine Death. This hee
obstinately rejecting, was presently beheaded, and the Emperor, upon the same condition, accepted a younger Sonne of
ten yeares old, and made him King in his Father's place.
This donne, hee tooke awaie the Crosse with him to Hierusalem, and sett it upp in it's former Place, whence [2] Cosdre had
taken it, and this is called the Exaltation of the Crosse.
From hence there is an easie prospect downewards, on both ^{Pag. 138.}
sides, haveing noething to be seene in it but the Towne Wall,
enclosing New Colledge on the right hand, and another faier
Wall enclosing Magdalene Colledge walke on the left. Re-

---

[1] Sic, cum lineola.   [2] Sic.

turning, therefore, back againe unto the North Gate, wee will take all the Streets and Lanes on the East side of the Towne in order as they lie. And, first, the Church of St. Michaell is hard by us on the left hand of Bocardo, and giveth entrance into a Lane of the same name, wherein there is noething observable, but a few small Cottages on the Towne Wall on the left hand, and the backsides of Houses and Gardens on the right, 'till wee come to Jesus Colledge, whose Garden

Pag. 139. haveing passed there lieth a faire Streete before us, crossing our way, and passing through a posterne Gate into the Suburbs over against Trinity Colledge. And here wee should proceed on our waie, but that the [1] now Chappell of Exeter Colledge hath stopt our passage. The next Lane from Bocardo in the Corne Market is called Jesus Colledge Lane, and bringeth us to the South side of that Colledge, and endeth in Alhallowes Streete, where wee were before, haveing noething but some few Tenements, Backsides and Garden Doores on either hand. And here betweene the Posterne Gate (which was mentioned before) and this Corner on the left hand, there are faire Entrances into two Colledges, opposite one to the other, *vizt.* Jesus Colledge [2] and Exeter Colledge on the right hand. This Streete lieth open unto

Pag. 140. the High Streete, haveing on the right hand dwelling Houses, among which one is called Mildred Hall, on the left hand Lincolne Colledge and the Church of Allhallowes; but wee follow on our waie directly betweene the Southside of Exeter Colledge and the Northside of Lincolne and Brasen Nose Coll. Att the end of which Lane there is an Entrance from St. Marie's into the common Schooles. But wee returne from hence unto the Conduit att Carefax, and there take [3] view Eastward of the High Streete, which is the fairest and

att
longest Streete of the Citty. For it beginneth [4]from the Conduit, and is continued, on both sides, with Cittizens

[1] F. *new.*   [2] Addend. forte, *on the left.*
[3] F. *a view.*   [4] Sic.

Houses all the length. Yet on the left hand, by Allhallowes Church, there is an Entrance into Lincolne Colledge Lane, whereof we spake before, and on the right the Lane called [1] Bear Lane, goeing downe to St. Edward's. From this Pag. 141. Church of Allhallowes, the Streete runneth on both sides, without interruption, till you come to St. Marie's Church on the left hand, and the Lane leading to St. Mary Hall and divers Colledges on the right. Att the West end of St. Marie's Church wee see the East side of Brasen Nose Colledge, and the Entrance of the Schooles, of which wee spake before. Opposite to Brasen Nose there are two old Halls, Black Hall and White Hall, now in their tenure, and serving for their use. Att the East end of St. Marie's is Catt Streete, leading to the Schooles, and opposite thereto a Lane leading downe to Martin Coll. In Catt Streete, towards the farther end, there is the back Doore of Hart-Hall on the right hand, and the great Front of the new Schooles on the left. On the Pag. 142. further end of the which Schooles, there is a passage leading to the North Doore of the Schooles, and that part of Exeter Coll. which hindered our passage before. Now for the Schooles, passing through the great Gate wee spake of before, wee see there is a goodly new Quadrant of faire building. 3. Stories high, the new and late worke partly of the Universitie, and partly of Sir Thomas Bodley, and other good Benefactors, builded upon the same Ground, whereon the old Schooles of Queene Marie's Building stood before, but now the Plott being enlarged, containeth a farr more noble and stately Fabrick. This Quadrant is equally devided into fower Parts, according unto the fower Entrances thereunto. On the East side standeth this great Front and lofty Tower where now wee are. Opposite thereunto the Entrance into the Divinitie Schoole. On the North the back waie leading toward Exeter Coll. On the South the waie leading toward Pag. 143.

---

[1] *Bran Lane* MS. Olim vocabatur *Judaismus Magnus*, sive *vicus Judæorum.* Sic enim Rossus, de Regib. Angl. p. 202. *Vicus ab hinc* [à Fano S. Frideswidæ] *tendens ad ecclesiam Omnium Sanctorum vocabatur Le Jury, id est, Vicus Judæorum.*

Brasen Nose. Betweene each of these Doores, in the Corners, there is a faire Staire Case, leading to the upper Schooles. The. 2. lower Stories of this Fabrick doe containe. 12. Schooles, thus distributed. Betweene the East gate and the Stare Case on the right hand, there is beneath the Meta-phisicke Schoole, above that [1]Geomitrie and Arithmatick Schoole. Betweene the same Stare Case, and the North Doore, there is beneath the Grammer and Historie Schoole, above that the Greeke Schoole. Betweene the North gate and the Stare Case towards the West gate, there is beneath the Morall Philosophy, and over it the Civill Law Schoole. Betweene the East gate and the Stare Case on the left hand there is below the Logick Schoole, and over it the Hebrew. Betweene the said Stare Case and the South Doore there

Pag. 144. is beneath the Rhetoricke Schoole, and over it Astronomie and Musick. Betweene the South gate and the Stare Case toward the West, there is beneath the Naturall Philosophy, and over it the Phisick Schoole. The West gate leadeth directly to the Divinitie Schoole, haveing on each side an open Gallerie to walke in. This side onely hath but. 2. Stories, the lower whereof containeth the said open Gallery, the upper is an addition unto the Publike Librarie, which Publike Librarie is over the Devinitie Schoole, and this upper Storie, which wee last spoke of, soe fitted, that with one stepp it answeareth to the Flower of the old Librarie, and with 4. or 5. stepps att each end ascendeth into the third storie of the Schooles, ordained likewise by Sir Thomas Bodley for an addition or augmentation of the said Librarie. The Divinitie

Pag. 145. Schoole was, att first, builded to the similitude of a Roman I, which Sir Thomas Bodley, by his addition of the open Gal-lerie, and the Storie over that, made to resemble a Roman T. Hee hath alsoe left meanes, for the building of the other End, next to Exeter Colledge, answearable thereunto, which Pos-terity maie, peradventure, see. The Divinitie Schoole it selfe was used for the lower House of Parliament in the yeare. 1625.

[1] Sic.

The upper Stories of the Schoole were employed, the North side for the upper House of Parliament, the East side for certaine Offices thereunto belonging, and the South for a Walk or Gallerie for the Lords.   But the intendment of Sir Thomas Bodley is, that all these Places should be filled with Bookes hearcafter, to the effecting whereof hee hath bestowed a yearely Revenue for the buying of such Bookes, as from tyme to tyme shall be thought worthy of that place.   And this is the noble Pag. 146. Fabrick and Building of the Universitie below, and Sir Thomas Bodley above. The Divinitie [1] Schooles were likewise builded by the Universitie, and the Library [2] above cheifely stored with Bookes att the charge of that noble and renowned Lord, Humfry Duke of Glocester.   Haveing thus taken a view of the Schooles, proceeding a litle further directly before us, wee come to a Posterne Gate of the Citty, commonly called Smith gate, and the round Synagogue of the Jewes, whereof wee made mention before.   On the right hand wee passe by Hart Hall, towards St. Mary Colledge, commonly called New Colledge.   [3] Leaveing the Colledge on the left hand, wee enter on a Lane on the right hand, which bringeth us directly to St. Peter's Church in the East.   This Church was builded by St. Grimbald, one of those learned men, whose help King Pag. 147. Alfred used in restoring of our Oxford Schooles (then much decayed by reason of the Danish Warrs) as wee have shewed before out of Asserius, and it was builded by him for that intent, that hee might laie his Bones therein after his death, but that unhappie Contention, which fell out betweene him and the auntient Schollars (as wee said before) made him returne to Winchester, where he ended his Life.   From hence there is an open passage into the High Streete, which wee leave, 'till wee have taken [4] view of those Places wee have not

---

[1] Sic.

[2] See what is said about the Divinity School and Library at Oxford in my Preface [§ 18] and Appendix [p. 300] to *A Collection of Curious Discourses written by Eminent Antiquaries,* &c.

[3] Hæc verba bis occurrunt in MS.

[4] F. *a view.*

yet touched. Therefore retourning to the Fish Markett, there is a Lane neare unto Ch.Ch. which is called St. Edward's Lane. This Lane hath Houses on the left hand, and the Wall of

Pag. 148. Christ Church, called Doctor Tresham's Wall (because unto him the oversight of the building that Wall was committed) on the right hand, till you come to Peckwater's Inn Corner, opposite whereunto is Beare Lane before mentioned. This St. Edward's Lane runneth on still, as before, with Houses on the left hand and the foresaid Wall of Ch. Ch. on the right. Then wee enter into the midst of [1] Mary Hall Lane, and turning on the right hand passe a long by Oriell Colledge on the left hand, and Corpus Christi Coll. on the right hand. Att the utmost end of Oriell Coll. there is that Lane, whereof wee spake before, commeing out of the High Streete, and opposite unto Catt-Streete Corner. This Lane is commonly called Pie Lane, but I will call it Winking Lane, because the first [2] Printing Presse, that ever came into England, was sett on

Pag. 149. worke in this Lane by Widdy kind, *alias* Winkin, de Ward a Dutchman. This Lane butteth upon [3] Martin Colledge Church, which Church is called by the name of St. John Baptist Church, and serveth not onely for that Colledge, but is the Parish Church alsoe of the fore named [4] Lane, and C. C. Coll. and those Houses that are over against this Church and Albane Hall, [5] and all the rest of the Lane till you come to the East gate of the Cittie. Over against Albane Hall there is a passage on the left hand leading unto the High

---

[1] F. *St. Mary.*

[2] This is a mistake. Winkin de Word did not set up the first Printing Press in England. 'Tis true, however, that he printed in this Lane, and 'twas called Winkin Lane from him (being before called Grope Lane) tho' now it bears the name of Magpie Lane, from the Sign of the Magpie. See § 6 of my *Occasional Remarks* at the end of Roper's Life of Sir Thomas Moore.

[3] Sic.

[4] It takes in only part of the Lane, the other part being in St. Marie's Parish. There is a Cross, to distinguish both Parishes, made, by the direction of Mr. Anthony à Wood, in the West Wall of the Lane by Oriel Colledge.

[5] *And all the rest of the rest of the Lane* MS. Here our Author also ascribes too much to St. John Baptist's Parish; tho' it must be allowed, that this Parish was larger formerly then it is at present. See the Appendix to this work, num. II.

Streete, and almost opposite to that of St. Peter's in the East,
besides that other which I last mentioned. And now beeing
come to the East gate of the Cittie, I make this observation,
that prudent Antiquitie provided, that the two Churches of
St. Michaell should be placed att the South and Northgate,
and St. Peter not farr from the West and Easterne gates, Pag. 150.
according to an old verse :

> *Invigilat portæ Australi Boreæque Michayell :*
> *Exortum solem Petrus regit atque* [1] *cadentem.*
> The North and South gates St. Michaell doth guard :
> The East and West St. Peter's care doth ward.

And this maie suffice for the Description of the Easterne part
of this Citty within the Walls. Noething now remaineth, but
onely the Suburbs of the East gate, which containeth on the
left hand a faire Front, all belonging and adjoyning unto
Magdalen Coll. on the right hand certaine poore Cottages and
scattering Houses, unto the Gate of Trinitie Lane. Beyond
this, the South side of Magdalen Coll. on the one side, and
a Tenement, adjoyning unto the Phisick Garden, bring us
unto the Bridge over Charwell, leading us into the Parish of
St. Clement, which hath Tenements likewise on both sides,
and two waies, the one leading unto Boltshipton Farme, which Pag. 151.
is called London waie, the other towards St. Bartholomew's
and the Countrie adjoyning. In this Parish St. Clement is
honored with a small Church, bearing his name. Hee was
the first Bishopp of Rome of that name, a Roman by
birth, borne in Mount [2] * Cælius. Though hee were nomi- * Cælius.
nated by St. Peter to be the first of all the Bishopps after
him, yet hee was content to give place unto Linus and Cletus:
soe that hee was the first after Peter by order of Nomination
and Election, though but the third by order of Tyme and
Succession. Hee suffered in the time of Trajan's Empire,
under Aufidianus a Captaine and Governor of his. The daie
of his Martirdome is noted in the Calender to be the 9th.
Calends of December, which in our Accompt is upon the.

---

[1] *Cadente* MS.   [2] Sic.

Pag. 152. 23th. of November. The manner of his Passion was on this sort. Aufidianus caused him out of a Shipp to be throwne into the Sea, haveing an Anchor tied to his Neck, least the People, knowing where his Body was, might honor him after his death.

The waie leading unto St. Bartholomewe's is a Causy leading directly thither, which is a poore [1] Hospitall, belonging unto Oriell Coll. and is counted the utmost Limitt of the Universitie Eastward. Unto the Chappell of this Hospitall, the Fellowes of New Colledge with their Quire did formerly, and doe formally, resort once a yeare, every May day Morning, and haveing made their Oblations, and sung Anthems for a space, they conclude this wholl Ceremonie and their Visitation with a passing along through the Grove

Pag. 153. to the Well, and doeing the like observance there.

Thus two parts of my Taske beeing performed, there remaineth onely the third, which is the Description of such Colledges and Halls as are now standing, which because almost every man knoweth, I shall not need to be long in discoursing thereof.

First, therefore, wee will speake of them in the order of their severall Seniorities.

Universitie Colledge　　　*　　　*　　　*　　　*　　　*
　　*　　　*　　　*　　　*　　　*　　　*　　　*

---

[1] See what I have said about this Hospital in p. 90 of the IId. Vol. of Leland's *Itinerary.*

APPENDIX I.

The Person referr'd to by Dr. Hutten (in p. 41) under the Title of A. M. is Anthony Munday, or Mundy, the same who continued Stowe's Survey, and writ a *Breif Chronicle from the Creation to this time. Lond.* 1611, 8º, and some other Things, among which must not be forgot that very scarce Thing of his intit. *A Discoverie of Edmund Campion, and his Confederates, their most horrible and traiterous practises, against her Majesties most Royall Person and the Realme.*

Wherein may be seene how thorowe the whole course of their Araignement they were notably convicted of every Cause.

Whereto is added, the Execution of Edmund Campion, Raphe Sherwin, and Alexander Brian, Executed at Tiborne the 1. of December.

Published by A. M. sometime the Popes Scholler, allowed in the Seminarie at Roome amongst them : A Discourse needfull to be read of every man, to beware how they deale with such secret Seducers.

Seene, and allowed.

Imprinted at London for Edwarde White, dwelling at the little north doore of Paules, at the Signe of the Gunne, the 29. of Janua.
1582. [In 12mo.]

I have given the Title of this Book at large for the sake of the curious, as it was sent me by my before mentioned learned Friend, the Reverend Mr. Thomas Baker, B.D., of St. John's Colledge in Cambridge, who found it in their Colledge Library. It is dedicated to the Rt. Hon. Sir Thomas Bromeley Knight, Lord Chanceller of England : William Lord Burleigh, and Lorde Treasorer, Robert Earle of Leicester, *&c.*, by *A. Munday.*

With an Epistle to the Reader, *&c.*, by *A. Munday.*

As soon as this Book was published, it gave great offence to the Roman Catholicks, and thereupon came out a little Book intit. 'A true Report of the death and martyrdome of M. Campion Jesuite and

Preiste, and M. Sherwin, and M. Bryan Preistes, at Tiborne the first of December 1581. Observid and written by a Catholike Preist, which was present therat. Wherunto is annexid certayne verses made by sundrie persons.' It consists of three sheets and a quarter in 8vo. Neither the name of the Place where, nor the year when, printed, is added. It is printed in the black Letter, and is so very scarce, that Mr. Wood tells us in Vol. I. of *Ath. Oxon.* col. 166, that he sought after it several years in vain. It was lent to me lately by a very worthy Friend in the Country, where I met with it as I was rambling about in Quest of Curiosities. The Author tells us, that this Book was chiefly occasion'd by, 'An Aduertisement and defence for truth against her backbyters, and specially against the whispering fauorers and colorers of Campions, and the rest of his confederates treasons,' which he calls 'a notable and most infamous libel.' At the end is, 'A caueat to the reader touching A. M. his discouery,' which 'Discouery' was no other than 'A Discovery of M. Campions and his confederates treasons,' which I have accounted for at large above, and is the same (as this Author observes) in effect and substance with the before mentioned Advertisement. In this Caveat we are told, that 'Munday was first a stage Player, after an aprentise, which tyme he wel serued with deceauing of his master, then wandring towardes Italy, by his owne report became a cosener in his Journey. Comming to Rome, in his short abode there, was charitably relieued, but neuer admitted in the Seminary, as he pleseth to lye in the title of his booke, and being wery of well doing, returned home to his first vomite, and was hist from his stage for his folly. Being therby discouraged, he set forth a balet against playes, tho' (o constant youth) he afterwards began again to ruffle upon the stage. I omit' (continues this Author) 'among other places his behaviour in Barbican with his good mistres, and mother. Two things however must not be pass'd over of this boyes infelicitie two several wayes of late notorious. First he writing upon the death of Everard Haunse, was immediately controled and disproved by one of his owne hatche. and shortely after seting forth the aprehension [1] of M. Campion, was disprooued by George (I was about to saye) Judas Eliot, who writing against him, proued that those things he did were for very lucers sake only, and not for the truthe, althogh he himself be a person of the same predicament, of whom I muste say, that if felony be honesti,

---

[1] This, I presume, is the same Book with that which Mr. Baker mentions to me in these words: *There is likewise,* A Breef Discourse of the taking of Edmund Campion and divers other Papists in Barkeshire *&c.* Gathered by A. M.

then he may for his behaviore be taken for a laweful witnes againste so good men.' Thus this Author, who, perhaps, may be thought by some as malicious, as the Author of the following verses, which I found, many years agoe, written in a spare Leaf (in a Hand of about the time of Queen Eliz.) at the end of a MS. *in Bibl. Bodl.* called *The Pricke of Conscience:*

> ' The grave counsell of Gravesend barge
> Gevethe Jhon Daye a privylege large
> To put this in prynt for his gaynes
> Because in the Legend of lyes he takethe paynes
> Commandinge other upon payne of Slavery
> That none prynt this but Jhon Daye the prynter of Foxe his knavery.

APPENDIX II. Seé p. 102.

E MS. penes Editorem.

Notes concerning the Foundation of Merton Colledge, and St. John Baptist's Church.

Memorandum,

I. That Merton College was Founded first by Walter of Merton at Meandon, or Maldon, in Surrey, *an.* 1264. in the Reign of Hen. 3. probably because the University of Oxford was then like to come to ruin, thro' the Scholars deserting it, and taking part with the Rebells at Northampton against the King.

II. That afterwards, upon Return of the Scholars to Oxford, he translated his College to this University, placing it where it now stands, and annexing certain Tenements to it, *viz.* one on the West side of St. John Baptist's Church, which he bought of the Abbey of Reading, to which the Advowson of the said Church belong'd, and three others on the East side, which he bought of the Priory of St. Frideswide, of James the Son of Master Mossey (a Jew of London) and Rob. Flixthorpe. All which Tenements made the Front of the College, and were in St. John's Parish.

III. As to the Church of St. John Baptist, it was of an ancient Erection, and belong'd at first to the Abbey of Reading, who, for the great respect they bore to Walter of Merton, and his Foundation carrying on at Oxford, granted it to him *An. D.* 1265. together with a Plot of Ground, belonging to the Tenement abovesaid, on the West side of the Church. So that being thus given, it was confirm'd to him and his Assigns by King Hen. 3. to the end that his Scholars might celebrate Divine Service therein. Afterwards, in the year 1292. it was appropriated by Oliver Bishop of Linc. to the Scholars of Merton College, and also made a Collegiate Parish Church, which to this day so continueth, being from that time stiled in ancient Evidences (which are reposited in the Treasury of the College) *Ecclesia Paro-chialis Sancti Joannis de Merton*, in others *Ecclesia S. Joannis de Merton* and *de Merton-Hall.* So that from that time all the Parochial Care was translated to them, and they were obliged to find a Chaplain (they having then a Chapell, on the South side of the College, dedicated to the Virgin Mary) to perform the Offices which were done before by the Rector.

IV. This Church in process of time coming to ruin, or being rather too little to contain the number of Students and Parishioners, 'twas pull'd down, and on the same Place was erected the present Church, which is a comely and decent Building, consisting of a fair Choir or Chancell, with an outward Church, and a stately well built Tower; half of which Church, containing the North Isle, was allotted for the Parish to burie their deceased. After 'twas quite finished, 'twas rededicated to the same Saint as before, *An. D.* 1424. in the Reign of Hen. 6. and at the same time was made a Description of the Parish, and an Account taken of the Number of Houses therein, most of which were Halls belonging to Scholars, which have been since totally destroy'd. But yet from their Names, mentioned in the Records to be seen in the College, it appears, that the Parish was much larger than 'tis at present; as, perhaps, may be also gather'd from a very old Map done in Wood, which was formerly in Mr. Ant. à Wood's Custody, as I have been several times inform'd by the learned Mr. Dodwell, to whom Mr. Wood had often shewed it.

V. For farther Particulars relating to this Parish, must be consulted Mr. Wyrley's Book of the Priory of Frideswide, the *Monasticon Anglicanum*, the Papers in Merton and Christ-Church Colleges, and those left by Mr. Wood at his death to the University.

THO. HEARNE 1703.

III

OF THE

ACTS DONE AT OXFORD

ON THE OCCASION OF

QUEEN ELIZABETH'S VISIT

IN THE YEAR

1566

JOHANNIS BEREBLOCI
COMMENTARII

COMMENTARII

SIVE

EPHEMERÆ ACTIONES

RERUM ILLUSTRIUM

OXONII GESTARUM

In Adventu Serenissimæ Principis

ELIZABETHÆ.

Ad Amplissimos Viros

DOMINUM GULIELMUM BROKUM

DOMINUM DE COBHAM,

Et

DOMINUM GULIELMUM PETREUM,

Regium à sanctioribus secretis Consiliarium.

Per J. B. Collegii ibidem Exoniensis socium.

E Codice MS. Editori donato à Thoma Wardo, de Warwico, Armigero.

I

'JOHANNIS BEREBLOCI

COMMENTARII

DE

REBUS GESTIS OXONIÆ

IBIDEM COMMORANTE

ELIZABETHA REGINA

A. D. ²MDLXVI.

DIE ultimo Augusti, quo nullum possumus recordari nobis ³Pag. 3. in vita illuxisse lætiorem, (Sabbati is dies fuerat, incredibili serenitate perspicuus) regia majestas à Woodstokio profecta, Oxonium versus iter habuit, multis comitata, inter quos præcipui fuere,

        Legatus Hispanorum.

        Marchio Northamtonensis.

Comes	Warwicensis. Sowthsexiæ. Huntingtonensis. Ruttlandensis. Oxoniensis. ⁴Warmondiensis.
Episcopus	Salisburgensis. Roffensis, ei ab Eleemosinis.

¹ *Adjeci.*   ² 1565 *B.*   ³ *Numeri marginales Codicis MS. paginas signant.*
    ⁴ *Wormondiensis B.*

<table>
<tr><td rowspan="10">Dominus {</td><td>Præfectus cubiculi.</td></tr>
<tr><td>[1] Vindelisorius.</td></tr>
<tr><td>Staffordiæ.</td></tr>
<tr><td>[2] Straunge.</td></tr>
<tr><td>[3] Sheffildc.</td></tr>
<tr><td>Mountjoye.</td></tr>
<tr><td>Henricus [4] Scymer.</td></tr>
<tr><td>Graye.</td></tr>
<tr><td>Paggett.</td></tr>
</table>

*Pag. 4. *Aderat etiam Guliclmus Cecilius cques inauratus, Reginæ à sanctioribus consiliis, et Cantabrigiensium Cancellarius, prætcr reliquam cquitum et Aulicorum turbam, solito frequcntiorcm ct copiosiorem. Comes Lccestrensis, cum suo famulitio, Oxonium antea accesscrat, ibi pro eo, quo apud nos fungitur, dignitatis ac officii muncrc, urbem cxornaturus, regiamque majestatcm nobiscum expcctaturus. Is hoc ipso die, doctoribus quibusdam, purpurato habitu, comitatus, aliisquc nonnullis collegiorum præfectis (qui propriis facultatum suarum vcstibus insigniti equis sublimiores vehebantur) in occursum principis fertur. Itaque ad duo milia passuum ab urbe progrcssi, (qui tcrminus nostræ authoritatis præfixus est) ibi per Marbcccum, suorum ac totius Academiæ verbis, serenissimam [5] principem, fausta ac eloquenti oratione, salutant. Inde Oxonium vcrsus movent, colonis agricolisquc cx villis et pagis hinc indc salutatum occurrcntibus, quorum sæpius itcrata vocc et [6] exclamationc, campi ferc et colles nihil jam, prætcr nomen numcnque regium, resonarc visi sunt. Jam vcro civitati propinquiorcs, in ipso limine et ingrcssu urbanæ ditionis, cis occurrit prætor urbanus, cum suis senioribus trabcatis, pallio & prætcxta purpuratis. Hîc tum prætor ab cquo dcsccndit, Rcginam orationc salutat, munus communi suorum nominc cxhibct, cratcram viz. ct nummos scxaginta, quos vulgo à figura *Angelos* appcllant. Finita oratione,

*Pag. 5. omnes *ad urbcm rectà proficiscuntur, campanis undiquc

---

[1] Windelisorius *B.*   [2] Strange *B.*   [3] Shefilde *B.*   [4] Semer *B.*

[5] Reginam *B.*   [6] Acclamatione *B.*

lætitiam ac gratulationem personantibus. Neque jam hoc loco vel dignitate regia vel amore nostro arbitror alienum esse, diversas hominum collocationes, ac inter eundum distributiones referre, quos Clarentius hodie rex fecialis non solum ordine miro, sed momento quodam et indicio disponere visus est. Is paludamento indutus erat, in quo principis ac regni propria insignia prætextis imaginibus exprimebantur. Primo itaque omnium præcessere lictores Achademici cum aureis baculis, tanquam itineris et viarum duces. Hos sequuti sunt principes nobiliores, maxima hilaritate, regio sumptu, supra quam credibile [1] videtur exornati, inter quos summi ordinis homines, Lecestrensis comes Academiæ Cancellarius, Prætorque [2]urbanus fuere. Deinde, miro pompæ ordine, lictores coronarii cum sceptris ingentibus, principi proximiores incedebant, quibus successit comes Southsexiæ, is gladium præferebat, gemmato capulo, aureis bullis, cœlataque vagina clarissimum. Inde non procul Augustissima princeps aurata honoratiori sede (lectica fuit undique aperta quam equi generosiores, purpura ornati, [3] temperato passu incedentes ferebant,) incessu raro ac nobili sequuta est. Ac ut vestitum curiosi minime desiderent, summo capite retiolum habebat, auro textile, bullis et unionibus conspicuum; toga deinde trabea muliebri serica ex clarissima purpura auro intexta fulgebat. Chlamis superior erat similis coccinia, conchilio *Pag. 6. tincta, cum subtegmine pellicio candore nitente, & maculis nigris triumphali more distincto. Illius sellam comitati sunt homines, cursores appellati, in quorum vestibus ex auro solido, regia viatorum insignia fuerunt, comitesque rei privatæ hinc inde ad dimovendam turbam discurrebant. Secundum lecticam pedissequis et ancillis locus fuit, quæ forma, pulchritudine, vestibus et equorum ornamentis summis principibus exæquandæ fuerunt. Traducti deinde fuerunt aliquot asturcones, sine sessoribus, auratis sericisque ephippiis instrati. Novissimum agmen clausere regii satellites, arcus ingentes,

---

[1] Est *B.*   [2] *Om. B.*   [3] Temporato *MS.*

clavasquc fcrreas, magnis sccuribus parcs, in humcris gestan-
tes, auro, scrico purpuraque spcctabiles, numero plus minus
ducenti, qui non tam custodiæ quam honoris causa, ncc ut
præsidio, scd ornamcnto, spcctaculo esscnt, principem [1]seque-
bantur.   Hoc comitatu summo honore, incredibili omnium
lætitia ad civitatcm contcndit, quo ubi pcrvcntum cst, ecce
autem nova facics, nova rcrum forma apparcbat.   Fracta
namque omnia ct dcbilitata refecta sunt, inclinata erecta,
prisca [2]rcstaurata, collapsa rcædificata, tecta ctiam, parictcs,
muri, fcnestrx, postes, porticus, ostia, januæ, valvæ, pavi-
menta, adcoque omnia principis advcntu, quasi novo vestitu,
fulgere & exultarc vidcbantur.   Ipsorum autem civium (Dii
immortales!) in vociferationibus suis quanta animorum de-

*Pag. 7. clarata cst voluntas?   Nec quisquam * tunc crat in tam
numcrosa illorum multitudine adeo aut voce aut spiritu
torpcsccns, qui non salutando [3]exclamabat, aut ita membris
claudicans, qui non pedibus ibat ut salutando adesset.   Porta
primo borcalis occurrebat, quam à communi carccre nomine
communiori *Bocardo* appcllant.   Hîc jam tum licuit totam
Acadcmiam serio exultantcm inspiccrc, omncs ordines, omnes
gradus, omncs dignitatcs, quasi uno intuitu triumphantcs con-
tcmplari, dicique vix potest, quanta in istorum animis voluptas,
quanta in vultibus alacritas, novo hoc luminc ac splendorc
effulsit, nihil in toto opido strepcbat, nihil [4]ex eis audirc fas
erat, præterquam, *vivat rcgina Elizabctha*, omniumque voces
unum illud personabant sæpius, *vivat Rcgina Elizabctha*.
Ingredienti, juvcnilis statim turba occurrcbat, hunc ci locum
primum ætatis tempus, primus vitæ actus disciplinæque suæ
tyrocinium dcdcrat.   Hîc tum placuit augustissimæ principi
paululum subsistcre, gratulantium vultus considcrarc, ac intu-
cntium animos jucundissimo suo aspectu reficerc ac [5]rccrearc.
Hæc mora nc [6]ci in offcnsionem cadcrct, junior [7]quidam Delus,
suorum æqualium ac commilitonum nominc, tempus protrahit
studio salutandi, tædium allevat suavitatc eloquendi, dum illa

---

[1] Sequibantur *MS*.   [2] Instaurata *B*.   [3] Acclamabant *B*.   [4] in *B*.
[5] Recreari *MS*.   [6] *Om. B*.   [7] *Om. H*.

interim benevolentiam sui apud omnes auget lenitate audiendi. Hinc jam [1] media per scholares movebat, qui ita frequentes ac copiosi plateas undique obsederant, ut coacti sunt advenæ, mulieres ac puellæ, visendi avidiores, * summis tectis ac fenc- *Pag. 8. stris insidere.   Plenæ itaque fenestræ, pleni parietes, ipsaque tecta insidentium ac gratulantium vocibus plena, adeoque plenitudine gravata fuerunt.   Ubi forum frumentarium præter- vecta est, ac ad ecclesiam Divi Martini pervenerat (qui locus ab insigni quadrivio, verbo parum Gallico [2] *Carfocks* appellatur) Laurentius quidam, idem Græcæ linguæ doctor optimus et interpres præclarissimus, moras dicendo facit, illius ad urbem accessum Græca oratione gratulatur, egregiumque studium in literis promovendis egregie collaudat.   Finita oratione, eam Bacchalaureorum ordo accepit, qui ætate provectiores, studiis- que jam ac disciplina maturiores, in occursum illius, singuli habitu et insignibus suis laureati, prodierant.   Isti ergo à scholaribus secundi viam hinc inde confertim claudentes, fausta ac felicia omnia præfabantur, quorum tam pia ac felici comprecatione ad ecclesiam Sancti Aldati brevi deducta est.   Ibi duo ex ista turba delecti juvenes, orationes duas, quas dicere temporis angustia prohibuit, reginæ in manibus offerunt, eas illa relatis gratiis accepit suavissime, ac benig- nissime complexa est.   Hiis proximi artium magistri fuerunt, sapientiæ studiosi, qui, inversis vestibus literariis, reginam pientissimam, tanquam alteram adventantem Minervam, ex- pectabant.   Istos tam excellenti animo, tam præstanti bene- volentia ac divino studio extitisse constat, ut accedentem Reginam, tanquam verum quoddam reipublicæ lumen, ac columen insigne civitatis nostræ, acceperint, acceptam vero non *aliter ac præcipuum Academiæ ornamentum decusque *Pag. 9. literarum maximum venerati sunt, illius majestatem, quibus potuerunt, verbis amplissimis ornantes, vitamque ac salutem, quanta fieri potuit [3] precatione, Diis immortalibus commen- dantes.   Homines profecto si contempleris, existimares digni- tate ac voce sua vel ipsos posse movere Deos, tantus in vestitu

---

[1] Medii *MS. et B.*   [2] Carfox *B.*   [3] Prefatione *B.*

splendor ac decentia, tantaque in vultibus amplitudo et majestas apparuit. Per hos itaque, tanquam Minerva quaedam, inter [1] medias Musas ferebatur. cui illi tanta cum laetitia ac vociferatione acclamaverunt, ut exclamare majus [2] nec potuit corpus sufficere, nec spiritus contentioni vocis inservire. Horum jam charitate ac benevolentia septa, ab ecclesia Sancti Aldati, quo loco bacchalaureorum ordo desiverat, ad interiora aedium Christi ad gradus fere [3] palatii pervenit. Nec hîc suis partibus magistri defuerunt. Duo namque reperti sunt, qui advenienti principi se offerre, ac ad pedes projicere gestiebant, quos studium commune ac benevolentia amplificare sonos voluit, quos tempus angustum & infantia eosdem deprimere compulit, tempori ergo ac taedio consulentes, totius facultatis suae incredibilem amorem scriptis profitentur, offerunt se, seipsos pollicentur, studium, labores, discrimina, vitam, mortem, ac si quid aliud charum habuerint, id inquam omne pollicentur. Cum ei ita gratulati essent, id serio gaudere serenissima princeps visa est, nec gratiarum immemor, grata admodum, gratias ex animo *egit humanissime. Hunc locum, in quo à Magistris jam desitum est, rursus Bacchalaurei sacrae theologiae ac Doctores ([4] eidem et discendi praeceptores et vivendi) [5] rursus [6] incepere. Horum gravitati et amplitudini vultus (qui sermo quidam non simulatus mentis illorum fuerat) respondebat; venerationem autem et aucthoritatem habitus ille eorum compositior et condecentior arguebat. Praeterquam [7] enim quod purpura et serico insignes fulgebant, natura etiam aetasque provectior, ac judicium in sua disciplina maturum, incredibilem eis opinionis et majestatis accessionem fecerat. Hii numero quinque supra viginti fuerunt.

*Pag. 10.

Doctores in sacra theologia.
{ L. Humfridus.
Godwinnus.
Overtonus.
Piersus.

---

[1] Medios *MS. et B.*   [2] Non *B.*   [3] Pallatii *MS.*   [4] *F.* iidem.
[5] *Om. B.*   [6] Incipere *B.*   [7] *Om. B.*

Doctores in sacra theologia.
- [1] Calfhillus.
- [2] Westfallingus.
- Elderus.
- [3] Cradokus.

Doctores in legibus.
- Kenallus.
- [4] Huesse.
- Whitus.
- [5] Awberius.
- [6] Griffethe.
- [7] Lluyede.
- [8] Langher.
- [9] Barber.

Pag. 11.

Doctores in re medica.
- [10] Masterus.
- [11] Frauncis.
- [12] Hinkus.
- Bailius se.
- Bailius ju.
- Barnes.
- [13] Attflowe.
- [14] Sliderst.
- [15] Gifford.

Non potuit certe istis non esse jucundum pabulum studii et doctrinæ suæ, ipsum honoris sui fontem præsentem contemplari et inspicere. Illorum ergo jam omnis actio, cogitatio, ratio, totus [16] denique vultus & apparatus, nihil aliud fuit, [17] quam constans, perpetua, fortis et invicta quædam testificatio amoris et voluntatis illius, quam [18] ei antea totus populus in apparatissimo suo spectaculo ostenderat. Sed quia meæ infantiæ non est, conari commemorare studia singulorum (quanquam etenim difficile est, ubi numerus gratulantium infinitior est, non

---

[1] Caulfhillus *B.*   [2] Westfalingus *B.*   [3] Cradocus *B.*   [4] Hues *B.*
[5] Aubericus *B.*   [6] Griffeth *B.*   [7] Lluied *B.*   [8] Langeher *B.*
[9] Barbar *B.*   [10] Masterius *B.*   [11] Ffrancis *B.*   [12] Hincus *B.*
[13] Atteslowe *B.*   [14] Sliderste *B.*   [15] Gyfforde *B.*   [16] *Om. B.*
[17] Nisi *B.*   [18] Illi *B.*

aliquem, omnes tamen, satis scio, nefas existimabunt quem-
quam præterire) ideo jam [1] universos dico, summos, medios,
infimos, hujus tum laudibus favisse, tum gratulationi se obtu-
lisse, eam ex animo coluisse, dilexisse, amasse, charam etiam
et jucundam habuisse. In ipso primo limine ac ingressu
palatii, quo tum forte Doctorum ordo sese protenderat, loco
aliquantulum, propter multitudinem, sublimiori, junior Kings-
mellus, orator Academiæ, constitit; is tum composite atque
ornate, cum quadam etiam actionis dignitate *splendida ac
grandi oratione Reginam excepit, cujus oratio tametsi fuerit
[2] aliquantulum longior (utpote quæ, quo ad longissime potuit,
spatium respexit præteriti temporis, ac Academiæ pueritiam
recordata est ultimam, inde usque eorum nomina repetens, qui
vel prima illius initia ac fundamenta [2] firmissima posuerint, vel
fundatam insigni aliquo beneficio coluerint et amplexi sunt)
ejusmodi tamen erat amplissimæ principis in audiendo lenitas,
in commorando humanitas, ut eousque attendendo facillime
[3] expectarit, quousque ille perorando tandem perfecerit. Deinde,
ut eadem, cujus toto hoc tempore incredibilis illa mansuetudo,
insigne nobis comitatis ac mansuetudinis documentum dederat,
posset idem etiam erga Deum relligione ac cultu divino præstare, templa statim piissima petiit, ibique religiosa totis precibus religiose adfuit. Postquam ad pulvinaria Omnipotentis
satis ab ea supplicatum est, palatium jam animo adhuc in-
defessa repetebat. Collegium Christi erat Domus [4] quidem
satis splendida et ampla, ita vero à suis præparata, ut inde
luce clarius apparuerit, quantum ea privatim semper luxuriam oderit, quantumque publice magnificentiam dilexerit.
Nihil namque ibi superbum, nihil fastu turgidum aut tu-
mescens, sed omnia ad illius majestatem apte & decore
fiebant, Diis immortalibus, eorum, quæ vel ad usum vel
ad victum pertinent, ubertate, copia, vtilitate, ejus adventum comprobantibus. Dumque illa jam maximas et anxi-
feras curas cessatione sua relaxavit, regii comites, *turpe
existimantes, hanc summam quietis facultatem longa solitu-

*Pag. 12.

*Pag. 13.

---

[1] Omnes jam *B*.   [2] *Om. B.*   [3] Expectaret *B*.   [4] *Om. B.*

dinc consumere, per plateas in opidum late varieque diffusi, magna [1] cum circumspectione animadverterunt, ejusque situm ac formam intuentes, vicos ibidem, itinerum perpetua quadam latitudine amplissimos, ædificiorum ornatu splendidissimos, collegiorum pulchritudine magnificentissimos, suspiciunt, admirantur, stupescunt. Vestibula, tum [2] primique aditus collegiorum carminibus exornati sunt, adeoque mille erant imagines optimorum versuum ad singulas eorum januas fixæ. Istorum ergo statim inspectione multum occupantur, lectione mirifice capiuntur, communique nostro erga principem studio (quod ex eis, tanquam clarissimo monumento, testatum habuerunt) incredibile prorsus est, quam statim delectantur.

Dies Dominicus.

Postero die quam in opidum introivit splendidissima princeps, laboribus jam assiduis ac gratulantium concursationibus aliquantulum confecta, parum belle se habuit, quod ex fructu illo jucundissimi aspectus sui nobis sublato intelleximus. Eo itaque die, propter illius absentiam, tum quia dominicus fuerat, in quo nihil [3] jam agi poterat, ab omni vacabant curatione et rerum administratione, cultui duntaxat divino ac sacris sanctissimorum hominum concionibus pie deserviebant. Nolo hîc prandiorum illustres apparatus referre, aut cœnas lautiores commemorare; consultum præcipue est in hac parte amplitudini, ut splendidiores fierent, non nihil etiam temperantiæ et modestiæ, ne forte in luxuriam caderent. Nocte adveniente, spectacula apparatissima data sunt, quæ nonnullis, qui ＊Pag. 14. eadem otiosi tota die expectarant, pro mercedis cumulo claritate sua fuerunt. Nihilque jam pretiosius vel magnificentius excogitari potuit illorum apparatione atque instructione. Primo ibi ab ingenti solido pariete patefacto aditu, [4] proscenium insigne fuit, ponsque ab eo ligneus pensilis, sublicis impositus, parvo et perpolito tractu per transversos gradus ad magnam Collegii aulam protrahitur; festa fronde cœlato pictoque um-

---

[1] Eum *MS. et B.*   [2] Primi *H.*   [3] *Om. H.*
[4] Procescenium *MS.*   Procestrium *B.*

braculo exornatur, ut per eum, sine motu et perturbatione prementis vulgi, regina posset, quasi æquabili gressu, ad præparata spectacula contendere. Erat aula laqueari aurato, et picto arcuatoque introrsus tecto, granditate ac superbia sua veteris Romani palatii amplitudinem, et magnificentia imaginem antiquitatis diceres imitari. Parte illius superiori, qua occidentem respicit, theatrum excitatur magnum et erectum, gradibusque multis excelsum. Juxta omnes parietes podia et pegmata extructa sunt, subsellia eisdem superiora fuerunt multorum fastigiorum, unde viri illustres ac matronæ suspicerentur, et populus circum circa ludos prospicere potuit. Lucernæ, lichni, candelæque ardentes clarissimam ibi lucem fecerunt. Tot luminaribus, ramulis ac orbibus divisis, totque passim funalibus, inæquali splendore, incertam præbentibus lucem, splendebat locus, ut et instar diei micare, et spectaculorum claritatem adjuvare candore summo visa sint. Ex utroque scenæ latere comœdis ac personatis magnifica palatia ædesque apparatissimæ extruuntur. Sublime fixa sella fuit, *Pag. 15.* pulvinaribus ac tapetiis ornata, aureoque *umbraculo operta, Reginæ destinatus locus erat. Verum illa quidem certe hac nocte non adfuit. Cum omnia jam hoc ordine præparata fuerunt, Domusque erat bene plena et completa, licuit statim in scena Geminum Campanum inspicere, à Duillio et Cotta apud Alexandrum Severum invidia ac æmulatione falso accusatum, servos, agricolas, et rusticos, corruptelarum illecebris irretitos, testes introductos ; nihilque tum magis ridiculum, quam istos contemplari, tanquam in certa victoria sordide triumphantes, de Gemini supplicio decernentes, de facultatibus dividendis rixantes, adeoque inter se pugnantes, deinde suum infortunium lamentis muliebriter lachrimisque deplorantes. Ubi satis [1]ita lusum est, libertini postea honestiores introducuntur, quos nec pœna nec præmium ad injuriosam accusationem potuit deducere. Istorum ergo chirographa, testificationes, indicia, quæstiones, rem manifestam fecere. Servi igitur tum accusatores, imperatoris mandato, cruci affiguntur,

---

[1] *Om. B.*

Duillius et Cotta debite plectuntur, libertini remunerantur, Geminus absolvitur, magnus ex omnibus plausus excitatur. Quo finito, cubitum disceditur.

Dies Lunæ.

Die [1]proximo per unum diem prætermissos jam labores repetimus, ac inchoata studia persequimur. Primò itaque bene mane in omni collegio prece ac obsecratione humili ad Deum utimur, ut nobis possint acta illius diei bene, fauste, feliciterque evenire. [2]Absolutis tandem precibus, matutinum tempus lectiunculis consumitur, *non publicis, sed iis, quas *Pag. 16. singulæ domus ac collegia aulis, aut loco alio frequentiori, solent juvenibus suis domi privatimque dare. Hora septima ubi advenerit, adjumentis externis et adventitiis quæque domus utitur. Ex domesticis enim vinculis emissa juventus, ad publicas Lectiones tum audiendas publice amandantur. Nec quasvis ista hora audire fas est. Soli namque ex omnibus hoc tempore legunt linguæ Græcæ et Hebraismi interpretes. Harum itaque Lectionum auditionem et inspectionem habere tum licet. Hora octava publice legunt decem scholis septem facultates tresque philosophiæ. Hic jam habent juvenes, unde discant congrue loqui per Grammaticam, ornate dicere per Rhetoricam, acute disserere per Dialecticam, expedite numerare per Arithmeticam, lineas et magnitudines per Geometriam, tonos & sonos per Musicam, sydera fixa, vagantes sphæras per Astrologiam, elementa rerum, concreta corpora per Philosophiam naturalem, Rem cujusque privatam, domesticam, publicam per Philosophiam moralem, ac denique res, quas, ab hominum sensu ac opinione remotas, suis ipse visceribus intellectus [3]recondidit, per Metaphisicen. Istis facultatibus studemus adolescentiores, iisdem solemus difficilem ac spinosam disciplinarum tramitem resecare, fallaciarum pestes contundere, imposturæ aditum præcludere, obicem errori ponere, ac iter ad majora postremo aperire. Hora nona, cum ab ista exercitatione juvenes cessant, *tum ad munera *Pag. 17.

----

[1] Postero *B*.   [2] Finitis *B*.   [3] Recondedit *MS*.

privatim singulis Domibus obeunda vel audiendo vel disputando coguntur. Hoc interim spatio Theologus prælector
publice, perfectiori jam sanctiorique disciplina, magnifico in
palatio, ac plena majestatis domo (opus id erat Humfredi,
Ducis quandoque Glocestrensis) pias hominum mentes instruit,
docetque, quo modo ex hac vita ad Deorum religionem
sanctimoniamque demigrari possit. Si quid vero in sacra
pagina, quam [1] interpretatur, occurrerit difficilius, si quid magis
arduum, ad sinceras & puras opinionum sententias inde enu-
cleandas, ad caliginem tenebrasque discutiendas, authorem,
lucem, ducem, se nobis præbet. Hæc dum ab illo perficiun-
tur, eodem ipso tempore jurisperiti à Duce et Lectore suo
commoditatem conficiendi negotii súi, et liberationem molestiæ
in legibus contrariis ac difficilioribus expectant. Interea etiam
necessaria ac fructuosissima illa [2] professio bonæ valitudinis
destinato ad id loco proprios auditores habet. Ibi tum dis-
cunt medici, quo modo humores, in corpore infusi aut intrin-
secus [3] illapsi, comprimi collidique debeant, quo modo eosdem,
si forte nimis acres, [4] purgare, nimis tenues digerere, nimis
concretos dissipare possint, ac quæ denique [5] unicuique morbo
applicanda sunt medicamenta et apta remedia. Hiisce lec-
tionibus decima hora singulis diebus finis terminusque consti-
tuitur.   Clamant continuo gymnasia atque omnes philosophorum scholæ magistrorum vocibus, quos publica Academiæ
campanella convocare solet, eosque *armare ad omnem dicendi controversiam ac disceptacionem. Duo ibi tum, inter
reliquos, præcipui (bacchalaurei sunt) pro philosophia summa
vi impetuque contendunt. Duo etiam, præ ceteris, magistri,
contra istorum vim gravitatemque, adeoque contra naturam
universam pugnant atque luctantur. Pugna summa [6] concer-
tatione pugnata, hora jam undecima, admonentibus eisdem
campanis, disceditur. Hoc interim spatio usitatum ac quoti-
dianum erat Cancellario nostro singulis diebus, postquam
lectiones inviserat, ante meridiem Legatum Philippi, regis

*Pag. 18.

---

[1] Interpretator, *MS.*   [2] Profectio *H.*   [3] Elapsi *B.*
[4] Spurgare, *MS.*   [5] Cuique *B.*   [6] Consertacione *MS.*

Hispanorum, amicissimi erga nostram rempublicam principis, aliosque reginæ proceres nobiliores, ad singula nostra collegia, aut saltem ad illustriora, circumducere. Eos igitur omni loco summo studio, incredibili benevolentia orationes hominum eloquentissimorum accipiunt, qui copiosa et ornata eloquutione magnam advenis suæ sapientiæ et ingenii admirationem mo- verunt. Post meridiem, nisi eorum motus conatusque alia negotia prohibeant, in scholis ab adolescentioribus exercitatio in Dialecticis sit. Hora itaque prima, postquam desierit campana, assident omnes, de vocibus subtiliter contendunt, inde admirabilem judicii maturitatem et acumen ingenii com- parant, intelligendi prudentiam acuunt, et eloquendi incredi- bilem celeritatem consequuntur. Qui in hujusmodi disputa- cione respondent, exinde *generales sophistæ* appellantur, nec cuiquam juniori licet ad [1]optatos bacchalaurei gradus provehi, nisi prius in hac luctatione respondendo contenderit. Verum hodie nihil actum est hujusmodi. Etenim toto hoc postmeri- diano tempore magna cum spe atque avidissime regiæ majes- tatis præsentiam in præparata solemniori disputatione expec- **Pag. 19.* tabamus. At illa hoc etiam die valitudini indulsit, qua quidem antea, dum nobis nimium humanitate sua servivit, sibi servivit vix satis. Itaque jam vicecancellarius noster, ceterique duces regendæ civitatis conabantur disputationes à destinato templo, cui quasi addictæ sunt et consecratæ, ad palatium traducere, ac à loco frequentiori sublatas, intra domesticos parietes con- cludere. Non tulit id augustissima regina, nec potuit ferre tantam causam, quanta nulla unquam antea in [2]disceptatione versata est, [3]loci [3]insolentia minui aut debilitari. Ad hæc, motum animi, impetum dicendi, contentionem disputandi, hæc omnia in actoribus leniora fore [4]suspicata est, ubi extra solitum conventum, et usitatam frequentiam coguntur. Placuit ergo eas ad crastinum rejicere, ac eousque authoritate sua differre. Nocte adveniente, ad præparata spectacula conveniunt. Quorum magnificus apparatus, cultusque elegantia, incredibili opinione sua ita omnium animos auresque compleverat, ut eo

---

[1] Aptatos *H*.   [2] Disputatione *B*.   [3] *Om. B*.   [4] Conspicata *B*.

infinita ac innumerabilis hominum multitudo, immensa et immoderata videndi cupiditate, confluxerit. Principis etiam præsentia, qua jam biduo destituti sunt, tantum sui desiderium omnium mentibus addiderat, ut inde [1] fuerat numerus longe auctior et infinitior. Vix jam cum proceribus, viris primariis, regina ingressa est, sellaque sublimiori consederat, cum tanta omnes *concursacione ad theatri aditus convolarent (aula ea collegii fuerat) gradusque jam [2] ita à plebe completi sunt, ut violentia sua commune gaudium fœda strage contaminaverint. Murus quidam [3] fuerat ex lapidibus quadratis ingentibus; [4] gradibus ex utroque latere propugnaculum opponebatur, ad ascendentium impetus sustinendos; concursus frequentior fit, impetus grandior; murus, tametsi firmior, sustinere non potuit, ex uno graduum latere concidit, ruina tres oppressi sunt, totidem vulnerati. Ex oppressis qui diutissime supervixit, non ultra biduum vixit. Vulnerati, adhibitis medicamentis, brevi convaluere. Hoc malum quamvis potuit communem lætitiam contaminare, nihilominus tamen eandem commaculare non potuit. Ad spectacula itaque omnes, alieno jam periculo cautiores, revertuntur. Duos ibi contemplari licuit adolescentes regios, Arcitum et Palamonem, quos eadem terra concordes diu habuerat, quos idem vitæ periculum [5] idemque carcer communis connexerat, quos affinitatis conjunctio ac jusjurandum fratres reddiderat. Unam isti eandemque virginem, Emiliam, sororem ducis Athenarum, misere deperierunt. Hîc tum in illis fas erat perspicere animos, retro contrarioque motu, pulsu ac impulsu, huc illuc agitatos, ac in carcere vix satis concordes, appetitu vehementiori perturbari, pugnare, digladiari. Quid multis? Mandato prohibentur, non curant mandatum: incarcerantur, erumpunt: exulant; amor non sinit longius *progredi, biduum nimium est, triduum ferre non potest. Regius itaque adolescens capitale supplicium non curat, habitu [6] indecentiori revertitur, ex Arcito, mutato nomine, Philostrates fit, ad omne genus officii scipsum instruit, nullum

*Pag. 20.

*Pag. 21.

---

[1] *F.* fuerit. [2] *Om. H.* [3] Fuit *B.* [4] Grandibus *B.*
[5] Periculum carcerque *H.* [6] Inde recentiori *B.*

tam vile munus, quod non exequitur, nihil tam à natura
molestum, quod non, Emiliæ præsentia, suave illi et mundum
facit ; sine ista jucundissima quæque laboriosa, gravia, odiosa
sunt.   Palamon interea custodem potione fallit, ex difficultatibus elabitur, nocte fugit, interdiu silvis latitat, fratri tandem
fit obvius.   Novos hîc tumultus Emilia commovet, adeoque
vehementes amor jam fecerat animi concitationes ac offen-
siones, ut mox [1] dimicarent, verum statim interventu Thesei
pugna sedatur.   Docet tum [2] Palemon qui fuit, quo proposito
pugnaverint, nec tamen mortem, quamvis graviter deliquerit,
deprecatur.   Dux, illarum prece commotus, quæ tum forte illi
inter venandum aderant, duellum statuit, jubet pugnam in
quadragesimum diem parent, præmium victori virginem pollicetur.   Dici non potest, quanta jam voluptate et lætitia adolescentes [3] discessere, nos etiam, postquam Deo ab omnibus pro
principe conclamatum erat, ea nocte discessimus.

Dies Martis.

Cum nobis proximus dies, qui Martis erat, illuxisset, studium Philosophiæ, à nobis nunquam intermissum, ad solitos
nos disciplinæ usus exercitationesque revocat, quibus maxima
* sedulitate in singulos dies invigilamus, donec ab eisdem ad *Pag. 22.
prandium vulgo vocati sumus.   Inclinato jam in postmeridia-
num tempus die, ad præparata publica progymnasmata festinantes vehementerque properantes confluimus.   In ore namque
omni populo fuerat, principem proceresque illorum nobilitatem
præsentia sua illustrare velle.   Hora jam secunda, aut non
multo secus, Lictores Academici, bedellos vocant, aureis torquibus ac novo habitu ornatiores assumptis fascibus, bacilli
[4] argentei sunt inaurati, magnitudine splendoreque suo insignes,
comitatum Cancellario novum præbuerunt.   Ubi locus paratior et instructior fuit, illustrissima princeps, stipata nobilibus,
septa pedissequis, ac omnium charitate et benevolentia munita,

---

[1] Demicarent, *MS.*   [2] *Sic.*
[3] Decessere *H.*   [4] Argenti *B.*

à palatio ad collegium Cantuariense, per hortulorum amoe-
nitates descendit. Inde ad templum [1] beatæ virginis, ubi tum
disputationes habebantur, quicquid spatii est, id omne pedibus
transmisit, totiusque jam multitudinis, quam tum capere potuit
urbs, concursus clamorque in hunc locum fit. Per istorum
acclamationes regina, cum ornatissimo procerum comitatu, ad
templi vestibulum sensim et [2] peditentim progreditur, fuitque
jam erectum intra columnas templi amphitheatrum ingens,
amplum et magnificum, gradibus excelsum. Classes et subsellia superius ædificata sunt. Ejus latitudo à meridie ad
aquilonem fuit, longitudo vero ab oriente ad occidentem pro-
tendebatur. Hinc viris feminisque licuit, honoratis et [3] illus-
trioribus, palæstras publicas jucundissime ex superiori loco
despicere, parte illius *orientali, [4] peramplus ligneus suggestus,
atque ibidem conclave extructum est, peristromatis et aulæis
ad loci dignitatem undique protectum, in quibus serico et auro
intextæ visebantur multæ vetustatis et antiquitatis historiæ.
Medio suggesto, loco celsiori, præalta sedes fuerat, auro ves-
tita et contecta, tapetiisque pretiosis ornata. Inferius theatri
septa magistrorum scabellis plena ac referta fuerunt, mediis
scabellis respondentis suggestum positum est. Ab aquilone
solenniorum ac scholarum comites (*procuratores* appellamus)
[5] reliquis sublimiores sedebant, istorum erat disceptantium
contentiones [6] dirimere, ac prudentia et gravitate sua tempus
unicuique moderari. Doctorum subsellia ex utroque Circi
latere altiora grandioraque fuerunt. Juxta istos à meridie,
qua parte Theatrum orientem respicit, alia sella prominere
visa est, coccinio serico, triumphali more, operta. Huc comes
Lecestrensis, Cancellarius noster, à lictoribus Academicis ses-
sum est perductus. Septa vero Amphitheatri exterius Artium
bacchaulaurei, scholares adolescentiores, advenæque, ingenti
ambitu ac longa comprehensione, [7] obsidere. Ipsa denique
ordinum collocatio conformatioque majestate sua splendidum
ac magnificum quiddam inspectantibus præ se ferebat. Post

* Pag. 23.

---

[1] Divæ *B.*   [2] *Sic.*   [3] Illustribus *B.*
[4] Per amplos ligneos *H.*   [5] Relequis *MS.*   [6] Dirimire, *MS.*   [7] *Sic.*

quàm jam, inter tantas precationes, longo tractu à regina processum est, eam reguli nobiliores lictoresque coronarii ad suggestum præparatum per gradus deduxere. Ubi vero à superiori loco omnium oculis prodiit, à theatro per Gimnasiarchas et celeberrimos artium professores iterum amplificata jam voce serio *reclamatum est. Dumque omnium oculi in [*Pag. 24.] doctorum imagines mente intenta defixaque intelligentia hærebant, subito vultu gestuque [1] adornatus composito habituque decentiori ad respondentis suggestum Campianus processit. Toga illi tum Dalmatica talaris fuit, manicis remissis ac largitate sua diffluentibus. Huic pallium inductum est undique consutum, præterquam qua dextro patebant aditus. Postremo erant humeri superius pellibus albis, candoreque lucentibus, redimiti. Atque hic tum habitus fuit omnium magistrorum, præterquam quod nonnulli, loco [2] palludamenti illius pellicei, serico utebantur, omni colore variegato. Statim procuratores voce sua pugnæ indicium ostenderunt et concertationis signum patefecerunt, quo excepto, Daius, quem sors principem primumque in adversa factione dederat, dum cupit omnes sententiæ suæ concordes conjunctissimosque efficere, quæstiones constituit, quibus quidque inter agendum referri debeat, quibus possint auditores intuendo respicere, [3] actores vero cursum suum disputando dirigere. Binæ fuerunt. Quæsivit prima, An aliqua superior causa existat, quam sint elementorum qualitates et vires, [4] que vi, lumine, motione sua ortus et interitus rerum dispensatur; hæc dispensatio, num à lationibus fiat, an in ipso mundo Deus est aliquis, cujus in arbitrio et nutu, tanquam in gremio parentis, hærere cetera omnia oporteat? Deinde, Neptunia prata, mareque illud profundum, quibus libratum sit ponderibus, qua vi agitari ac turbari soleat, quo motore sic in immensum æstu quodam aliquando fervescat, ut nobis propius jam accedere, *ac continuo mutato [*Pag. 25.] cursu à nobis recedere videatur? Hiis hoc modo pr positis, Campianus, postquam principem salutaverat, ac, quantum

---

[1] Adornatum *MS.*, ad ornatum *B.*   [2] *Sic.*

[3] Actoris *MS.*   [4] *Sic MS An* qua vi, *&c.?* quæ *B.*

potuit dicendo consequi, mercedem præsentiæ suæ gratiis cumulatissime reddiderat, cum brevitate respondet, 'Vices opinor et mutationes eorum, quæ ex primis initiis turbida mixtione conflantur, ad vires et qualitates elementorum ascribendas non esse, sed à conversione sempiterna ac latione omnium perfectissima principium motionis ac volubilitatem habere, certoque aliquo cœli signo commoveri. Et quamvis nulla certa, et nobis cognita ratione hoc fieri existimamus, non dubia tamen causa, et à cœlesti dispensatione definita concitari ista certum est. Hinc æstus [1] maritimos fretorumque angustias, ac totius maris accessum ac recessum, lunæ motibus gubernari, ejusdemque ortu et obitu commoveri novimus. Siquidem ea ultima cœlo [2] citima terris, lumine lucens alieno, tantam ac talem vim commoditate loci, qualitate [3] sui, ac differentia luminis, optimo jure sortita est. Luna ergo [4] accedente propius, mare, solutis et liquefactis vaporibus, quibus undique refertum atque commistum est, rariori materia mirabiliter auctum diffluit ac incitatur; ubi vero ejus radii iterum defervescunt, rursus se [5] colligit, fluctioneque sua reflectitur.' Hujus orationi vehementer à Daio reclamatum est; qui ubi paucis docuerat, naturam istiusmodi suspicionibus repugnare, adversarium suum, quasi intentantis loco, producendo, interrogando, arguendo premit, impellit, urget; sed cum armato ac bene *parato pugnavit, quem nec subita et fortuita argumentatio facile vincere, nec longa ac diligens oratio superare potuit. Tandem procuratores signum dedere, quo audito cessit Daius invitus de certamine. Ei succedit continuo Mericus vicarius in isto munere. Post hunc, curam et cogitationem prœlii Bristollius suscepit, cui ad eandem pugnam surrogatus est Squierus. Isti tum omnes primam catervam fecere. In hac luctatione contradicentium, quorum argumentationes accepit Campianus, omnesque in venis atque visceribus inclusas suspiciones penitus introspexit, statimque in ipso congressu facillime expedivit. Jam nunc, cum non longe tempus

*Pag. 26.

---

[1] Maritemos *MS.*   [2] Sitima *MS. et B.*   [3] *Sic et B.*
[4] Accidente *MS. et B.*   [5] Collegit, *MS.*

alterius muneris abesset, appellant procuratores Belleium, ac appellando urgent, ut huic certamini disceptator, id est, rei sententiæque moderator, adesset. Id cum audivit, nullam moram interponendam putavit, quin statim, consilio suo, seposita omni rejectione officii, quod tunc forte habebat, repentinus judex consedit, brevique oratione singulas argumentationes conclusit, ancipites variosque illorum casus explicavit, ac ad extremum, magna auditorum voluptate, exitum et determinationem totius controversæ disputationis complexus est. Et Campianus, labore suo jam perfunctus, à suggesto descendit, ceterisque omnibus hæc visa sunt satis. Reginæ vero tam mirifica fuit in audiendo delectatio, ut ei nequaquam satis videri potuerunt. Coacta jam [1] ergo est princeps literarum philosophia pro ea, quæ illi cum * literata principe necessitudo *Pag. 27. intervenit, iterum uno loco, uno die et uno quasi aspectu seipsam patefacere. Ea ergo jam habitu illo prodiit, quo solet modestissimos mores docere; sine quibus nec civitas unquam esse, nec homines ita [2] esse, ut ratio postulat, bene morati possunt. Hujus propugnationem authoritas Cancellarii, benevolusque ceterorum consensus, Wolleo detulit. Eum igitur præcedens Lictor ad suggestum ducit. Quem Lechus statim inter adversarios homo primarius primo à fronte aggreditur, ac, ut eum facilius sede sua commovere ac convellere possit, de gravissimis et implicatissimis controversiis dimicationem proponit. Nihil ibi humile aut depressum erat. Imo vero [3] hoc majus erat totum magnificum et regale. De regno namque adipiscendo et administrando quærebatur, Utra consuetudo probatior, quæ Disciplina melior, quis usus utilior, eorumne, qui hereditario et paterno jure [4] quod successione certum et definitum est, alicui non dubio principatum deferunt, an successioni præferenda sit electio, quæ in plurimorum judicio ac virtute posita, non solet plerumque, nisi quem ex æquo et bono optimum cognoverit, æstimatione sua comprobare? Dehinc quæsivit, Si optio naturæ nostræ detur, si nobis potestas electioque facta sit, utrum velimus in civitate

[1] *Om. H.*   [2] *Om B.*   [3] Hoc etiam *B.*   [4] Quo successore.

illius rectam administrationem ac justam gubernationem, qui cum purpura, sceptro et insignibus regiis benemoratus sedeat, an potius vinci istum ceterosque omnes publico jure patiemur, ita ut sine ea nihil facere, nihil mutare, nihil [1] cuiquam condonare

*Pag. 28.   debeant? *Sed nihil tam implicatum [2] est, quod non potest homo philosophus explicare. Tanta namque erat Wollei memoria, tanta observationis magnitudo ac rerum incredibilis [3] pene animadversio, ut non solum ad singula interrogata aptissime respondere, sed objecta omnia penitus videre, et secum videndo reputare, et reputando discutere, et discutiendo indicare, et indicando refellere, redarguere, dispellere potuerit. Postquam [4] Lechus desiverat, secundus ad certamen accessit Thorntonus, cui successit [5] Bustus, deinde Tobias Matheus, qui ultimum in eo oppugnando locum sortitus est. Isti omnes studio majore, acerrima etiam atque attentissima cogitatione, successionis vim elevare, ac regiam in republica gubernanda authoritatem debilitare conati sunt. Id interim agunt, id moliuntur, ut possint in rege deligendo electionem molestius persuadere, in civitate regenda illum tacitum et elinguem magistratum maxima assiduitate præferre. Ubi vero per istos ancipiti disputatione in utramque partem copiose certatum esset, Cooperus, procuratorum admonitu, suo officio prospexit. Eloquenti igitur oratione involutæ rei notitiam definivit, ac modum quæstionibus ex uniuscujusque vitæ commoditate ac reipublicæ salute imposuit. Non licere scilicet hominibus privatis prædicationem nobilitatemque paternam in filio despicere, sed illum effigiem potius pristinæ et antiquæ claritudinis existimare, nec eum quovismodo paternorum bonorum exheredem

*Pag. 29.   reputare, sed institutum liberaliter, ac ad spem regni politiori disciplina imbutum [6] censere. Neque [7] enim caret electio sua offensione, in qua sæpius videmus magnum odium cum crudelissimo dissidio, ac inter optimos viros de summo jure summas dissentiones, præter legum vacationes, ac inter regnum, quod hoc modo crebro ac frequenter contingit, quæ omnia difficile

---

[1] *Om. B.*   [2] *Om. H.*   [3] *Om. B.*   [4] *Leachus B.*
[5] *Buscus H.* (male).   [6] *Sensere MS.*   [7] *Om. B.*

est dicere, num eis magis calamitosa sint, quibus sunt sub-
eunda, quam omni reipublicæ perniciosa, ubi sunt aliquando
introducta. Deinceps docuit, quam magnum ac sanctum in republica regis nomen esse debeat, quamque omnibus jucundum
et optabile, qui sua auctoritate legis disceptator, ac in rebus
difficilioribus moderator quidam existit, nec id solum videre,
quod jam agitur, verum etiam [1]quid futurum sit providere ac
prospicere, cum lex nullam habeat rationem aut hominum aut
temporum, verum muta nimium est, ac sæpius crudelior, quam
ut [2]eam virtus liberi populi ferre [3]poterit. Sero jam acto hoc
negotio, paulo post sextam Regina pedibus ad palatium revertitur, jam undique strepentibus scholarium vocibus, eoque
magis, quod jam didicere regii satellites ac plebs advena,
maximas istorum salutationes Latine cum eisdem sonare.
Nulla spectacula hac nocte data sunt, quod Regina, longiori
antea disputatione impedita, non potuit eisdem sine salutis
suæ aliquo discrimine adesse.

Dies Mercurii.

Die consequenti, Mercurium appellamus, post meridiem
templum Divæ virginis novas palæstras novo apparatu ac
præparatione sua pollicetur. Concursus itaque omnium frequentior fit, ac brevi tempore tota academiæ multitudo in
eum locum convenit. Regina ornatiori jam lectica, cum ingenti procerum *caterva, cui major illius [4]amplitudo, ancillas *Pag. 30.
pedissequasque adjunxerat. Omnes repente in equis conspicui
visuntur. Tota continuo civitas, solita jam acclamatione,
strepitu, salutatione personabat. Eam acclamationes istæ ad
templum deducunt. Nova inde reclamatio oritur, quo finito,
suggestum [5]ascendit sellaque consedit. Fenestræ statim,
gradus, loca Theatri eminentiora, summa, media, infima,
omnia denique intuentium vultibus complentur. Procuratores
[6]ilico novam dimicationem, sine ulla mora, canunt. Rursus ad

---

[1] Quod *B.*   [2] Eā *H.*   [3] Potuit *B.*

[4] Multitudo, ancillulas *B.*   [5] Assendit *MS.*   [6] Om. *H.*

pugnam homines, natura sua minime profecto contentiosos, impellunt. Tum [1] Awberius (qui, propter juris civilis cognitionem, summo semper in honore fuit) imperium non recusans, locum certaminis, suggestum scilicet, bene paratus [2] conscendit. In hunc Whitus (homo in prosequutionum cautionumque præceptionibus perquam acutus & cautus, ac in communi societate vivendi integerrimus) sine ulla dilatione involat. Ei vestis Dalmatica fuerat, talaris ex electiori et clarissima purpura ; lato clavo coccinio superius induebatur, additum postremo humeris paludamentum est, ejusdem coloris, cum serico subtegmine, similique tum vestiti habitu omnes Doctores sedebant. Inter [3] istos certamen de jure et æquitate fuit. [4] Primo ex   arripiunt causam ad agendum. Quærit Whitus ab [1] Awberio, cum Anteacutenses privilegia quædam authoritate principum nostrorum publicis literis consignata habeant, si integræ gentes nationesque, agitatæ aliqua belli contentione, [5] principis mandato certaverint, [6] ecquid æquum [7] censeat, bello jam confecto, et pace undique stabilita, nulla adhuc per principem nova immunitatum *[8] concessione facta, Anteacutenses istos jure privilegii antiquo et vetusto gaudere? Alteram certationem Bart. ll. Paulus. ff. de solutionibus dabat. Titius à familiari Sempronio mutuatione viginti coronatos Gallicos acceperat, singuli tum novemdecim drachmarum æstimati sunt. Post mutationem, antequam persolutum debitum est, principis edicto (cui omnis potestas æstimationis habendæ permittitur) uniuscujusque coronati pretium diminuendo remittitur. Facit jam pretium mutatum quæstionem, numquid ex æquo et bono debeat Sempronius viginti solos coronatos rependere, an difficiliori conditione solvendi nummi sint, ea scilicet æstimatione ac pretio, quo fuerunt inter mutationem recepti? Multa hinc inde in utramque partem [9] strenue disputata sunt. Proceres jam voluptate capiuntur, ipseque Whitus, impetu ac

*Pag. 31.

---

[1] Auberius *B.*   [2] Ascendit *B.*   [3] Ipsos.
[4] *Sic, cum spatio in MS. et in B.*   [5] Principi *MS.*, principum *B.*
[6] Equid *MS. et B.*   [7] Sentiat *B.*   [8] Accessione *B.*   [9] *Om. B.*

cupiditate vincendi, omnes in admirationem sui traxit, adeoque
fuit huic summo viro ad res magnas bene gerendas divinitus
adjuncta fortuna, ut Reginam ipsam studio suo præ ceteris
suaviter commovere, ac jucunditate quadam perfundere visus
est. Sed hostem, tot legum præsidiis non munitum modo,
sed etiam ornatum, tantoque comitatu virtutis septum, vincere
aut expugnare non potuit. Quamobrem magnum adhuc sui
desiderium proceribus relinquens, Lhuido cessit, qui ab illo
proximus huic militiæ obligatus fuerat. Ille ergo jam respondentem suo more gravius urget, insectatur, et, quocumque se
verterit, persequitur. Sed hunc impellunt procuratores, nec
progredi longius sinunt, Langherum vehementius inclamantes,
quem jam postremo jubent aliquid in aspectum lucemque ex
recondita et inclusa sua legum commentatione proferre. Hic
ergo et leges * et libros testes protulit, protulit inquam res   *Pag. 32.
occultissimas, ac quamplurimis potuit argumentis oneravit
respondentem, sed nihil illum commovere potuit. Ita undique
legum propugnaculis, quasi muro firmissimo & sanctissimo,
septus est. Quamobrem ornatissimum virum vicecancellarium
nostrum altiori voce clamant jam sæpius, ut advolet, ut [1] ex-
peditus accurrat, finem huic certamini suo judicio impositurus.
(Kenallus is erat) quo nemo quisquam est legum, et consuetudinis illius qua utimur, aut ad respondendum, aut ad agendum, aut ad cavendum peritior. Nunc ergo aliquando ab
illo fas erat [2] discere, quanti semper privilegia æstimanda
sunt, quæ secum nimiam vivendi licentiam plerumque tra-
hunt ; quæ jus suum et impunitam omnium rerum libertatem
vendicant, ita ut plerumque et principi et populo odiosa sunt
et molesta, et eo magis quod nunquam soleant, sine publici
juris maxima offensione, contingere. Ita vincula quodammodo revellunt, non modo judiciorum, sed etiam utilitatis
vitæque communis ; ea ergo semel deleta excitare (nisi novo
forte concessu princeps illa speciatim promulgaverit) nihil
erit aliud, quam effigiem quandam spirantis mortui intro-
ducere, qui halitu suo omnia turbat et confundit. In secunda

---

[1] Expiditus *MS.*   [2] Dicere, *MS. et B.*

quæstione illius sermo multus erat de interiori et præstantissima rei mutuatæ bonitate, quod ea in pecuniis ab
æstimatione, non à numero pecuniarum; à pretio, non à
forma; ab usu, non à materiæ qualitate petendą sit. Non
debet ergo Sempronius pro viginti aureis, quos mutuatione
acceperat, * numerum restituere, sed æstimationem, nec formam, sed pretium, maxime cum illos aliunde sumpserat, non
tam propter materiæ qualitatem, quam propter usum, qui
præcipuus in pretio ac æstimatione cernitur. Hac illius oratione, hora jam sexta, disputationes eo die absolutionem per-
fectionemque [1] consequutæ sunt, Regina per solitos applausus,
nos solito cursu domum revertimur. Hac nocte, ludis inter-
missis, instaurativi constituti sunt. Theatrum ergo jam summa
contentione alta nocte repetimus, regina proceresque invitan-
tur spectaculo, invitati accedunt. Consedere omnes, ingens
silentium consequutum est. Jam tum in scena milites ambo,
Arcitus et Palamon, ad diem certum præsto fuere, firmissimo
præsidio uterque septus. Erat ab uno latere Emetrius, In-
dorum rex, cujus in tutela Arcitus fuit. Hunc centum milites
sequuti sunt. Totidem habebat ex altera parte Threicius
Licurgus, cujus virtuti, fidei, felicitati commendatus est
Palamon. Visum est Theseo, [2] pugnam singulari certamine
agi oportere, cum illo virginem futuram, cum quo victoria
fuerit. Haud displicet consilium regibus, nec fratres recusant.
Fiunt igitur in silvis septa marmorea. Tria ibi extruuntur
religiosissima altaria, ad [3] unum, quod Dianæ fuerat, supplex
accedit Emilia. Hic tum illa vitæ solitudinem et perpetuam
castimoniam precatur, infelix nimium non potuit exorare.
Dea matrimonium prædixit. Ex altera parte Arcitus ab eo,
cujus sint in tutela præsidia bellicæ virtutis, victoriam petiit.
Continuo ei Mars intonuit victoriam. Venerem Palamon
altari suo pro virgine precatur, cui illa statim virginem pollicetur. Hic jam inter * Deos contentio facta est. Eam
disrumpit Saturnus. Interea uterque princeps armorum cura-

**Pag. 33.* **Pag. 34.*

---

[1] Consequuti *MS. et B.*   [2] Pugnam . . . futuram *om. B.*
[3] Unam, quæ *MS.*

tionem pro suo milite suscepit, quo finito, tubarum cantus
strepitusque audiuntur. Consertis deinde manibus, ferocius
pugnant. Ut primo statim concursu increpuere arma, mican-
tesque fulsere gladii, horror ingens spectantes perstringit, et
neutro adhuc inclinata spe, bis lassitudine defatigati pugnantes
requiescunt; tertio cum jam non motus tantum corporum
agitatioque anceps telorum, sed vulnera quoque et sanguis
spectaculo omnibus erant, corruit Palamon, et victori objicitur
fratri. Arcitum gaudio omnes conclamant ovantes, gratulan-
tesque accipiunt. Palamonem exanimatum spes jam tota, non
tamen cura, deseruerat. Quamobrem altiori jam oratione actio-
neque ardentiori furit, et Venerem, cui ab infantia serviverat,
quasi nullius jam aut voluntatis aut potestatis execratur. Non
tulit indignantem Venus, nec potuit æquo animo[1] Martem, sibi
præpositum, ferre. Suam causam lamentis agit muliebriter,
fletuque. Ejus lachrimis commotus Saturnus, victorem, in-
signiori laurea triumphantem, igne ferit subterraneo. Ita
confestim Arcitus moritur. Ingens tum apparatus sepulturæ
fuit, publico honestatur funere, subeunt lecticam optimates,
sequuntur reges, corpus solemniori pompa crematur. Postremo regio consilio, communique omnium consensione, Pala-
moni virgo traditur, idque factum frequentissimo jam theatro,
incredibili spectatorum clamore et plausu comprobatum est,
atque hac ista nocte proposita spectacula fuerunt.

Dies Jovis.

*Posterus dies summos homines, doctissimos medicos, sanc- *Pag. 35.
tissimos theologos, contentè pro se quisque [2] dimicantes habuit.
Elapso igitur meridie, hora prima, consueto more, solito loco,
frequentiores convenimus. Regina etiam proceresque ad publicas et forenses exercitationes iterum contendunt. Ei inter
eundum in collegii hortis T.[3] Nelus occurrit, prælector Hebræus.
Is Rabbinorum in duodecim prophetas [4] commentariis, quos

---

[1] *Om. B.*   [2] Demicantes *MS.*
[3] Nealus *B. et sic semper.*   [4] Commentarias, *MS.*

ex Hebræo Latinos fecerat, Regiam majestatem donavit. Paratus etiam gratulatione Hebraica, quam in adventum illius conscripserat, eam salutare, addidit præterea Dialogum versibus conflatum, totius Academiæ topographiam [1] continentem, cum singulis scholarum ac collegiorum genuinis picturis, naturalem eorum situm ac formam indicantibus. Eas formas [2] Berblokus ex collegio Exoniensi calamo suo fecit, opus admirantur omnes. [3] Regina vero, Neli benevolentia, istoque illius dono magnopere commovetur, nec antea unquam visa est ullum munus majus meliusve accepisse, ita amplissimis et singularibus verbis ei gratias egit. Postquam ad templum pervenit, omnesque jam maxime intentis oculis, ora, vultusque eruditissimorum hominum contemplabantur, procuratores solitum dicunt, usitato more loquuntur. Interea [4] Fraunciscus animo certo et confirmato suggestum conscendit, pro medicina fortissimis ac peritissimis ducibus seipsum opposuit. Telis hostium, dimicationi capitis, omnium furori atque ferro seipsum opposuit. Ei initio Huicus, medicus nobilissimus atque optimus, minas jactare ac formidines opponere conatus est. Jam vero vitane [5] *prorogari artis medicæ beneficio queat, ejusque termini [6] proferri, id primo sententiis ac rationibus pugnaverunt. Deinde, num [7] cibi graviores et ad concoquendum difficiliores primo stomacho objiciendi sunt ; secundo vero loco addendi, si qui facilius digeruntur? Proximus in opponendo erat Bailius senior. Si nunquam alias, ab isto tamen homine, Frauncisco licuit et exemplo id demonstrare, quod prima quæstione docuerat, et revera ita esse firmissimo quasi testimonio confirmare. Ita namque suis medicamentis delibutus, itaque [8] seipsum Bailius arte sua levatus est, ut non solum Charontem [9] altera sua pede jam diutius, quam adversa illius valitudo ferre visa est, fefellerit, sed omnium fere [10] expectationem incolumitate sua superarit. Hac de causa, id unum à serenissima principe rogavit, ut, quicquid dicturus esset

*Pag. 36.

---

[1] Contenentem, *MS.* [2] Bearblockus *B.* [3] *Om. B.* [4] Franciscus *B. et sic semper.* [5] Prorogare *MS.* [6] Proferre, *MS.* [7] Sibi *MSS.* [8] *Sic. An,* ipse? [9] *Sic. An,* altero suo? [10] Exercitationem *B.*

contra artem medicam, cujus beneficio vitam ipse suam tam
diu prorogaverat, id omni prorsus fide careret. Cum hîc
uterque post longam concertationem se recepisset, Fraunciscus jam visus est quasi in extrema fortuna consistere. Alter
namque Bailius, qui quasi custos apud nos est rerum medica-
rum, cujusque est in arte medendi interpretanda evolutio,
quasi quoddam oraculum nostræ civitatis, Hic, inquam, pos-
tremus contra Fraunciscum magna vi summo impetu fertur,
opponitur tum scripto scriptoris voluntas, et authoritas, quæ
bene paratum commovere poterat, contraria authoritate mi-
nuitur, quod est objectum tepore quandoque elevatur, quod
est responsum iterum nova contentione frangitur. Procuratores statim, ad hæc hominum tam diversa studia coërcenda, *Pag. 37.
Masterum, quanta voce possunt, alliciunt excitantque. Continuo ergo divisit ille in prima quæstione vitæ terminos, alios
supra-naturales appellavit, à summo Deo admirabili prudentia
multo ante provisos, quos nullo consilio, arte nulla prorogari
fas est. Deinde adduxit accidentarios, qui nullis præsidiis
produci et difficillime præcaveri possunt, quod ab inopinato
casu in singula momenta evenire soleant. Novissimos natu-
rales dixit, naturæ beneficio nobis attributos, futurosque, pro
temperamenti bonitate, corporis structura, victus ratione, salu-
britate cœli et soli, aut longiores aut breviores; istos solet
Medicina prorogare, calidum nativum ne ab humido extin-
guatur fovendo, naturale humidum ne à calido consumatur
reficiendo. In secunda quæstione, esculentorum delectum
atque discrimen fecit, alia primo alimenta esse dixit, alia
deinde medicamenta, alia vero inter hæc media. Eorum
igitur, quæ pura alimenta sunt et duntaxat [1] nutricantur, principio crassiora sumenda [2] sensit, et quæ difficilius concoquun-
tur in intima et calidiori stomachi parte recondi voluit, quod
illa profundior et æstu semper ferventior sit. Debemus tum
levia secundo loco, post hæc tenuissima extremo jam illius
[3] ore et quasi palato collocare; ocius enim ista concalescunt,

---

[1] Nutriantur *H.*   [2] Censit *MS.*   [3] Om. *B.*

et ubi stomachus [1] hebetat, magis ibi tenuitate sua quam [2] mox facillime digeruntur. Sed omnium horum una summa cautio est atque firmissima provisio, hominem bene sanum *cum esse oportere, cui istum vivendi modum ratio et doctrina præscribit. Qui enim infirma sunt et ægra valitudine, hiis alia, eaque paulo incertior lex et regula definita est. Cum ista illius oratione instituta medicorum Disputatio mox absoluta est. Et Fraunciscus tandem, onere ac munere respondendi liberatus, à suggesto discessit. In extrema jam parte hujus operis atque negotii homines integerrimi, quorum existimamus pietatem, quasi lumen aliquod ingens et insigne, elucere, accepta per solenniorum comites tesserula, in aciem contentionemque venerunt. Humfridus illico, cujus labore et assiduitate aditus illi in Theologia difficiles longe lateque se pandunt, nec inimicitias nec vitæ dimicationes pro sanctitate nostræ religionis sibi defugiendas existimans, ex primis doctorum subselliis, ad suggestum respondentis præeunte cum bacillo lictore deductus est. Eum statim sanctissimi illius fratres, eidemque filii, diligenti præparatione aggrediuntur, convellere tentant, quem tamen non possunt commovere. Primos istorum ordines duxit Godwinus, qui percontando atque interrogando binis quæstionibus certo sibi in illo certamine fines terminosque limitavit. Primo igitur quæsivit, *An jus fasque sit homines, sine potestate ac imperio, privato consensu aut communiori aliqua* [3] *consolatione et conciliatione, arma sumere, conducere milites, trahere exercitus, ac vi, quasi tamen vindices tyrannoctoni, sibi arripere potestatem corrigendi, emendandi, puniendi reges suos sceleratos, nefarios, impios?* Iterum deinde rogavit, *num sanctiores *rerum sacrarum ministri, qui in Dei ministeriis vehementius laborant, debent æquali inter se conditione vivere, an potius tenere potestatem et imperium, et usque ad extremum spiritum dominari in suos?* Humfridus continuo utrumque fidenter negavit, [4] Godwinus contra inimicissime et infestissime contendit. Godwinum

*Pag. 38.

*Pag. 39.

---

[1] Hebitat, *MS.*   [2] Mora *malit nonnemo.*
[3] Consacratione *B.*   [4] Godwinus . . . contendit *om. B.*

statim sequutus est Westfalingus, post illum Overtonus, deinde
[1] Calfchillus, deinde [2] Piersus, omnes profecto consecratiori legis
scientia, ac vitæ singulari sanctimonia [3] religiosissime, in quibus
par jam idemque erat voluntas, studium æquale, et simile
veritatis desiderium. Sed non fuit controversia hæc [4] discep-
tatio sola, fuit et cognitio veritatis. Hinc igitur istos videre
licuit plura conari, illum vero ex adverso omnia perficere,
istos infinita voluisse, hunc contra omnia potuisse. Nec cuiquam mirum esse debet, homines istos tam in hac causa
adversus illum impotentes fuisse. Neque [5] enim quod fecerunt,
id omne arbitrio suo fecerunt; sed officio ac necessitate
adducti, timide, verecunde dubitanterque istam causam receperunt. Et quos inter agendum investigatio veri fecerat
vehementiores, eos fecit sanctitas atque religio in eventu
[6] remissiores. Tandem vero, ubi, omnibus urgentibus, contentione, gravitate et argumentorum pondere nihil labefactari
potuit Humfridi sententia, scholarum tum comites, justi comi-
tiorum rogatores, adhibita sanctitatis suæ debita reverentia,
D. Juellum, Salisburgensem Episcopum, etiam atque etiam
[7] orant, ut sua velit authoritate multitudinem litium, et varietatem illam causarum inter homines tam pios ac religiosos
judicio suo componere. Dixit ergo doctissimus Præsul, sine
omni *cunctatione ac tarditate, quod sensit, non licere *Pag. 40.
nobis, nec posse homines privatos, sine summo scelere ac
maximo maleficio, sui principis perditos ac impios conatus
vindicare. Neque enim subditos suppliciorum metus à domi-
norum potestate liberare, nec ab hujus imperio vel nostra
innocentia, vel mortis terror, vel res gestæ illius sceleratæ,
vel alius quicunque metus avocare debet. Quinetiam eis
obedire ac parere debemus, neque solum parere, verum [8] etiam
eos colere atque diligere, illud unum scientes, cujus toties in
sacra pagina admonemur, quod idem ille, qui eis resistit, nihil
videtur aliud, quam summi ac omnipotentis Dei ordinationi
ac constitutioni resistere. Id manifesto ita esse, exemplis

---

[1] Caulfhillus *B.*   [2] Piersius *B.*   [3] *An,* religiosissimi?   [4] Disputatio *B.*
  [5] *Om. B.*   [6] Remitiores *H.*   [7] Rogant *B.*   [8] *Om. H.*

docuit et firmissimis rationibus confirmavit. Deinde ministerium, laborem quidem majoris operis atque muneris esse
dixit, attamen ut jucundior nobis esset illius functio, ei tribuit
omnem divinitatem, principatum et dominationem inde sus-
tulit, ac ab omni cum servitute et molestia liberavit. Jusque
ministris omnibus æquabile et unum esse dixit, opusque æquabiliter inter eos dispartiri voluit, neminem intollerantius sese
[1]jactitare, aut præstantiam doctrinæ, dignitatis, laboris vel
fortunæ [2]magnifice gloriari: sed simili [3]consentione ac conflatu
summo conspirantes, omnem offensionem fugere, simultatem
depellere, ac tandem inter se fraterna æqualitate vivere. Com-
prehensionem postremo orationis, sanctiori jam ad Deum
precatione pro principe nostra, clausam et terminatam habuit.

*Pag. 41. Eam sequuta ex tota multitudine consentiens vox, applau-
susque frequentior mirifice comprobavit. Ac ne hîc quidem
videtur mihi silentio prætereundum, quod in extrema parte et
conclusione disceptationis nostræ ab illustrissima Regina,
summa benevolentia ac suavitate, factum est. Illa namque
statim humanissima (ne gravissimo indicio taciturnitatis suæ
videretur labores nostros in contemptione ac despicientia
posuisse) [4]consessum intuens, nosque omnes circumspiciens
atque considerans, incredibili statim facilitate incepit Orato-
rem agere, dicendo peragrare per animos omnium, ac sensus
mentesque nostras oratione sua pertractare. Muliebris verecundia atque modestia cunctantem eam primo atque diffiden-
tem fecit, pudoreque virginali, quantum illius ætas ac educatio
patiebatur, erubuisse visa est, ac à dicendo timiditate quadam
ingenua aliquandiu refugisse, cunctantem vero ac verecun-
dantem amor incredibilis nostrorum omnium mirum sane est
[5]quantum eam statim commovit. Ita namque tota multitudo,
omniumque tum vultus ex illius ore et sermone avidissima
spe atque expectatione pendebat, ut inde excitata, animo
[6]corroborato [7]ac [7]confirmato, orationem apud nos, in hanc
ferme sententiam, pronunciaverit.

[1] Jactare *B.*   [2] Mirifice *B.*   [3] *Sic et B.*   [4] Concessum *MS. et B.*
        [5] Quam *B.*   [6] Corroborata *B.*   [7] *Om. B.*

Qui male agunt oderunt lucem, et idcirco quia ego conscia sum mihimet male acturæ causam meam apud vos, puto hoc tempus tenebrarum mihi fore aptissimum. (Hoc tum initio usa est, quia nox erat, omniaque jam latere visa [1] sunt, crassis occultata et circumfusa tenebris.) *Magna vero me diu tenuit dubitatio, taceremne an loquerer. Si enim loquar, patefaciam vobis, quam sim litterarum rudis. Quod si tacerem, defectus hic videretur esse contemptus. Quod igitur attinet ad ea, quæ *vidi aut audivi, ex quo veni in hanc Academiam, fuerunt ea* *Pag. 41. *omnia (meo [2] quidem judicio) pereximia. Quia vero tempus breve est, quod superest ad dicendum, duo duntaxat vobis in genere jam dicere institui; quorum alterum est laudare, et alterum vituperare. Laus autem ad vos pertinet. Non possum namque non laudare et vos, et quæ à vobis dicta sunt et facta, eaque probare omnia, quasi pereximia et excellentia. Ceterum nonnulla, quæ imperfectiora in se erant, quæ in prologis vestris vos ipsi excusastis, quatenus sum Regina probare non possum. Quia tamen in exordiis cautionem habuistis, in suo genere tanquam perfectissime acta et disputata non improbo, sed alterum illud vituperare ad me proprie pertinet, quia cum omnibus notum sit, me aliquam operam impendisse bonis disciplinis et linguis addiscendis, Pædagogi tamen mei in terram tam sterilem et infœcundam operam suam posuerunt, ut non possim jam cum maxime velim, fructus ostendere, aut dignitate mea, aut illorum laboribus, aut vestra expectatione dignos. Quamobrem, cum vos me supra modum laudatis, ego, quæ mihi optime conscia sum, quam sim nulla laude digna facile agnosco. Finem igitur faciam huic orationi meæ, barbarismis plenæ, si duo vota prius addidero, quæ in animo habeo, ut me vivente sitis florentissimi, me mortua beatissimi.* Dixi.

Audita est magno silentio, ac summa omnium attentione. Deinde maximæ ad [3] eam acclamationes, ac pro illa comprecationes sequuntur. Parietes, adeoque fenestræ, ac subsellia, vocibus nostrorum hominum visa tum sunt resonare vehementius, ac iterum nobis verba nostra perfectiori quodam *Pag. 43.

<hr>

[1] *Om. B.*   [2] Sane *B.*   [3] Eum *MS.*

sono referre. Et quamvis erant jam acta in serum hujus diei protracta, ita ut multa nocte domum remeare coacta sit, pedibus tamen per confertissimos homines patientissima remeavit. Hic sextus ab adventu principis dies in civitatem fuit. Is jam quartam in theatro noctem ludorum nostrorum dedit. Tum munus amplissimum et apparatissimum, quod communis expectatio desiderabat, communi opera restituitur. Ejus elegantia ac scenæ magnificentia Regina proceresque mirum in modum ac impense admodum delectati sunt. Fabulam sexto humanarum conversionum libro Ovidius dedit. [1] Ex eo libet, quantum possumus, eandem referre. Primo ibi exauditus est strepitus quidam subterraneus, reconditus & formidabilis. Hinc sese infernis è partibus erigit Diomedes. Illud vero tum fuit horribile, spumas agere in ore, caput, pedes, brachia, flagrantia habere, non fortuito, sed insito et innato [2] incendio, ipsum vero misere nimis perterreri, ac agitari furiarum tædis ardentibus, ad facinus immane ac nefandum impelli, domo scilicet propria virus acerbitatis suæ evomere, ad nepotum thalamos omnia dira canere. Sed Dæmonem [3] istum tam tetrum, tam horribilem, tam infestum suis consistere nusquam longius patiuntur, ad inferna iterum maximo luctu laboreque tanquam in pistrinum aliquod, eum furiæ detrudunt. Tereus interea ab Athenis domum revertitur, commentaque sororis Philomelæ funera uxori Progne subdole et versute refert.

> *Lachrimæ fecere fidem, velamina Progne*
> [4]*Deripit ex humeris, auro fulgentia lato.*
> *Induiturque atras vestes,*
> *Et luget non sic lugendæ fata sororis.*

*Pag. 44.

Neque enim sensu et vita caruit tum Philomela, sed fratris Terei, viri petulantis et impuri, vi compressa, libidines, contumelias, turpitudinesque subierat. Nec tamen ita conquiescit homo audacissimus. Nova [5] enim voluptatis libido ad aliud insanum facinus suscipiendum eum continuo impellit: taciturnitatem namque crudelitate ac sanguine firmavit,

---

[1] Ex eo . . . referre *om. B.*   [2] Fulmine *B.*
[3] *Om. H.*   [4] Derepit *MS.* diripit *B.*   [5] Etenim *B.*

Arreptamque coma, flexis post terga lacertis
Vincla pati cogit.
Luctantemque loqui comprensam forcipe linguam
Abstulit ense ferox.
   De scelere hoc possit ne miseranda queri.
Os mutum facti caret indice.
                    fugam custodia claudit.

Saxis tum facta ejus lapidatio est.   Ibi ei pro cubiculis stabula, pro tricliniis carcer, pro strato stramen fuit.

                         Grande doloris
         Ingenium est, miserisque venit solertia rebus.
         Indicium sceleris filis intexuit albis.
                         Tradidit uni,
         Vtque ferat Dominæ [1]gestu rogat, illa rogata
         Pertulit ad Prognen.
         Evolvit vestes sævi matrona tyranni,
         Fortunæque suæ carmen miserabile legit,
         Et mirum potuisse (silet!) dolor ora repressit.

Pœnasque [2]expetere domestici sanguinis mirum est quam desideraverit.   Pergit ergo peccata ulcisci peccatis, et [3]injurias injuriis, nec scelera jam sceleribus addere quicquam verita est. Omnium itaque primum modum excogitavit, quo ereptam *sororem recuperare possit.   Liberi patris sacrificia simulat, *Pag. 45. multisque bacchantibus comitata

               Venit ad stabula avia tandem,
         Exululatque, evoeque sonat, portusque refringit,
         Germanamque rapit, raptæque insignia Bacchi
         Induit.
         Attonitamque trahens, intra sua mœnia ducit,
                    fletumque sororis
         Corripiens, Non est lachrimis hoc, inquit, agendum,
         Sed ferro, seu, si quid habes, quod vincere ferrum
         Possit, in omne nefas ego me, germana, paravi.
         Aut ego cum facibus regalia tecta cremabo,
         Aut linguam, aut oculos, aut quæ tibi membra pudorem
         Abstulerunt, ferro rapiam, aut per vulnera mille
         Sontem animam expellam.
                    Peragit dum talia Progne,
         Ad matrem veniebat Itis.   Quid possit ab illo
         Admonita est, oculisque tuens immitibus, ah! quam
         Es similis patri, dixit, nec plura loquuta,
         Triste parat facinus.
         Mater Itin puerum, visu miserabile! mactat,
            Apponitque fero viscera cocta patri.
         Ipse sedens solio Tereus sublimis avito,
         Vescitur, inque suam sua viscera congerit alvum.

[1] Precibus *B.*   [2] Repetere *B.*   [3] Injuria *MS. et B.*

Vescenti Philomela caput cervice resectum
Misit in ora patris, nec tempore maluit ullo
Posse loqui.
Thracius ingenti mensas clamore repellit,
Et sequitur nudo genitas Pandione ferro.

Eratque spectaculum istud in pravis actibus insignis humani
*Pag. 46.   generis similitudo, fuitque intuentibus * quasi fabula quædam
illustris eorum omnium, qui vel amori, vel iracundiæ nimium
indulgent, quorum utrumque, etiamsi ad meliores veniunt,
inflammant tamen appetitione nimia, eosque longe quam
antea ferociores impotentioresque reddunt, atque voce, vultu,
spiritu, dictis et factis, à temperantia et moderatione plurimum
dissidentes.   Finito spectaculo, cum jam populus [1] ingenti
[2] assensione principis nomine plausum atque probationem
dedisset, domum festinantes [3] revertuntur.

Dies Veneris.

Insequens jam Veneris dies, antecedentibus calamitosior,
[4] nobis illuxit.   Ut enim nos antea principis adventus mirifice
levarat, sic hodie subitus illius discessus, præcepsque profectio, multo gravius vehementiusque afflixit.   Sed æquo
animo ferre necesse erat.   Fuit ita [5] enim gravi fato et prius
fundatum et constitutum.   Primo igitur diluculo, lictores
nuncii procul ad singula collegia amandantur, Doctores omnes
præpositi collegiorum ab eisdem citantur, denunciant magistris consilium statum, et solenne, majorem convocationem
vocamus, campana.   Deinde quasi certo indicio [6] monemur.
Nemo tum [7] obsurdescit.   Multitudo omnis in sanctiori et
secretiori [8] parte templi Divæ virginis confestim [9] congregata
est, Domusque illa jam erat non communi conventu, sed
electiori magistrorum turba referta.   Referente ibi doctissimo
vicecancellario nostro, ac Comitibus solenniorum tredecim ex
proceribus, tanquam maximum et certissimum nostræ erga
illos benevolentiæ indicium, muneribus Academiæ amplissimis
*Pag. 47.   ornamus, donamus magisterio.   Honestissimos etiam homines,

---

[1] *Om. H.*   [2] Ascensioni *H.* assentione *B.*   [3] Revertimur *B.*   [4] *Om. B.*
[5] Enim ita fixum *B.*   [6] Monentur *B.*   [7] Obsurdescet *H.*   [8] Parti
MS.   [9] Congreta *MS.*

quos gymnasii nostri soror germana Cantabrigia celsiori magisterii titulo, aut sublimiori Doctorum gradu collocaverat, pro illa, quæ nobiscum intervenit, fraterna necessitudine, amoreque incredibili, eodem apud [1] nos dignitatis honore ac gradu collocamus. Isti hora nona, frequenti magistrorum congregatione, ab hiis, quibus, annua quadam commutatione imperii nostri, procuratio ac civitatis gubernatio permissa est, summo omnium consensu, in numerum collegiumque nostrum cooptantur. Quod vero negotii erat in proceribus admittendis, illius omnem curationem procuratores, eorumque deputati comites suscipiunt. Domo regia communiore, scilicet Collegii Christi Aula, [2] perficiunt. Hora nona, [3] Peirsus, sacræ theologiæ Doctor, in augustissimo palatii templo De functione curaque regia, Latine concionatus est. Hora post meridiem tertia, prope jam occidente sole, pientissima princeps discessionem parat. Mora, cunctatio, ejusque tam sera abitio, indicia nobis manifesta fuerunt, quam voluit mansisse; sed famulitium immensum erat, ac concursationis multitudo infinitior, nec civitas eam sine majori apparatu habere aut capere potuit. Ita ergo nobis discessit, ut invita, ac [4] necessario illud fecisse videretur. Exeunti statim in ipso palatii vestibulo Tobias Matheus occurrit, eam eloquentia suæ orationis commorari diutius cogit, communi suorum nomine gratias agit, fausta ac felicia omnia precatur, ac denique collegarum verbis ei dixit vale. A palatio, modico ad dextram flexu, ad ecclesiam Sancti Martini, insigne illud quadrivium, urbis [5] umbilicum, profecta est. Hîc nova, eaque iterum dextra, ad orientem flexione utitur. Inde ad templum *omnium Sanc- *Pag. 48. torum contendit, tum ad ædem Deiparæ virginis. Incredibilis tum fuit fori strepitus, fremitus, clamor à suspensis et pendentibus speculis, ab ædium projecturis, à periculosissimis locis, unde, cum ingenti omnium admiratione, salutantes ac vale dicentes, homines, pueri feminæque prospiciebant. Hoc jam loco, ne novissima nostra facta inconvenientia forent

---

[1] *Deest in MS.*   [2] Perficiant *MS.*   [3] Piersus *B.*
[4] Necessario . . . statim in *om. B.*   [5] Umbelicum, *MS. et B.*

primis, tota Academiæ multitudo, ad utrumque vici latus æquabiliter dispartita, in conspectu principis pulcherrime stetit. Licuit ibi ex uniuscujusque habitu, quo quisque tum apud nos, dignitate, gradu, honore fuisset facillime indicare. Nec aliquis tum fuit ex tanta frequentia, qui non se totum, nervos viresque omnes, hujus salutationi dedit vovitque. Illa interim, mœsta ac tristis, mœrorem animi nostri dolore suo [1]adjuvavit. Visa namque est abitionem istam gravate ferre, ac ideo molestius inter equitandum fortunam suam accusare. Dicitur de iniqua, sua sorte gravissime conqueri, quod antea coacta sit à nobis discedere, quam aut collegium aliquod inviserit, aut alicujus sacrati hominis concionem audierit. Nec unquam aliàs hospitio suo magis mœstam exisse ferunt, quam hodie civitate nostra exierit. Hæc accusans, sæpiusque ad nos suavissime respiciens, per portam orientalem, collegiumque Magdalenæ, ad præscriptos Academiæ fines terminosque pervenit. Ibi tum iterum [2]Marbeccus docuit, quam reipsa et animo grata Academiæ fuisset sua præsentia, quantam ad [3]studendum alacritatem omnibus attulisset, quanta calcaria adhibuisset, quantos in omnium mentibus igniculos accendisset. Deinde gratias illi, quantas maximas animo orationeque sua capere potuit, nostrorum nominibus egit cumulatissime. Post *istam orationem, singuli Doctores ad illius pedes provoluti, gratias immortales egerunt, multamque ei salutem dixerunt. Eos illa statim ad dextræ osculum humanissime erexit, vultuque ac verbis [4]eis declaravit, nullum nostrum aut dictum aut factum, ex quo ad Academiam accessisset, intervenisse, quod illa non illustri gratia acceperit, adeoque animo suo coluerit, ut sit inde longe jam paratior vel dignitatem vel vitam dimittere, quam custodiam capitis nostri, aut commemorationem nominis deponere. Hac in optione à nobis illa statim sine ulla mora discessit, nosque domum revertimur, reliquum jam [5]nihil esse existimantes, quam ut illam proficiscentem amore prosequamur, redeuntem spe expectemus, absentem omni memoria, officio, fide, pietateque colamus.

Pag. 49.

---

[1] *Sic et B.*   [2] *Marbeckus B.*   [3] Studiendum *MS.*   [4] *Om. H.*   [5] *Om. B.*

ACADEMIÆ OXONIENSIS
TOPOGRAPHICA DELINEATIO

Per *THOMAM NELUM*

COLLEGIORUM

Scholarumque Publicarum

ACADEMIÆ

OXONIENSIS

Topographica Delineatio

Per Thomam Nelum

E Codice MS. in Archivis Bibliothecæ
Bodlejanæ descripsit ediditque

Tho. Hearne, A. M. Oxoniensis

OXONII

E Theatro Sheldoniano

MDCCXIII

COLLEGIORUM

SCHOLARUMQUE PUBLICARUM

ACADEMIÆ

OXONIENSIS

TOPOGRAPHICA DELINEATIO

[*Plate omitted.*]

ASPICIS, ut viget hæc fixis radicibus arbor?
  Hac illac patulis frondibus aucta suis?
Arbor Hebraismi typus est, quæ frondibus auctam
  Se gaudet nummis, Elisabetha, tuis.
Plantavit Deus hanc primus sator in Paradiso,
  Verbaque mortales jussit Hebræa loqui.
Transtulit huc olim Pater hanc tuus inclytus; ejus
  Tu pia radices, Elisabetha, rigas.
Par est ergo tibi fructus hos proferat arbor,
  Sumptibus (o Princeps maxima) culta tuis.

Serenissimæ Augustissimæque Principi Dominæ
ELISABETHÆ REGINÆ Angliæ, Franciæ, ac
Hiberniæ, Christianæ Fidei Propug-
natrici, &c. Fausta feliciaque
sunto omnia.

Habes en (illustrissima Princeps Elisabetha) Oxoniensis
Academiæ tuæ Collegiorum Scholarumque publicarum qua-
lemcunque topographicam delineationem, calamo partim scrip-

torio, partim carmine poetico sub Dialogi forma utcunque
expressam, ejus ut universam imaginem præsentem, quasique
ob oculos expositam, pro tuo arbitratu habeas, cujus incolæ
bonarum artium omnium studiosi sub auspicatissimo hoc
regno tuo, haud aliter ac sub Minervæ cujusdam clypeo tuti,
ardentius nihil obnixiusve a Deo Opt. Max. contendunt, quam
ut omnes ac singuli suam tibi, quam summam debent, obser-
vantiam, fidem, industriam certatim præstare possint. Cujus
quidem delineandæ ratio tametsi crassiore quadam Minerva
& impolitiore tum stilo, tum carmine constet quam ut regiæ
Majestatis tuæ aspectu digna videri possit, dabis tamen (ut
spero) veniam primis hisce conatibus in re nova, qui non
alio, quam gratulandi animo Serenissimæ Majestatis tuæ quam
exoptatissimo huic ad nos adventui instituti sunt.   Illud vero
in universum quam fieri potest humillime supplex regiam Majestatem tuam rogatam velim (Princeps augustissima) ut quae

————— pictoribus atque poetis

Quidlibet audendi semper fuit æqua potestas,

eam mihi nequaquam hic interclusam esse velis, interea temporis dum regiæ Majestatis tuæ nomini amplissimo Dialogi
partem alteram interlocutoriam attribuo, alteram vero honoratissimo Domino Roberto Dudlæo, Comiti Lecestrensi
nostroque Cancellario dignissimo vicissim accommodo. Ser-
vato tamen utrobique (quod spero) utriusque tum tuæ, tum
illius personæ decoro. Argumentum porro Dialogi tale fingi-
tur, quale ex abrupto, vel e re nata desumptum videri
possit. Perinde ac si te (Regina nobilissima) Woodstochio
discessuram Cancellarius interrogaret, ecquo tandem proficisci
luberet, ut ex eo arrepta deinceps occasione, futuræ narrationi
topographicæ via quasi sterni videatur. Quæ si Regiæ tuæ
unius præstantiæ quoquo modo grata esse poterit, eadem tum
aliis multo gratior, tum mihi quoque qualiscunque hæc opera
quam gratissima fuerit. Faxit Deus Opt. Max. ut quam
diutissime valeas.

Serenissimæ Majestatis tuæ obsequentissimus Alumnus,

THOMAS NELUS, Hebraicæ linguæ Professor Oxon.

Dialogus in adventum Reginæ Serenissimæ Dominæ
Elisabethæ gratulatorius, inter eandem Reginam
& Dominum Robertum Dudlæum Comitem
Lecestriæ & Oxoniensis Academiæ
Cancellarium.

Interloquuntur Regina & Cancellarius Oxon.

Cancell. Siccine (chara tuis, regnique columna Britanni
      Elisabetha) domo pergis abire tua?

Regina. Non ego pergo domo peregre procul hospes abire,
      Sed quo pergo, mea est urbs ea tota domus.

Cancell. Quod res est loqueris, (Princeps ter maxima,) tota
      Nam Regni sedes est domus ista tua.

Regina. Quum sint ergo domus mihi plures, pluraque tecta,
      Quid ni mutarem tecta subinde mea?

Cancell. Sed si pace tua liceat mihi scire, lubenter
      Hoc equidem scirem quo tibi tendat iter.

Regina. Oxonium versus pergo, Musisque dicata
      Tecta peto, Musis concomitata meis.

Cancell. Et quæ tanta subit Musas ibi caussa videndi,
      Quum sit Musarum præsto caterva domi?

Regina. Ipsamet illa domi Musarum præsto caterva
      Has sibi sacratas suasit adire domos.

Cancell. Næ tu digna tuis persolvis præmia Musis,
      Dum loca Musarum visere sacra paras.

Regina. Ecquid enimvero rerum spectabo novarum?
      Dignumve adventu Principis ecquid habet?

Cancell. Urbs antiqua tuis visenda patebit ocellis,
      Et manibus cives oscula fida dabunt.

Regina. Num quid præterea dignum aut memorabile cernam?
      Quod merces tanto digna labore siet?

Cancell. Cernes præcipue Musarum quinque ter ædes,
      Urbs quibus Europæ non habet ulla pares.

Regina.   Tune ergo has ædes nosti, quas Thamisis, amnis
              Inclytus, alluvio cingit utrinque suo?
Cancell. Quidni pernoscam? quarum Dux esse lubenter
              Jampridem cœpi, nec piget esse ducem.
Regina.   Siccine tu subito Musis Dux esse volebas,
              Qui Lecestrensis diceris esse Comes?
Cancell. Non minor est studiis, quam castris, fama [1]præesse,
              Et Ducis & Comitis nomen utrumque juvat.
Regina.   Quin harum breviter mihi nomina pande domorum,
              Quis, cui, quam tulerit fautor & author opem.
Cancell. Hoc equidem faciam quanta brevitate licebit
              Paucula metiri pluribus apta metris.

Ecclesia Christi.

[*Plate omitted.*]

Prima stat australis Domus ampla, Ecclesia Christi,
    Primo jam duplici nomine digna loco;
Tum quia te, patremque tuum sit nacta patronum,
    Tum quia sit reliquis auctior ista cohors.
Cœpta quidem Thomæ Wulsæi sumptibus olim,
    Sed patris Henrici censibus aucta tui.

Cœpit sub Henrico octavo, per Thomam Wulsæum Archiepiscopum Eboracensem, Anno Domini 1529; absoluta est ab
eodem Henrico octavo, Anno Domini 1546.

Regina interloquitur.

Regina.   Unde fit, ut, posset quam plures illa fovere,
              Non foveat numeros undique plena suos?
Cancell. Tot fovet illa quidem, quot par est census alendis;
              Et plures aleret pluribus aucta bonis.
              Invida sed Musis mors immatura Patroni
              Fecit, ut hic possit pluribus esse locus.
Regina.   Est ergo cui quis possit prodesse : paratæ
              Materiæ citius debita forma datur.

[1] Sic in MS.

Collegium Oriall.

[Plate omitted.]

Cancell. Sed pergam in reliquis. Stat Musis septima sedes
       Orial, o vere regia dicta domus.
     Annis illa valens, Edwardi tempora vidit,
       Qui rex illius nominis alter erat.
     Condidit hanc Adam quidam cognomine Brownus,
       Et regi nomen detulit ille suo.

Cœpit sub Edowardo secundo per Dominum Adam Browne,
Eleemosynarium ejusdem Edouardi, Anno Domini 1323.

Collegium Corporis Christi.

[Plate omitted.]

     Quinta jubet nostræ memores nos esse salutis,
       Quo modo, & unde salus parta sit illa docens.
     Quam Deus assumpto quia Christus corpore donat,
       Corporis a Christi nomine nomen habet.
     Censibus hanc amplis Richardus Foxus abunde
       Sustinet, & Musis apta dat esse loca.

Cœpit sub Henrico Septimo per Richardum Fox, episcopum
Wintoniensem, anno Domini 1516.

Collegium Mertonense.

[Plate omitted.]

     Nec procul hinc distat, quæ sexta est ordine,
         Merton,
       Seu Mertonensis dicta perampla Domus.
     Gualterus Merton Præsul (quo Præsule Roffa
       Floruit) huic Domui fautor & author erat.
     Quæ quamvis multos foveat pia mater alumnos,
       Ædes sacra tamen pluribus apta foret.

Cœpit sub Edouardo primo per Gualterum Merton episcopum Roffensem, anno Domini 1276.

Collegium Novum.

[Plate omitted.]

Cancell. Proxima mox sequitur satis ampla frequensque
   studentum
  Turba, novi cœtus nomen adepta diu.
  Turribus hæc altis toto micat æthere, raris
  Doctrinæ gemmis vitis onusta suis.
  Condidit hanc Præsul Guilielmus, in urbe Wykama
  Proles ter fausto sydere nata, Wykam.

Cœpit sub Richardo secundo per Guilielmum de Wykham
episcopum Wintoniensem, anno Domini 1375.

Collegium Magdalenense.

[Plate omitted.]

  Nec minus est celebris domus ampla, dicata Mariæ,
  Cujus sacra fidem Magdala castra docent,
  Splendida munificum testantur tecta patronum,
  Æmula splendoris digna, Wykame, tui.
  Indidit huic nomen Guilielmus Waynflet, alumnus
  Unus & ipse gregis, magne Wykame, tui.

Cœpit sub Henrico sexto per Guilielmum Waynflet episcopum Wintoniensem, anno Domini 1459.

Cancellarius interloquitur.

Cancell. Debebant paribus Collegia cætera verbis
  Describi, mora ni tædia longa daret.
Regina. Perge modo, & reliquis data nomina prima recense,
  Auribus hæc parient tædia nulla meis.

Collegium Omnium Animarum.

[Plate omitted.]

Corpora præpropero studio plerique saginant,
  Nec curant animas sedulitate pari.

Id ne Musarum faceret studiosa juventus,
    Admonet apposito nomine quarta Domus.
Sumptibus Henrici Chichlæi structa, juvandæ
    Ceu foret hæc animæ tota dicata Domus.

Cœpit sub Henrico Sexto per Henricum Chichlæum Archiepiscopum Cantuariensem, anno Domini 1437.

Collegium Reginale.

[*Plate omitted.*]

Huic itidem similis Pastor Robertus Eglisfild
    Reginæ munus donat & ipse suæ.
Nam Reginalem quum Magnis sumptibus ædem
    Fundasset, vocat hanc (clara Philippa) tuam.
Femina quo Musis nutrix, non dura noverca,
    Pergeret, & studiis Mater adesse pia.

Cœpit sub Edowardo Tertio per Dominum Robertum Eglysfild, Sacellanum Dominæ Philippæ, uxoris ejusdem Edowardi, anno Domini 1340.

Collegium Universitatis.

[*Plate omitted.*]

En tibi jam prodit speciosa Academia, quæ quum
    Sit species, generis nomen adaucta tenet.
Ut Logice species generatim sæpe vocatur,
    Et pars pro toto corpore sæpe venit.
Huic Dunelmensis Guilielmus presbyter ædi,
    Communi studiis nomen ab urbe, dedit.

Cœpit sub [1]Aluredo, per Dominum Guilielmum Archidiaconum Dunelmensem, anno Domini 873.

Regina interloquitur.

Regina. Illud in his summa puto dignum laude, quod ipsi
    Noluerint titulis luxuriare suis.

[1] Lege potius, Cœpit sub Aluredo rege A.D. 873. Restaurat. per Guil. Archid. Dunelm. circa A. D. 1249.

Cancel.   Omnibus hæc eadem laus est communis, habetque
             In reliquis itidem laus ea vera locum.
Regina.   Summæ laudis erat, gestis tot rebus honestis,
             Laudibus authores abstinuisse suis.
Cancel.   Tres aliæ restant inclusæ mœnibus ædes,
             Quas nullo fas est præteriisse modo.

Collegium Ænei Nasi.

[*Plate omitted.*]

Æneus his nasus prælucet, ut insula ponto
   Prominet, aut reliquo nasus in ore nitet.
Quæ domus impensis Guilielmi structa Smythæi,
   Æneo & æterno nomine digna manet.
Multis illa quidem turbis conferta studentum,
   Spes ut sit messis magna futura bonæ.

Cœpit sub Henrico 7° per Guilielmum Smythe episcopum
Lincolniensem, anno Domini 1513.

Collegium Lincolniense.

[*Plate omitted.*]

Huic latus occiduum claudit Lincolnia sedes,
   Quæ sibi Patronos gaudet habere duos.
Alter erat Thomas Rotheram, Richardus & alter
   Fleminge, ejusdem Præsul uterque loci.
Quos ubi ditarat Lincolnia, gratus uterque,
   Non sibi, sed sedi dona dat ista suæ.

Cœpit sub Henrico 5° per Richardum Fleminge episcopum
Lincolniensem, anno Domini 1420. Auctum per Thomam
Rotherham, episcopum Lincolniensem, anno 1479.

Collegium Exoniense.

[*Plate omitted.*]

Distat ab Oxonio spatiis Exonia multis,
   Et procul occidui vergit ad ora maris.

Attamen Oxonii sedes Exonia fixas
      Invenit, & Musis jam fit amica quies.
Condidit has Præsul Gualterus Stapleton ædes,
      Indidit & sedi nomina digna suæ.

Cœpit sub Edouardo 2° per Gualterum Stapleton episcopum Exoniensem, anno Domini 1316. Auctum sub Elisabetha Regina per Dominum Guilielmum Petræum ordinis equestris militem inauratum 1566.

Regina interloquitur.

Regina.   O pia pontificum mens hæc! o tempora fausta
      Quæ tantos clero progenuere viros!
Cancell. Clerica sic olim concors concordia clero
      Certatim voluit ferre libenter opem.
      Sed ne sola suos videatur clerica turba,
      Et Musas opera velle fovere sua,
      Arctica si lubeat pomœria pulchra videre,
      Hisce parem laicos ferre videbis opem.
Regina.   Siccine conjunctis certatum est viribus, urbs hæc
      Ut fieret studiis tota dicata sacris?
      Quin age dic laico quot habemus in ordine, Musas
      Auctas hic opera qui voluere sua.
Cancell. Illud ego (Princeps ter magna) lubentius addam,
      Tota quod hic nostræ laudis harena patet.
      Sed mihi restat adhuc prædictis ædibus, intra
      Muros, appendix adjicienda prius.
      Quæ tua quum laus sit, (Guilielme Petræe) lubenter
      Reginæ dabis hic nonnihil ultro tuæ.
      Quod te præcipue videatur amare, suisque
      Consiliis præsto semper adesse velit.
      Patria te jactat genuisse Devonia, & urbs hæc
      Gaudet se studiis instituisse suis.
      Sumptibus ergo tuis tu gratus utrique parenti,
      Auxiliatrices reddis utrinque manus.

Ut quas exiles prius hic Oxonia habebat,
    Has habeat plenas jam satis aucta domos.
Aucta quidem numero, sed & amplis censibus aucta
    Clara sub imperiis Elisabetha tuis.
Quæ quales, quantosque tibi promittat alumnos,
    Ex uno disci cætera turba potest.
Is Berblokus erit, cujus dexterrima dextra
    Has formas mira dexteritate dedit.
Quin age, macte tua virtute (Petræe) fovendis
    Fœtibus hisce tuis quam potes adfer opem.

Collegium Trinitatis.

[*Plate omitted.*]

Urbis at egressæ jam mœnia, proxima sedes
    Occurrit Thomæ sumptibus aucta Popi.
Quam sacrosanctæ Triadis cognomen habere
    Jussit inauratus Miles, equestre Decus.
Hujus adhuc teneros fœtus, pia mater adauget
    Conjunx, tam digno conjuge digna suo.

Cœpit sub Maria Regina per Dominum Thomam Popum,
ordinis equestris militem inauratum, anno Domini 1556.

Collegium Balliolense.

[*Plate omitted.*]

Sed minus hoc mirum est, nostrates hactenus urbem
    Hanc juvisse, suam cui Scotus addit opem.
Clarus Ioännes regali stemmate natus
    Balliol, hic Musis atria clara locat.
Qui patria pulsus, patriæ jam redditus, Anglis
    Hos fidei testes obsequiique dedit.

Cœpit sub Edwardo primo per Joannem Ballioll Regem
Scotiæ, anno Domini 1265.

Transitio ad descriptionem ultimi Collegii.

Ultima postremo jam commemoranda triumpho,
  Restat Ioänni sacra dicata domus.
Quæ licet extremo claudatur fine laborum,
  Chara vel in primis est tamen illa mihi.
Sicut Iäcobo Patriarchæ Benjamin olim
  (Excepto Joseph) primus amore fuit.

Collegium Joannis Baptistæ.

[Plate omitted.]

Cancell. Has Thomas Whitus, Londini gloria, raras
  Mercator merces donat, emitque suis.
Qui Londinensi bis Prætor in urbe, superstes
  Vivit adhuc, equitum non mediocre Decus.
Faxit ut ille diu vivat, valeatque superstes
  Musis, ac demum cœlica regna petat.

Cœpit sub Maria Regina per Dominum Thomam White, ordinis equestris militem inauratum, anno Domini 1557.

Cancell. Quod si plura libet paucis audire, superstes
  Restat adhuc sacris sacra dicata schola.
Regina. Quin age sacra mihi schola summe audita placebit:
  Et reliquis colophon ædibus aptus erit.

Schola Theologica.

[Plate omitted.]

Cancell. Eminet, & mediæ fastigia suspicit urbis,
  Dux Humfrede, tuis sumptibus ista schola.
Surgit in immensum turritis undique pinnis,
  Sectaque perpulchro marmore, quadra Domus.
Splendida luminibus crebris laquearia fulgent,
  Artificumque nitent pendula saxa manu.

Cœpit sub Henrico Sexto per Dominum Humfredum Du-cem Glocestriæ, anno Domini 1447.

Scholæ Publicæ.

[Plate omitted.]

Imminet huic series bis quinque instructa domorum,
　　Semita qua studiis omnibus una patet.
Sumptus hoc fecit Regina Maria, deditque
　　Unde novas possis hasce videre Scholas.
Elisabetha soror tu digna sorore Maria,
　　Pro pietate tua, quas dedit illa, foves.
Gratia ut æqualis jam detur utrique sorori,
　　Altra quod has foveat, quod dedit altra Scholas.

Transitio ad Aulas, seu hospitia litteraria.

Cancel.　Hiis sed adhuc arctis nolens contenta videri
　　　　Finibus, est aliis urbs quoque culta locis.
　　　Scilicet hæc aulis olim plenissima, Musis
　　　　Parturiit fœtus urbs populosa novos.
　　　Quæ nova progenies urbisque Colonia ducta,
　　　　Crevit in immensum viribus aucta suis.
　　　Tempus edax rerum multas absumpsit, & aulæ
　　　　Quædam dant dictis ædibus apta loca.
　　　Aulas jam tot habet, quot habent sua nomina Musæ,
　　　　Et par est numero turba novena novem.
Regina.　Quin age ne pigeat, quum sis Præfectus & Aulis,
　　　　Aularum nobis nomina trita dare.

Descriptio Aulæ Cervinæ.

Cancell.　Harum quæ forma est pulcherrima, proxima tectis
　　　　Aula, Wykame, tuis ordine prima subit.
　　　Quæ licet hic primas videatur habere, sororum
　　　　At nulli laudem detrahit illa suam.
　　　Inclyta nobilium numerosa pube referta,
　　　　Cervina a cervi nomine dicta domus.

Eminet hæc aliis formæque situsque nitore,
    Ut cursu canibus cerva præire solet.
Unde suo merito Cervina hæc dicitur Aula,
    In media Cervi cornua fronte gerens.

Epitome aliarum Aularum.

In reliquis sermo fiet contractior, octo
    Quæ restant variis undique sparsa locis.
Aulica duntaxat vulgataque nomina paucis
    Attingam, & brevibus puncta notabo metris.
Regina. Sed cave, ne nimium dum tu brevis esse laboras,
    Obscurus fias hac brevitate tua.
Cancell. Candida, Lata, Nova, studiis civilibus apta,
    Porta patet Musis, Justiniane, tuis.
Quæ restant, aliis discendis artibus Aulæ
    Sunt propriæ, quibus hæc nomina prisca manent.
Sacra Mariæ, Alburnensis, Glocestria, divi
    Edmundi, ac demum Magdalis aula frequens.

Peroratio Cancellarii.

His inclusa modis en qualiacunque Ducatus
    Septa mei, Princeps Elisabetha, vides.
Regina. Ex his jam tandem, Roberte, intelligo, cur tu
    Dux magis hic, alibi quam Comes esse velis.
Næ tu præclarum nactus videare Ducatum,
    Cui sunt tantorum tot monumenta virum.
Siccine currenti (quod vulgo dicitur) istis
    Carminibus properas subdere calcar equo?
Ut magis hæc lubeat præsentia cernere, quæ tu
    Magnifico narras ore stupenda loca?
Cancell. Quod si audita placent, multo magis ista placebunt,
    Si præsens oculis hauseris ista tuis.
Regina. Quin age tu comitem mihi te (Comes inclyte) præbe,
    Ut monstres digitis quæ modo lingua docet.

Cancell. Hoc equidem faciam promptus, gratesque laboris
  Hujus suscepti nomine gratus agam.
Quin & tota cohors mecum prostrata studentum
  Advolvet genibus se resupina tuis.
Quæ cum multa tibi (Princeps præclara) tuisque
  Debeat, hoc uno nomine tota tua est.
Quod Musis olim Mæcenas alter adesse,
  Quum pater Henricus cœperit illa tuus,
Et dederit studiis stipendia digna fovendis,
  Publica lectorum vox quibus ore præit,
Tu proles tali tantoque simillima Patri
  Hæc larga foveas continuata manu.
Dum quas radices pater hic plantavit, easdem
  Æmula munifico filia rore rigas.
Sic sic perge tuo non impar esse parenti,
  Patrizans Patri par pietate pari.
Nec dubita quicquam, quin incrementa daturus
  Sit Deus, & sumptu præmia digna tuo.
Interea vero communi nomine grates,
  Quas summas habet, urbs hæc tibi tota refert.
Privatimque sacræ linguæ prælector Hebræus
  Privato grates nomine gratus agit.
Qui tibi ne sterilis maneat, vel inutilis arbor
  Fructus, quos potuit plantula ferre, tulit.
Tu quales quales fructus (clarissima Princeps)
  Oblatos hilari fronte, manuque lege.

Gratulatio Hebraica in adventum ejusdem Principis illustrissimæ Dominæ Elisabethæ ab eodem Hebraice Conscripta.

[Hebrew Speech and Verses omitted.]

III c

OF THE

ACTES DONE AT OXFORD
WHEN THE QUEEN'S MAJESTY WAS THERE

By NICHOLAS ROBINSON

OF THE

ACTES DONE AT OXFORD

When

THE QUEEN'S MAJESTY

WAS THERE

SO COLLECTED AND NOTED

By NICHOLAS ROBINSON, at Oxford,

Now being Bishop of BANGOR.

ACTES DONE AT OXFORD,

WHEN THE QUEEN'S MAJESTY WAS THERE;

SO COLLECTED AND NOTED

BY NICHOLAS ROBINSON[1], AT OXFORD;

NOW BEING BISHOP OF BANGOR.

[From Brit. Mus. MS. Harl. 7033. fo. 142.]

Viri nobilitate infignes, qui Oxon. aderant:

Marchio Northamp.	Epūs. Sarum.	D. Sheffield.
Comes Oxon.	Epūs. Roff.	D. Windsor.
Comes Sussex.	D. W. Howard.	D. Stafford.
Comes Lecester.	D. Lestrange.	Mr. Rogers, Miles Aur.
Comes Warwic.	D. Graye.	Mr. Cecill, Miles Aur.
Comes Rutland.	D. Patchet.	Mr. Knolles, Miles Aur.
Comes Hunt.	D. Russell.	
Comes Ormund.		

Doctores in Disputat. presentes:

Theolog.	Juris. Civ.	Medicin.
Dr. Humfrey[2].	Dr. Kennall[10].	Dr. Huicke[14].
Dr. Godwin[3].	Dr. Lloyde[11].	Dr. Masters[15].
Dr. Calfild[4].	Dr. Loocher[12].	Dr. Bayle[16], Sen.
Dr. Overton[5].	Dr. Abre[13].	Dr. Bayle[17], Jun.
Dr. Westfaling[6].		Dr. Archlo[18].
Dr. Peers[7].		Dr. Barons[19].
Dr. Cradocke[8].		Dr. Stithurst[20].
Dr. Yelder[9].		Dr. Gifford[21].

[1] [See Preface.]

[2] Lawrence Humphrey, born at Newport Pagnell, admitted a Demi of Magdalen

Disputatores in Phil.

Moral.	Natural.
Mr. Wollye [22], Resp.	Mr. Campion [27], Resp.
Mr. Leche [23], Oppo.	Mr. Dee [28], Oppo.
Mr. Thorneton [24], Op.	Mr. Mericke [29], Oppo.
Mr. Buste [25], Opp.	Mr. Bristow [30], Oppo.
Mr. Matthew [26], Op.	Mr. Squyer [31], Oppo.

1547, A.B. and Perpetual Fellow there, and A.M. 1552, expelled from his fellowship in the reign of Mary, and restored at his return after her death. In 1560 he was constituted Queen's Professor of Divinity; and 1561 elected President of his College. 1562 D.D. 1570 Dean of Gloucester. 1580 Dean of Winchester. Wood, A. O. I. 242. He died 1589, aged 63, and was buried in Magdalen College Chapel. [Boase, Register, p. 218.]

[3] Thomas Godwin, a native of Okingham, in the county of Berks; sent to Oxford about 1538, admitted Probationer-Fellow of Magdalen Coll. 1544, and next year Perpetual-Fellow, being then A.B. Dean of Christ Church 1565, and of Canterbury 1566, Bishop of Bath and Wells 1584. He died aged 73, 1590; and was buried at his native place. A. O. I. 700. [Boase, p. 205.]

[4] James Calfhill, of Shropshire. Admitted at Oxford 1545, Student of Christ Church, 1548, A.M. 1552, Second Canon of Christ Church 1560, D.D. Dean of Bocking, and Archdeacon of Colchester, and nominated to Worcester 1570, but died before consecration. He died 1570. A. O. I. 163. [Boase, p. 216.]

[5] William Overton, born in London, Demi of Magdalen 1539, Perpetual Fellow, and A.B. 1551, D.D. 1565. Bishop of Lichfield and Coventry 1579, died 1609, and was buried at Eccleshall. A. O. I. 350. [Boase, p. 221.]

[6] Herbert Westphaling, of German origin, admitted of Christ Church 1547, A.M. 1555, Canon and Rector of Brightwel about 1561, Canon of Windsor 1577, and Bishop of Hereford 1585, where he died, and was buried 1601–2. He learnedly disputed before Queen Elizabeth at Oxford 1566. A. O. I. 314. Hist. & Ant. Univ. Ox. II. 305. [Boase, p. 217.]

[7] John Piers, born at South Hinxsey, near Abingdon, admitted a Perpetual Fellow of Magdalen 1546, and Student of Christ Church, Rector of Quainton, in the county of Bucks, Prebendary and Dean of Chester about 1558, Master of Baliol and Dean of Christ Church 1570, Dean of Salisbury 1571, Bishop of Rochester 1576, of Salisbury 1577, Archbishop of York 1588. He died at Bishopsthorpe 1594, aged 71. A. O. I. 713. [Boase, p. 210.]

[8] Edward Cradock, of Staffordshire, Student of Christ Church 1552, Margaret Professor 1565, D.D. resigned his professorship 1594. Ath. Ox. I. 277. [Boase, p. 230.]

[9] Arthur Yeldard, A.M. of Cambridge, incorporated at Oxford 1556, President of Trinity College, B.D. 1563. Ath. Ox. Fasti I. 85–92. [Boase, p. 233.]

[10] John Kennall, LL.D. 1553, Canon of Christ Church, Chancellor of Rochester, Archdeacon of Oxford 1561, Canon Residentiary of Exeter, where he died 1591. Ath. Ox. Fasti I. 79. Commissary of Oxford, ib. 93. [inf. p. 185.] He was Vice-Chancellor this year. Boase, p. 185.]

[11] Q. Hugh Lloyd, born in Carnarvonshire, educated at Winchester, Fellow of New College 1564, Chancellor of Rochester 1578, Chief Master of Winchester School, LL.D. 1588, died 1601, buried in the outer chapel at New College. Ath. Ox. I. 310. [Boase, p. 260.]

EST locus qua itur ab Oxonia Wodstokum, nomine Wol- ^{f. 142ᵛ.}
vercote, ad tria milliaria ab Academia, in ipsis finibus jurisdic-
tionis ac libertatum quibus Scholares utuntur. In hunc locum
convenerunt Commissarius Universitatis, Doctoresque aliquot,

[12] Robert Lougher, or Loffer, of All Souls, LL.D. 1564, Principal of New Inn, Professor of Civil Law, and Chancellor of Exeter, died 1583. Ath. Ox. Fasti I. 93. [Boase, p. 237.]

[13] William Awbre, of All Souls, Principal of New Inn; born at Cantre in Brecknockshire, Professor of Civil Law, Judge Advocate of the Queen's army at St. Quintin's, Advocate in the Court of Arches, one of the Council of the Marches in Wales, Master in Chancery, Chancellor of Canterbury, one of the Masters of Requests in Ordinary; died 1595, and was buried in St. Paul's, London. Ath. Ox. I. 73–81. [Boase, p. 225.]

[14] Robert Huicke, Fellow of Merton, M.D. of Cambridge, Fellow of the College of Physicians, incorporated M.D. at Oxford 1566, when the Queen was there. Ath. Ox. I. f. 98. [Boase, p. 264.]

[15] Richard Master, descended from a family of that name in Kent, admitted of All Souls, Prebendary of Fridaythorpe in the church of York 1562, being about that time Physician of the Chamber to Queen Elizabeth. Ath. Ox. I. f. 81. [Boase, p. 173.]

[16] Henry Baylie, of New College, Proctor 1547. Ath. Ox. I. f. 72. M.D. 1563. Ibid. 92. [Boase, p. 192].

[17] Walter Baylie, M.D. Professor of Physic, 1563. Ibid. 92. [Boase, p. 219.]

[18] Astlo. Nichols. Archlo or Archto MS. [v.s. p. 121 *n*. From Boase, p. 229, it appears that the real name is Atteslowe, as given in the note just cited.]

[19] [Robert Barnes, Barne, or Baron. Boase, p. 174. v. s. p. 121.]

[20] [Should be Slithurst (Richard). v.s. p. 121. Boase, p. 188.]

[21] John Gifford, of New College, M.D. 1598. He died in a good old age, and was buried at Hornchurch, Essex. Ath. Ox. I. f. 155.

[22] Francis Wolley, a native of Shropshire, of Merton College, A.M. 1557, Latin Secretary to Queen Elizabeth 1568, Prebendary of Wells 1569; and though a layman, Dean of Carlisle 1578, and Chancellor of the Garter 1589, one of the Commissioners to try the Queen of Scots, knighted 1592, and one of the Privy Council; died at Pyrford, Surrey, where he had an estate, and was buried in St. Paul's, 1595. Ath. Ox. I. f. 86. [*John* Wolley acc. to Boase, p. 222.]

[23] James Leech, of Merton College. Ibid. 101. William Leech, of Brazen Nose, was Senior Proctor this year. Ath. Ox. I. f. 96. [The former is meant, inf. p. 182. Boase, pp. 220, 233.]

[24] Q. Thomas Thornton, Vice-Chancellor, Canon of Christ Church, Worcester, and Hereford, Chanter of Hereford, and Master of Ledbury Hospital; died 1620, buried at Ledbury; D.D. 1583. Ibid. 480. F. 124. 126. [Boase, p. 243.]

[25] Henry Bust, of Magdalen College, Proctor 1567, M.D. 1578, Superior Reader of Lynacre's Physic Lecture; died at Oxford 1616. Ib. f. 100. 117. [Boase, p. 242.]

[26] Tobie Mathew. (Peck.) [Inf. p. 190.]

[27] Edmund Campion, of St. John's, A.M. 1564. When Queen Elizabeth was entertained by the University of Oxford, he did not only make an eloquent oration before her at her first entry, but also was respondent in the Philosophy Act in St. Mary's Church, performed by him with great applause from that Queen and the learned auditory. He afterwards turned papist. See Ath. Ox. I. 207. [Boase, p. 244.]

[28] Of Magdalen College. [John Day, Dey, or Deus. Boase, p. 226.]

ac Collegiorum Præpositi, ut Reginæ adventui gratularentur in ipsis terminis. Quæ ubi accessit, Marbecus [1], homo apud suos disertissimus, et Ecclesiæ Christi prebend. facunda oratione eam accepit. Qua finita ad manus oscula sunt omnes isti admissi, Honoratissimo Leicestriæ Comite, et Acad. Oxon. Cancellario, eorum [2] et dignitatem et nomen Regiæ Maj. significante.

Ubi progressum est paulo ulterius et urbi propinquius, Major Oxon., cum 13 Senioribus, qui omnes purpureis amicti erant togis, una cum tipetis holosericis, obviam Reginæ fiunt, se fascesque suas illi subjiciunt. Etiam Major pauca quædam dixit, quod qui illis est in Jure consultus, *Recorder* dicimus, per hosce dies ægrotabat. Tandem Reginæ oblatus est crater argenteus, in significationem obedientiæ ac gratitudinis.

Introiit Regina in urbem per portam Aquilonarem, in qua carcer publicus est, qui Bocardo dicitur, intra duas turres quæ portam utrinque claudunt, quæque dealbatæ [3] erant, medium spatium Insignia Regni urbisque depicta habuit. Urbis hoc Insigne erat, Bos viz. vadum pertransiens. In superiori quasi frontispicio hujus Portæ, hoc literis majusculis erat scriptum, *Decet Regem regere Legem.*

Statim ut est ingressa Reg. Maj. in oppidum, porrigunt illi Sophistæ quidam orationem gratulatoriam ; sic etiam postea et Baccalaurei et Mri Artium fecerunt ; ubi recta platea per populi ac scholarium multitudinem in medium urbis venit Regina, quod vulgo dicitur Caerfax, Laurentius [4] qui est

[20] John Mericke, a native of Anglesea, educated at Winchester School, admitted of New College, Proctor, 1565, Vicar of Hornchurch, Essex, 1570, and Bishop of Man 1573 ; died 1599. Ath. Ox. I. 718. [Boase, p. 238.]

[30] Richard Bristow, of Christ Church, A.M. 1562. Ath. Ox. I. f. 91. And Junior of the Act celebrated July 13, this year. Promoted to one of Sir William Petres' Scholarships at Exeter College 1567, turned papist ; died 1581. Ath. Ox. I. 211. [Clark, p. 11.]

[31] Adam Squyre, of St. John's, D.D. 1576, Master of Balioll College, Archdeacon of Middlesex ; and Prebend of Totenhale, in St. Paul's, 1577, married Bishop Aylmer's daughter, and died before 1580. Ath. Ox. I. f. 113. Newcourt, I. 82. [Boase, p. 243.]

[1] Of him see below, p. 235.   [2] Ejus, MS. (M.)

[3] Qui ... quique dealbati, MS. ; but *duas* corrected from *duos*. (M.)

[4] Giles Lawrence, a native of Gloucestershire, admitted of Christ Church College

Regius Interpres Græcæ linguæ Oxon., Græce verba fecit, f. 143ʳ. quo ejus adventum Academiæ gratum intelligerit, prædicabatque Reg. laudes. Huic ubi se Regia Maj. parabat ut responderet, vel impetu imperitæ multitudinis, vel ferocia mulorum, e suo quasi loco paululum propellitur lectica, qua vel propter frequentes imbres, vel ægritudinis metum, delata fuit. Itaque relicto cum gratiis Laurentio, per Baccalaureorum et Magistrorum medium in Collegium dictum Christi Ecclesiam, præeunte magna nobilium turba, una cum Legato Hispano[1] devenit, siquidem in hoc Collegio Hospitium Reginæ erat paratum, magno societatis sumptu, commoratique sunt ibidem per hosce dies Comites Leicestriæ, Oxon, Warwic., D. Will. Haward, D. Sheffield, Mr. Will. Cecill Secretarius, Mr. Francis Knolles, atque alii, quia studentes omnes sese receperunt in alia loca vicina, præter præbendarios quosdam.

Hujus Collegii tres sunt partes fere exædificatæ, at quarta quæ Boream spectat vix fundamenta jacta ostendit. Ex his tribus quæ ad orientem est, tota erat in varia cubicula distincta, ad similitudinem Aulæ cujusdam Regalis, in quibus Regina toto hoc tempore conquievit. Ubi igitur ad fores hujus ædificii, novo opere extructas, Maj. Regia fuisset delata, pompa certe ut decuit regia, Academiæ orator ætate juvenis, sed prudentia virili, ex sellula quadam posita Reginam est affatus, dixit de timore suo, de excellentia tantæ Principis, Regum beneficia in Academiam, ab Aluredo restauratore (ut voluit) percensuit, viz. Richardi primi et Eduardi primi tum Henrici 8ᵛⁱ et Edovardi sexti, qui Buccrum ac Martyrem in hoc regnum vocarunt, ejus vero hoc esse immortale beneficium, quod Academiam inviseret. Sermonem cum præcatione pro Regina absolvit.

Fores istas architectura insignes ornabant hinc inde car-

1539, Probationary Fellow of All Souls 1542, Archdeacon of Wells 1564, which he resigned 1580. He was living 1584. Ath. Ox. I. f. 100-117. [Boase, p. 231.]

[1] Gusman, dean of Toledo. Wood, Hist. and Ant. Univ. Ox. I. 286. Ath. Ox. I. 157.

mina omnis generis : etiam in superiori harum parte pinge-
bantur versus isti :

Vive diu, splendor gentis, Regina, Britannæ,
Et quæ das pacis commoda, perge dare.

f. 143ᵛ.   Ad preces recta in Sacellum quam primum itur, variis
musicis instrumentis Psalmi canuntur, et oratione Latine
absolvuntur per Decanum. Ad extremum in Hospitia omnes.
Spectacula nulla hac nocte.

Dies 2. viz. Domin.

Sunday,
Sept. 1.   Sequenti die, qui Dominicus fuit, conveniunt Consiliarii
omnes in Ecclesiam Christi, ubi post preces matutinas, Dr.
Overton [1], Præbendarius Winton., concionem habuit ad Regni
magnates, populumque reliquum. Thematis loco selegit illud,
Psal. 118. *Hæc est dies quam*, &c.

[Sequitur Concionis brevis Epitome hic omissa.] [2]

Hæc postquam isto modo dixisset, surrexerunt Consiliarii,
reliquique honorati viri, discesseruntque in sua.

A prandio hujus diei nihil egregii actitatum, nisi quod
Concionator quidam Harris [3] nomine in eadem Ecclesia
Christi ad populum dixerit ex eo capite D. Petri, *Sobrii
estote et vigilate, &c.* Partitus est orationem in mores
hominis Christiani, tum in adversarii considerationem, postremo in defensionem contra adversarium. Dixit itaque de
sobrietate et vigilantia, dixit de adversario nostro, ejusque
accessu ad nos; dixit denique de fide qua illi resistimus,
cum exortatione ut vere fideles simus.

Hunc diem clausit Historia quædam Gemini [4] cujusdam,
quam Historiam studiosi quidam Collegii Christi in formam
redigerant Comœdiæ, sed oratione soluta, qui eandem in

---

[1] His prebend of Winchester is not mentioned by Wood, among his other
preferments. Hist. and Ant. Univ. Ox. I. 287.

[2] Sic in MS. (M.)

[3] Thomas Harrys of New College, Archdeacon of Cornwall 1500. Ath. Ox.
I. 654.

[4] Marcus Geminus. Hist. and Ant. Univ. Ox. [v.s. p. 124.]

scena peregerunt in Aula ejusdem Collegii, ubi omnia erant
ad splendorem et ornatum satis illustria, sumptibus regiis, et
adjumento Mͬi Edwards[1], qui duobus fere mensibus in Academia mansit, ad opus etiam quoddam Anglicum conficien-
dum, quod sequenti nocte edidit.   Huic historiali comœdiæ
interfuerunt Consiliarii Regii, nobiles viri ac fœminæ, una f. 144ͬ.
cum Legato Regis Hispani.   Aberat Regina[2] vel ægritudinis metu, vel aliis impedita negotiis.   Sonuerat jam prima
a media nocte, cum huic spectaculo esset impositus finis.

3 *Dies Act. die Lunæ.*

Hora septima hujus diei Hebraicus Prælector[3] interpre- Monday,
tatur ; ad octavam Mͬi Artium ordinarias lectiones auspica- Sept. 2.
bantur ; ubi nona fuerat audita, Academiæ Cancellarius
habens in Comitatu Legatum Hispan. et alios Proceres
Regni venit in Scholam Theologicam ad audiendum Doct.
Humfridum Regin. Professorem exponentem ex 6 Cap. Esa :
Væ qui justificatis impium, &c.   A decima ad undecimam,
totus fere hic auditorum numerus se recepit in Scholas
Philosoph. ad disputationem audiendam.   At hinc Collegium
Novum perlustrat, ubi orationem gratulatoriam habuit Mr.[4]
* * * * Tandem ubi Bibliothecam pervidisset, itum est ad
prandium.

Ab hoc tempore ad noctem nihil publice in Academia
est gestum, nisi quod Dr. Cradocke[5] in Theol. Schola alteram Lectionem Theol. sit auspicatus, legebat enim ex primo
capite Lucæ Evang.

Ut superiori nocte, sic et ista Theatrum exornatum fuit

---

[1] Richard Edwards, of Somersetshire, admitted Scholar of Corpus Christi College, under the tuition of George Etheridge 1540, and Probationary Fellow 1544,
Student of the Upper Table at Christ Church, and A.M. 1547.   Ath. Ox. I. 151.

[2] Wood says she was there.   [Sed v. s. p. 124.]

[3] Thomas Neale.

[4] The name here omitted is supplied in Wood, Hist. and Ant. Univ. Ox. I. 288
with that of George Coriat, father of the mad traveller, who was admitted Perpetual Fellow of New College 1562, and presented to the Rectory of Odcombe
1570, where he died 1606.   Ath. Ox. I. 335.   [Boase, p. 254.]

[5] Of whom see before, p. 174.

splendide, quo publice exhiberetur Fabula Militis (ut Chaucerus nominat) e Latino in Anglicum sermonem translata per Mr̃um Edwards et alios ejusdem Collegii alumnos. Postea quam ingressa fuerat Regia Maj. in Theatrum, clausique essent omnes aditus, nescio quo casu nec qua ratione, cecidit muri cujusdam pars, qua in Aulam itur, oppressitque Scholarem Aulæ B. Mariæ[1] et oppidanum nomine Penny, qui ibidem mortui sunt, ac etiam alterius cujusdam Scholaris crus fractum fuit, cocique[2] utrumque crus conquassatum, faciesque confecta quasi vulneribus fuit lapidum ruina. Veruntamen non fuit intermissum spectaculum, sed ad mediam noctem prorogatum.

f. 144ᵛ.

4 *Di., viz. dici Martis.*

Tuesday, Sept. 3.

Lectiones ordinarias Mr̃i repetunt, Medicinæque Professor Regius in Schola Theol. Aphorismos Hipocratis est interpretatus. Tum Disputationes quodlibiticæ (ut vocant) fiebant, quibus interfuit D. Secret. Cecillus. Postea Cancellarius Acad. adiit Legatum Hisp. in Collegio Mertonensi commorantem, eumque primum in Collegium Corporis Christi, tum in Collegium Aureol. deducit, ubi in ipsis Portis Mr. Belly[3], Præpositus ejusdem Collegii, eos oratione accepit, sed laudibus tantum Cancellarii referta. Mox Collegium Omnium Animarum, et Aulam et Bibliothecam lustravit: tum quod est ex adverso Collegium Universitatis invisunt, in quo et Aululam et Sacellulum spectant. Tandem recta Magdalenense Collegium adeunt ex improviso ut videbatur, nam nulli illis obviam processerunt, nec ullius voce salutati erant priusquam in ipsam sunt ingressi Aulam, ubi Præsidens ad illos venit: ubi hortos, pomeria, bibliothecamque fuissent contemplati, discesserunt.

A meridie circa tertiam Regia Majestas magna comitata

---

[1] . . . . . . Walker. Wood, Hist. and Ant. Univ. Ox., ubi supra.

[2] John Gilbert. Ibid.

[3] John Belly, LL.D. 1567, Chancellor of the Diocese of Lincoln, and one of the Masters in Chancery. Ath. Ox. I. f. 101. [Boase, p. 227.]

nobilium turba in Ecclesiam B. Mariæ jamdiu expectata
venit. Hic sedes erant hoc tempore apparatæ, ad Canta-
brig. Theatri similitudinem, ubi facultatum omnium Disputationes publicæ fierent. Regia sedes cum Regali Cathedra
ab oriente in occidentem spectabat, ad dextram Consiliarii,
aliique Primores Regni, ad sinistram fœminæ nobiles una
cum Legato Hisp. Reliquam superiorem sessionem occupa-
bant alii quinque. Doctores considebant medio quodam loco,
infimi erant Artium M̃ri ; inter Doctores etiam sedebat
Cancellarius. Cum omnia isto modo fuerant constituta,
Senior Procurator, Lechus[1] nomine, expressit paucis gaudium universæ Acad. ob adventum tanti Principis ; tum
petiit, ut illis liceret suo more disputare. Ubi Latine satis
perorasset, ad Magistros opponentes dixit, ' Mr. propone f. 145ʳ.
quæstionem.' Duæ itaque sunt propositæ quæstiones ex
naturali philosophia desumptæ ; viz. ' An inferiora regantur
a superioribus ? ' 2. ' An Luna sit causa fluxus et refluxus maris ? '

Qui Respondentis locum occupavit, viz. Mr. Campion, ex
Collegio D. Joannis, ubi totidem verbis et 4 versibus has
quæstiones repetisset, adjunxit rationes quasdam suæ defen-
sionis, idque non longa oratione.

Surrexit ad oppugnandam primam Quæstionem Decus
Magd. Coll. qui contendebat superiora fieri propter genera-
tionem et corruptionem inferiorum, atque ita hæc inferiora
præstantiora fore. Hunc sequutus est Mr. Mewricke Novi
Coll., qui animarum affectiones sequi corporis temperiem
voluit probare, ut necessitatem actionum nostram induceret.
Tertius disputavit Mr. Bristow, non tangere superiora hæc
inferiora, et ideo non agere. Postremo Mr. Squier D. Joannis
Socius, de gemellis dissimillimis egit. Atque ita ad deter-
minatorem res delata fuit, qui proprium quendam locum sibi
assignatum habuit. Hic Mr. Belly vocatur, viz. Præpositus
Coll. Aureol.: conclusit paucis superiora agere in hæc inferiora. De secunda Quæstione nihil est dictum[2].

---

[1] See before, p. 175.   [2] [Sed v. s. pp. 131-2.]

Secuta est statim in eodem loco Disputatio Moralis Philos. In qua ubi Procurator jussit Magistrum Quæstiones proponere, Mr. Leche Mert. Coll. quæsivit, 'An Princeps declarandus esset electione potius quam successione?' Tum, 'An præstaret regi ab optima Lege, quam ab optimo Rege?'

Ad has respondebat Mr. Wolly Coll. Mert. uno verbo, verum longius præfatus est in Politices laudem vel admirationem potius, cujus exactum exemplar proposuit Reginam præsentem. Ad extremum petiit, ut Leges nostrates colligerentur in unum codicem a R. M. Atque sic ad disputandum ventum est.

Mr. Leechus Mertonen. petita a Regia Maj. venia, elegantem orationem habuit contra successionem et pro electione in creando Rege. Tandem ratiocinatus est sic, quod natura justius, Reipub. utilius, et naturæ magistratus convenientius, hoc sequendum. Qui Lechum secutus est, viz. Mr. Thorncton, voluit de 2da Quæstione agere, quod instructior ad illam venerat; verum revocatur jussu Regio ad primam; in qua nihil fere dixit, nisi electionem non esse postponendam propter incommoda. Successit 3tio in loco Mr. Buste, Magd. qui urgebat adversarium interrogationibus et quasi dialogismo quodam contra successionem verba habuit, sæpe se ad Reg. Maj. convertens, quasi queritans quod adversarius de sententia dimoveri noluit. Hic a Procuratore revocatus, contendebat hoc argumento, viz. 'Beatam fore Civitatem, si ex electione Reges crearentur.'

Ultimo Mr. Matthew contra successionem dixit suaviter et distincte, et cum summa laude, cujus erat hæc ratio, 'Plus tribuendum consilio quam fortunæ, et in successione fortuna dominatur.' Hæc ille hoc modo.

Ad extremum Mr. Cooper[1] Magdel. pro successione determinavit, cum adjectione maximi periculi si Regnum

---

[1] Thomas Cooper, A.M. B.M. 1556, Master of Magdalen College Free-school 1546, Bishop of Winchester 1584, Dean of Christ Church 1566, of Gloucester 1569, Ath. Ox. I. 158. Bishop of Lincoln 1570, died at Winchester 1594. Ib. I. 265. [Boase, p. 194.]

relinqueretur de successione incertum.   De altera Quæstione nihil est dictum.

His peractis, Reg. Maj. in palatium se recepit, sibi nihil illa nocte actitatum.   Silebat enim Comœdia.

Habuit Mr. Neele 4 ex minoribus Prophetis[1] ex Hebr. in Lat. versos, quos voluit Canc. Oxon. dedicare, sed visum est consultius ut Reginæ commendaret.   Idem Mr. Neele Prælector Linguæ Heb. depinxit quasi in tabulas quasdam singula Collegia separatim, adjunxitque dialogi in morem exordia, fundationes, numerum, &c. cujusque Societatis, inter-locutoribus Reg. et Acad. Cancell.   Hunc librum obtulit Regiæ Maj.

Mr. Jacobus Sanford transtulit Epictetum in Angl. Ser-monem, Reginæque dedicavit.   Huic libro nomen fecit, 'The Manuell of Epictetus.'

Mr. Keis[2] Præpositus Collegii Universitatis scripsit de f. 146r. Antiquitate Oxon. Academiæ libellum, quem per Cancel-larium Oxon. voluit Reg. Majestati presentari.

Di. 5. viz. Merc.

Mr. Harris in Ecclesia S. Petri concionatus est, eodem Wednes-assumpto themate quo in die etiam Dom. viz. *Sobrii estote*, &c. day, Sept. 4. 1 Petr. 5.   Egit de crudelitate adversarii, tum [de] adulatione adversarii, postremo de fide, qua illi resistitur.   Crudelitas apparet in membris ejus, ut in Pharaone, &c., de Tyrannis et Rom. Pont.[3], ejus crudelitas in homines et pecora.   2 De adulatione ex historia gentium, tum de Joab. Præterea hunc adversarium cavendum tempore prosperitatis.   Postremo, quo-modo si occupemur rebus divinis et sacris, adversarius a nobis fugiat, quomodo possumus resistere, quoniam nihil ille potest, nisi facultas illi concessa fuerit : sic clausit hanc concionem.

---

[1] All the prophets.   Hist. and Ant. Univ. Ox. I. 288 [but see the Preface].

[2] Thomas Key, or Cay, wrote 'Assertio Antiquitatis Oxoniensis Academiæ,' which drew him into a controversy with Dr. John Cay of Cambridge, of which see Ath. Ox. I. 173.   Brit. Top. I. 211.   He died at University College 1572, and was buried in St. Peter's in the East, Oxford.   [Boase, p. 143.]

[3] In the MS. thus :—'Ro. Pont. [Re pot.].'   (M.)

Lectiones ordinariæ celebratæ et Disputationes quotlibeticæ. Lectio nulla Theol. ut nec superiori die.

A prandio ubi in Ecclesiam B. Mariæ Regina venisset, Procurator Jun. ordiri disputat., Dr. White[1] proposuit 2 Quaest. (verum paucis est Reg. Maj. allocutus, quæ dignata sit Academiam adire, quod ejus Pater tantum quasi in transcursu egit, cum pollicitatione recordationis perpetuæ): Primam, 'An privilegium bello extinctum facta pace revivisceret, nulla facta speciali mentione in fœderibus pacis?' Secundam, 'Utrum creditor vel debitor sustineret damnum et incommodum diminutæ pecuniæ, si ante diem solutionis moneta fuerat diminuta?'

Dr. Abre[2] Responsor prætermisit laudes Juris Civilis, quod erat in his Quæstionibus defensurus comprehendit paucis verbis. Tum Dr. White cum rationibus aggreditur, primum satis esse ista privilegia in generali conventione pacis contineri, ut in mutuo, ut in dote, quæ non egent speciali mentione : tum pacis ac belli contrarios esse effectus, at bellum destruere privilegia, pacem quasi e mortuis revocare. Has rationes legibus et authoritate confirmavit.

f. 146ᵛ.   Dr. Lloyd[3] secundam aggreditur, de qua nihil dixerat Dr. White, contendebatque satis esse, si debitor restituat pecuniam eadem bonitate, quum æque bon. reddit, tum quod ejusdem quantitatis reddit, quod erat in moneta unice spectandum.

Dr. Lucher[4], omissa prima Quæstione, disputavit eandem rationem fuisse partis ad partem quæ totius ad totum; at totum si interiret, debitor non teneretur ad damnum, quum speciei interitus erat. Et quum Respondens hic debitorem ad quantitatem non ad speciem teneri dixit, conatus est etiam ostendere, et quantitatem etiam interire, proposito exemplo ejus, qui ad diem constitutum, adhibitis testibus numerasset

---

[1] Thomas Whyte, of New College, Prebendary of Winchester, LL.D. 1553, Warden of New College 1553, Archdeacon of Berks 1557, Chancellor of Sarum 1571, died and was buried there 1588. Ath. Ox. I. f. 79. [Boase, p. 202.]

[2] See before, p. 175, n. 13.

[3] See before, p. 174, n. 11.

[4] See before, p. 175, n. 12.

pecuniam, et in sacculum conclusisset, quod postea perdidisset.

Dr. Kenall[1] Commissar[i]us Universitatis determinavit privilegia mortua non renasci sequente pace : tum debitorem teneri ad damnum et incommodum diminutæ pecuniæ. Hinc post Disput. hanc in Jure Civ. Reg. in Palat.

Hac nocte quod erat reliquum de Historia vel Fabula Palæmonis et Arcitis[2] actitatum est, Regina ipsa in scena præsente.

Tribus illis diebus quibus in Ecclesia B. Mariæ disputatum erat, multi Scholares carmina, variis de rebus conscripta, per parietes suspenderunt. Unus omnes Reges Angliæ a Willelmo Mag. ad hæc tempora versibus comprehendit : Alius Martyrum Oxon. combustorum historiam est persequutus. Erat qui ipsum oppidum Oxon. depingendum charta quadam curavit, atque ibi spectatum proposuerat.

Fertur quodque Collegium conscriptum Libellum habere Lat. versibus, de origine, fundatore cujusque, de viris illustribus, qui ibidem enutriti erant, &c., ac præterea cujusque Collegii alumnos carminibus animi sui lætitiam significasse, quod[3] ad singula Collegia visenda Regina non iverit.

Di. 6. viz. Jovis.

f. 147ʳ.

In Scholis ordinariæ Lectiones. In Collegio Merton. Disputatio in Phil. morali repetita fuit, vel potius absoluta coram Cancellario, Legato Hisp. cæterisque Nobilibus ; eodem Mͬo Wolleo respondente, opponentibusque eisdem Mͬis, viz. Leche, Thorneton, Bust, et Mathew ; Determ. Mͬo Cowpero. Sed præcipue 2da Quæst. de legibus et regibus agitata fuit.

Thursday,
Sept. 5.

A prandio venit Regina in Ecclesiam B. Mariæ ad Disputationes. Hic proponuntur a Dͬe Huic una Quæstio in re Medica, viz. 'An vita humana arte medica prorogari possit ?'

---

[1] See before, p. 174, n. 10.   [2] Arcis, MS. (M.)
[3] Licet, Nichols.

Ubi Dr. Fraunces[1] dixisset, quibus in rebus vita constaret, quousque prorogaretur, addidissetque ad causas valere artem med.; longiore oratione Dr. Huicke egit de perfectione naturæ, et imperfectione artis, ex Galeno; tandem ratiocinatus est sic: 'Natura per se satis perfecta est: Ergo non indiget arte, ut in cervis et corvis, qui longissime vivunt.' Respon. Naturæ vocem distinxit.

Dr. Bayle sen. est sequutus, qui, omissa præfatione, disputavit hoc modo: 'Conservare vitam non est medici, quum infiniti morbi sunt, et infinitorum nulla sit ars.'

Dr. Bayle jun. gratias egit Principi, et Acad. nomine et suo, quod Regius Professor in Med. erat, egitque hac ratione. Ars Med. non potest retardare senectutem: Ergo nec mortem. Quod probavit quoniam solidæ partes non poterant humectari. Reliqui Doctores, viz. Dr. Archlo[2], Dr. Barons, Dr. Stythirst, Dr. Gifford, non disputarunt; verum determinavit Dr. Masters, distinxitque humidum in humidum aereum, exsangue, et radicale. Hoc significari dixit tribus illis Parcis, quæ Clotho, Colon, Atropos dicuntur.

Cum finita fuerat Disput. Med., Dr. Humfrey Cathedram occupat Theol. Cui proposuit hanc Quæst. Dr. Godwyn, 'An privato homini liceret arma sumere contra malum Principem?' Dr. Humfrey præfatus est de Reginæ præsentia ad audiend. Theologiam, de ejus regno pacifico, de se Doctoribusque caeteris, quod non faverent seditioni, quod abhorrerent ab omni tumultu; atque tandem conclusit, ex præcepto divino obediendum esse Principibus etiam malis.

Dr. Godwyn rursus explicavit primum apud Ethnicos licuisse, tum apud Judæos, interficere Tyrannos, viz. ex honoribus illis decretis, ex felici successu, ex turpissima vita Tyrannorum, tum exemplis; verum pressius egit isto modo: 'Quod apud Judæos licuit privato, licet et nobis. At privato licuit,

---

[1] Thomas Francis, of Christ Church, after he had taken the degree of A.M. in Divinity, entered in the physic line 1550, King's Professor of Physic, as Deputy for Dr. Warner, 1552, M.B. 1553, Provost of Queen's 1561, Physician to Queen Elizabeth, and much respected by her. Ath. Ox. I. f. 81. [Boase, pp. 198, 299.]

[2] ? Archto. (M.)

viz. Jephthæ, qui erat privatus, sic : Non potuit eligi, quum non potuit ingredi Templum, et hoc ideo, quum filius erat meretricis, et homines malos collegerat ut patet.' Resp. est 'nec majorem nec minorem firmam esse ; quum, Ethnicis non licebat ingredi templum, et tamen erant Principes ex illis. Sed minor erat incerta, quoniam verbum Hebr. significat et stabulariam mulierem et meretricem.'

Dr. Calfild promisit se probaturum (præfatione habita, viz. se tantum habere quædam figmenta contra veritatem), Primo, ' Nullum debere esse principem, tum malum posse interfici.' Incepit a secunda, hac ratione, 'Eum licet interficere qui ad Idola ducere vult. At potest hoc facere Princeps, ergo a privato interf.' Major. probavit ex hoc loco Deut. Resp. est 'alios locos indicare judicandi modum, viz. ut seductor in portas ducatur, &c.' 'Quod nullus deberet esse Princeps, ostendit, ex eo quod ad Noe, nemo legitur vel Cain vel Lamech puniisse ob homicidium, et quod juxta Epiph. Barbarismus erat ad Noe, &c.' Resp. ' Etiam Aristotelem ostendere a primordio fuisse Reges.'

Disputavit breviter Dr. Overton ad hunc modum : ' Licet cuique privato Reipub. consulere, at optime consulitur, si interficiatur malus Princeps.' Resp. ' Non consuli Reipub. si privatus interficiat principem.' Adjecit dictum Hieronimi de f. 148ʳ. feriendo malo principe, quod Respondens interpretatur de gladio Excommunicationis.

Dr. Westphaling hic paucis verbis egit sic : ' Quod odisse licet, licet et interficere. At odisse licet. Ergo. Major, odium est homicidium, ex Epist. Joan. Resp. odium cordis, linguæ, fact. ex. Argumentum fallax, quod non de eadem specie agat.' Minor. ' Licuit Davidi odisse.' Resp. ' Non vivimus exemplis.'

Dr. Peerse promisit se partes suas confirmaturum, a causa efficiente et finali. Orsusque est ad hunc modum : ' Cujus facti Deus autor est, id licitum est. Deus autor est, ut privatus interficiat malum Principem. Ergo. Minor, Hieron. non est hominis via ejus : Deus operatur in nobis, &c. Operatur omnia in omnibus.' Resp. ' Actio divina duplex : cum efficaciter operatur : cum permittit, sic aliquo modo operatur. At quod Deus efficaciter operetur omnia constat ex Aug. de lib. arbitr. ubi ostendit Deum inclinare ad bonum et malum.' Resp. ' Hoc fit justo judicio prop er corruptam naturam.'

Eр̄us Sarum [1] determ.   Petita venia a Regia Maj. collaudavit Respondentis orationem ; tum ostendit et autoritate verbi Dei et piorum exemplis, quantum obedientiæ debeatur Reg. potestati, ex sacra scrip. protulit illud Ro. 13. 1 Pet. 2. tum etiam, *Ego dixi Dii estis.*   Tractavit exemplum Pauli multis verbis, viz. quo modo se gessit erga Neronem, quodque esset Nero crudelis Tyrannus ; subjunxit de Saule et Davide.   De secunda Quæstione, quum proposita non fuit, dixit se nolle loqui, nisi a Maj. Regia jussus esset.   Hinc de observantia Academiæ in Reginam deque laudibus Reginæ multis est persecutus.

Cum finisset acclamatum ab universis, *Vivat Regina.*   Nobiles quidam Reginam suppliciter rogant, ut Academiam alloqui dignaretur ; illa diu reluctatur, quod ex improviso subeundum esset tam eruditum negotium, et coram tam curiosis testibus, imo coram Legato Hispaniæ, homine peregrino, qui fortasse in alienas terras spargeret quod tam temere fuisset susceptum. Veruntamen instant multi, ac etiam Hisp. Legatus, ut saltem unico verbo dimitteret Academiam ; tandem evicta precibus suorum, ad dicendum in Regale solium venit. Quæ ex submissa ejus voce arripere potui, hæc erant [2]:

Oratio Regiæ Majestatis.

' Qui male agunt oderunt lucem.   Hoc et ipsa tempus vestra expectatione indignissimum, aptissimum meæ ignorantiæ duxi.   Sed tamen ne defectus videatur contemptus, pauca

---

[1] John Jewell.

[2] The Queen's speech as here given differs from that in Wood's Hist. and Ant. Univ. Ox. I. 289 ; but, as the Bishop acknowledges he could not hear her Majesty, we must make due allowance. [v. s. pp. 144-5.]

f. 148ᵛ.

dicam. Hæsitatio in animo meo magna est, et dubiam facit, laudare debeam an vituperare, loqui aut tacere, omnia hæc præstare tempus non sufficit, Duo tantum facere in animo habeo, viz. laudare ac vituperare.

Quantum attinet ad laudem, revera haud ita aut stupida sum, etsi indocta aut ingrata ... Si saltem quæ pereximia sunt non laudem, aut quæ præstantissima sileam.   Ex quo in hanc Academiam veni, audivi multa, probavi omnia, quæ vero sunt per se[1] ... cum cautione et exceptione semper addita nec mea autoritate ut Regina, nec judicio ut Christiana probo.

Et hæc de laude. De vituperatione hæc pauca. Quanquam multi Philosophi scribant, rem difficillimam esse cognoscere seipsum, tamen in hac causa fateor me non ... Notum est omnibus et perspectum, quod multis annis in linguarum cognitione versabar. Idcirco hoc quamvis verecunde tamen vere dicam, quod tempus potius meum consumpsi in audiendo; pædagogi mei, qui me docuerunt, in tam sterilem terram semina jecerunt, ut fructus producere vestra expectatione dignos non possum, nec quales a dignitate mea requirantur. f. 149ʳ. Idcirco maxime semper in meipsa vituperavi.

At cum expectationi vestræ honeste verbis meis satisfacere non possum, cum optione finiam breviter : optio mea hæc est ; ut me vivente florentissimi sitis, me vero mortua beatissimi.'

Hæc ubi dixisset, universi illi gratias egerunt.

Postea Regia Maj. in Aulam deducitur, accensis tædis cereis, quod octava jam hora sonuerat. In hujus noctis silentio in scena exhibetur quomodo Tereus Rex comedit filium necatum apparatumque ab uxore Progne ob stupratam sororem suam, omnia certe prout oportebat summo apparatu, cultuque vere regio. Cum hæc Tragœdia[2] plausum suum accepit, itum est cubitum.

---

[1] Sic in MS. Q. *per vosmet ipsos excusata,* or *excusatione digna reputata.*
[2] This tragedy was written by Dr. Calfhill, before mentioned, p. 174, n. 4.

Di. 7, viz. Veneris.

Friday,
Sept. 6.

Ad octavam in Ecclesia B. Mariæ congregantur Mꝫi Regentes ac non Regentes[1]. Post maturam deliberationem decernuntur honores ; viz. viris nobilibus prout Cancellarius, Doctoresque 3 aut 4 statuerent. Deinde Cantabrigiensibus Mꝫis ibi præsentibus conceditur idem gradus ac locus quibus apud suos fuerant. Tandem circa nonam quidam Cantabrigienses admittuntur ad id honoris.

Nondum hæc sunt isto modo peracta, cum ecce pulsatur campana, in Ecclesia Christi pro Concione ad Clerum. Regia Maj. non venit. Cancellarius aliique viri nobilitate præstantes accesserunt : quibus consedentibus, Dr. Peerse, Comitis Leicester Capellanus et Præbend. Ecclesiæ Cath. Cestriæ, ad prædicandum paratus, orditur illo Prophetæ dicto ; *Et erunt Reges nutricii tui et Reginæ nutrices tuæ.*

[Sequitur concionis brevis epitome hic omissa[2].]

Circa quartam a meridie erant omnes Doctores, Mꝫi, ac Bachalaurei sparsi per plateas, expectantes Reginæ discessum, viæque omnes rusticorum villicorumque multitudine refertæ erant. Etiam Collegiorum Præpositi, una cum Commissario, f. 149ᵛ. equos paratos habebant, ut Reginam in fines suos deducerent, quod observantiæ genus præstiterunt suis quoque togis insignibusque scholaribus ornati.

Mox ubi Regina ad conscendendum equum auratis phaleris insignem videbatur apparata, præsto erat ad fores Mr. Mathew[3], Collegii ejusdem socius, qui oratione perpolita ac numerosa illa quidem, totius Academiæ nomine, gratias illi ageret, utque benigne conservaret Collegium, quod pater inchoavit, frater ornavit, soror auxit, rogaret.

---

[1] After *Regentes* MS. adds *ac non Reg.* probably by an error. (M.)

[2] Sic in MS. (M.)

[3] Tobie Mathew, admitted Probationary first of University College 1559, soon afterwards Student of Christ Church, A.B. 1563, A.M. 1566, elected Public Orator 1569, Canon of Christ Church 1570, and Dean 1576, Vice-Chancellor 1579, Chaunter of Sarum and Dean of Durham 1583, Bishop of Durham 1595, Archbishop of York 1606, died 1628. Ath. Ox. I. 730. [Boase, p. 252.]

Hujus approbavit studium, laudavitque orationem ; sicque summo splendore, pompa certe suspicienda, votisque omnium resonantibus, per orientalem portam, versus *Ricotum* iter arripuit, quod illi faustum fœlixque sit Deum Opt. Maximumque supplicitur oramus.

A BRIEF REHEARSALL, &c.

By RICHARD STEPHENS

()

A

BRIEF REHEARSALL

Of all such Things as were done

IN THE

UNIVERSITY OF OXFORD

During

THE QUEEN'S MAJESTY'S

ABODE THERE

This exhibited by RICHARD STEPHENS

As an Extract

DRAWN OUT OF A LONGER TREATISE

Made by Mr. NEALE

Reader of Hebrew

AT OXFORD

A BRIEF REHEARSALL

Of all such Things as were done

IN THE

UNIVERSITY OF OXFORD

DURING

THE QUEEN'S MAJESTY'S

ABODE THERE.

This exhibited by RICHARD STEPHENS,

As an Extract

DRAWN OUT OF A LONGER TREATISE

Made by Mr. NEALE,

READER OF HEBREW AT OXFORD.

[From Brit. Mus. MS. Harl. 7033. f. 150.]

THE 28 day of August, being Wednesday, three dayes before the Queen's Maj. coming to Oxford, the Earle of Lei-cester, Chancellor of the University, came to Oxford, accompany'd with Secretary Cecill and others, to see how the University was provided to receive the Queen. One Mr. Pottes[1] made an oration before them at Christ's Church, in Dr. Kennal's the Commissarie's lodging, enduring the space of a quarter of an houre or thereabout, for it rained that day so vehemently, that the oration could not be made abroad, as

---

[1] John Potts, of Merton College, *insignis philosophus & medicus satis peritus.* A.M. 1561. Ath. Ox. I. f. 20. [Boase, p. 234.]

it was appointed, and that all the graduates should be present. Thus done, there they dined in Christ's Church; and after dinner returned to Woodstocke again, to the Queen's Majesty.

31 Augusti.

Saturday,
Aug. 31.

This day, being Saturday, the Queen's Majesty, with the Nobility, came from Woodstocke to Oxford, and in the ways betwixt these two places, at the uttermost of the University liberties, besides a village named Wolvercote, was first received by the Earle of Leicester (who, for that purpose, came to Oxford before the Queen's coming this day) with four Doctors; viz. Dr. Kennalls Commissary, Dr. Humfric, Dr. Godwin, Dr. White, and eight Masters of Art, with the three Esquires Bedells, which delivered their staves to the Chancellor, and by him were they surrendered up to the Queen, and so she redelivered the same. Then an oration was there made unto her by one Mr. Marbecke, during a quarter of an houre, or thereabout, which she accepted very thankfully; and afterward they kissed her hand proffered forth unto them. This being done, she came from thence, with her Nobility (the three Esquires Bedells on horsback carying their staves before

f. 150ᵛ.

her) within a mile of Oxford, where the Maior, named Mr. Williams, with his brethren the Aldermen, all in scarlet gowns, and with the rest of the Citizens, received her Majesty; where the Maior delivered unto her first his mace, which was redelivered unto him; and afterwards he made an oration in English unto her, and presented, in the name of the whole city, a cupp of silver double gilt, in value 10*l.* in the which cup was about 40*l.* in old gold, as it was thought. After this, when she entred into the city of Oxford at the north gate, called Bocardo, from which place untill Christ Church Hall doore, all the University standing in order, according to their degrees, First, Scholers, of the which two, in the name of the rest, exhibited to the Queen an oration in writing, and certain verses. Then Bachelors, of the which two did in like sort, in the name of the rest

of the bachelors. Afterwards Masters of Art. And lastly
Doctors, every degree in his habit and hoode.

A short oration by a scholer named Deale[1] was made unto
her ; from whence she coming passed through the street ;
where the scholers (and as at this time, so did they at all
times, at the Queen's Majesty coming abroad) in order
kneeling, cryed, ' Vivat Regina : ' which she taking very
thankfully, with a joyful countenance sayd oftentimes, ' Gratias ago.'

When she came to the top of Carfax, being the midst of
the city, an oration was made unto her in Greek by Mr.
Lawrence, Publick Reader of the Greek Lecture, during the
space of a quarter of an houre, which she very well accepted, and gave him thanks in the Greek tongue. From
thence passing still through the scholers, she came to the
hall doore in Christ's Church, where an oration was made
unto her by one Mr. Kingsmell, Orator of the University, f. 151ᵛ.
whome she thankked for his pains. And afterwards, with
a canopy over her, carryed by four Senior Doctors, she
entred into the church, and there abode while the quyer sang
and play'd with cornetts, *Te Deum* : and so went from
thence, through a garden, to her lodging. There were set
upon the college gate, the hall doore, and walls adjoyning
thereto, where the Queen entred, diverse verses in Latin
and Greek.

Primo Septembris.

This day being Sunday, Dr. Overton made an English Sunday,
sermon in Christ's Church, in the forenoon. After that, in Sept. 1.
the afternoon, another was there made, by one Mr. Harris.

This night was played, in the Common Hall at Christ's
Church, (a fair large scaffold being provided, with lights all
of wax, prince-like) a Latin play, named ' Marcus Geminus,'
at which divers Noblemen were present ; but the Queen's
Majesty came not abroad all this day.

---

[1] [Robert Deale of New College, Wood, Hist. & Ant. ii. 156, Clark, Register,
p. 21.]

Furthermore, there were at sundry times, after dinner and supper, private disputations in philosophy by Masters of Art, before the Earle of Lecester, and the rest of the Nobility, during the Queen's abode in Oxford.

Secundo Septembris.

Monday,
Sept. 2.

This day, being Munday, the Noblemen, and the Embassador of Spain, came abroad in the forenoon, to hear the public lectures, and other ordinary lectures and disputations, all which were kept, during the Queen's Majesty's abode in Oxford, as otherwise in full term ; and after that, they rode to see the New College, where there were made, before the Earle of Lecester Chancellor of the University, the Embassador, Secretary Cecill, and others, two orations.

This day at night, the Queen heard the first half of an English play called ' Palæmon and Arcite,' made by one Mr. Edwards, of her Chappell, and played in the common or great hall at Christ's Church.

f. 151ᵛ.

At the beginning of the play there were, by a mischance, three slain ; the one a scholer of St. Mary's Hall named Walker, the other a cooke named John Gilbert, and the third a brewer named Mr. Pennie (and more hurt), by the press of the multitude, who thrust down a piece of the side wall of a stair upon them, which the Queen understanding, was very sorry for that mishappe ; and then forthwith sent her own surgeons to help them, but by that time they were passt remedy.

3 Septembr.

Tuesday,
Sept. 3.

This day, being Tuesday, afternoon about two of the clock, were, in St. Mary's, the University Church, from that time untill six of the clock, disputations in naturall and morall philosophy, at the which the Queen with her Nobility was present from the beginning to the end.

As the Queen entred into the church, there were divers schedes of verses in Greek, Latin, and Hebrew, set upon the doore and walls of the said church; and so there were in like sort the Wednesday and Thursday following, even a little before the Queen's coming to hear disputations.

The questions in Naturall Philosophy were,

1. 'Corpora inferiora reguntur a supernis Lationibus.'

2. 'Luna est causa fluxus et refluxus maris.'

Mr. Daye,   Mr. Bristow, ⎫ were opponents in the
Mr. Mericke,   Mr. Squier, ⎭ said questions.

Mr. Campion was Respondent. And Mr. Bellie was Determiner.

The questions in Morall Philosophy were,

1. 'Princeps declarandus est successione, non electione.'

2. 'Præstat gubernari ab optima Lege, quam ab optimo Rege.'

Mr. Leche, jun.   Mr. Bust,   ⎫ were Opponents in the
Mr. Thornton,   Mr. Mathew, ⎭ said questions.

Mr. Wollie was Respondent. And Mr. Cooper was Determiner.

This done, at night was thought should have been played f. 152ʳ. the other part of 'Palæmon and Arcite;' but it was deferred untill the night following[1].

4 *Septemb.*

This day, being Wednesday, after dinner were disputations Wednesday, the space of foure houres in Civill Law, in St. Mary's Church Sept. 4. as is aforesayd, before the Queen's Majesty.

The questions in Law were,

1. Privilegium per Venetos Florentinis concessum, et per bellum inter utramque Rempublicam superveniens extinctum,

---

[1] Concerning orders in disputation, and other academical exercises, they agreed much with those which the University of Cambridge had used two years before. Comedies also and tragedies were played in Christ's Church, where the Queenes Highnes lodged. Among which the comedy, entituled Palæmon and Arcet (made by Master Edwards of the Queen's Chappell) had such tragicall successe as was lamentable. For, at that time by the fall of a wall and a paire of staires and great prease of the multitude, three men were slaine. Stow, Ann. p. 659, a. b.

pace postea secuta non censetur esse restitutum, nisi in ipsis pacis conventionibus expresse sit cautum, ut restituatur.'

2. 'Si post acceptam mutuo pecuniam, ante diem solutioni præstitutum, acceptæ monetæ valor sit imminutus edicto Principis, debitor pecuniam ejus æstimationis, quæ tempore contractus fuit, creditori reddere tenetur.'

Dr. White,   Dr. Lowgher, } were Opponents in the said
Dr. Loyde,   } questions.

Dr. Awberie was Respondent. Dr. Kenalls, Commissary of the University, was Determiner.

This day, at night, the Queen heard the other half of the forenamed play, 'Palæmon and Arcite,' in the Common Hall at Christ's Church; and the same ended, gave Mr. Edwards, the maker thereof, great thanks for his pains.

5 *Septembr.*

Thursday, Sept. 5.

This day, being Thursday, were disputations in Physick and Divinity, in St. Mary's, the University Church, from two of the clock, or thereabout, untill seaven, before the Queen's Majesty; who gave very attent care unto them, and tarryed till the full end thereof.

The questions in Physick were,

1. 'Vita potest prorogari arte medica.'

2. 'Cibi tardæ concoctionis præferendi sunt cibis facilioris concoctionis.'

f. 152ᵛ.

In the which questions,

Dr. Huicke,   Dr. Barnes,   } were ready to oppose;
Dr. Baylie, sen. Dr. Slethurst,   } but for lacke of time
Dr. Baylie, jun. Dr. Gifford,   } only the three first op-
Dr. Atslo,   } posed.

Dr. Francisce was Respondent. Dr. Masters was Determiner.

The questions in Divinity were these,

1. 'Non licitum homini privato arma sumere contra Principem, etiam injustum.'

2. 'Ministerium verbi non est Dominatus.'

Dr. Godwin,   Dr. Westphaling, ╲ were ready to oppose;
Dr. Calfhill,   Dr. Yelder,   ⎰ but for want of time
Dr. Overton,   Dr. Cradocke,   ⎱ the two last were ex-
Dr. Pierce,   ╱ cluded.

Dr. Humfrie was Respondent.   And Dr. Jewell, bishop of Sarum, was Determiner.

After these disputations ended, the Queen's Majesty, at the earnest request and entreaty of the King of Spain's Ambassador (who was present at the foresaid exercises) the Earle of Leicester, the Earle of Ormund, Secretary Cecil, and others of the nobility, made a very comfortable and eloquent oration, in Latin, before the whole University, to the great comfort and delectation of them.

This day, at night, was played in the Common Hall at Christ's Church a Tragedy in Latin named 'Progne.'

6 *Septembr.*

This day, being Friday, Dr. Pierce made a sermon in Latin, before dinner, in Christ's Church, divers of the Nobility and others being present.   But the Queen's Majesty, by reason of great pains-taking and watching the former day and night (as it was supposed), did not come to this sermon.

His theme was taken out of the 49 chap. of Esai. the prophet,

'Reges erunt nutricii tui, et Reginæ nutrices tuæ.'

This day, the Commissary and Proctors, in the name of the whole University, presented unto the Queen's Majesty six pair of gloves, that were very fine; and to diverse of the Noblemen, and to the Officers of the Queen's House, some two pair, some one; which were accepted thankfully.

Also this day, about nine of the clock in the forenoon, was a Convocation, wherein the Honorable and Worshipfull Men were incorporated Masters of Arte; which, after the said Convocation, took their oath in Christ Church Hall, before the Earle of Leicester, Chancellor of the University,

Friday,
Sept. 6.

f. 153^r.

Dr. Kenalls his Vice-chancellor, the bishop of Sarum, the two Proctors, and certain other Doctors appointed in the name of the whole University for the same purpose, in this sorte, ' Ad observandum statuta, privilegia, libertates, et consuetudines hujus Universitatis.'

Their names are these as followeth :

Dñs. Gul. Howard, Magnus Camerar.
D. Edward Veir, Comes Oxon.
D. Ambr. Dudley, Comes Warwic.
D. Edw. Manner, Comes Rutland.
D. Tho. Butler, Comes Ormund.
D. Stafford.
D. Strange.
D. Sheffield.
D. Gul. Cecill, Eques Aur., Secretar.
D. Franc. Knolles, Eques Aur., Vice Camerar. et Præfectus Satellitum.
D. Nich. Throgmorton, Eques Aur.
D. Edw. Rogers.
Tamworth Arm. a cubiculo R.

This done, after dinner, even at the departure of the Queen's Majesty, Mr. Mathew made an oration before her in Christ's Church ; which done, she, with her Nobility and very many Gentlemen, coming from Christ's Church over Carfox, and so to St. Mary's, where divers schedes of verses were pasted on the doore and walls, and on the gates and walls of houses of scholers as she passed by : passing by the scholers standing in order from St. Mary's to the east gate, four Doctors of the University riding before her in their scarlet gowns and hoods, with foot clothes, and four Masters of Arte riding in like manner, but in black gowns and hoods, according to their degree (the Maior, with certain of his brethren to the number of 14 or 15, riding before her in their scarlets, to the end of Magdalen Bridge, where their liberties ended : which being told to the Queen's Majesty

by their Steward, Sir Francis Knolles, she bid them farewell,
with thanks) even unto Shotover, a mile and more out of
Oxford; where the Queen, understanding by the Earle of
Leccester, Chancellor of the University, that their liberties
ended there, after an oration made to her by Mr. Marbecke,
she held forth then her hand unto them, which they kissed;
and so, with thanks to the whole University, bid them all
farewell.

A little after this, a scholer named Deale, made an oration
unto her; which she accepted very well, and gave him thanks.
And so she rode that night to Ricot, to Mr. Norris' house,
eight miles from Oxford.

[Then follows the Queen's speech to the University, almost
exactly the same as printed in Wood's Hist. et Antiq. Univers.
Oxon. lib. I. p. 289[1].]

Numerus Studentium et Servientium omnium in Collegiis
et Aulis in Academia, Oxon. repertus et exhibitus 12 Augusti, an. 1568. viz.

Studentium   1764
Servientium   78
Summa totalis   1842

----

[1] Sic in MS.   (M.)

APPENDICES.

Oxoniensis Academiæ Gratulatio de Adventu Sere-
nissimæ Reginæ Elizabethæ ad ædes clarissimi
Comitis Leicestrensis ejusdem Academiæ
Cancellarii per Thomam Cooperum[1]
Magdalanensem.

Mirum fortasse tibi videri possit (Illustrissima Regina) quid Oxoniensis Academiæ studiosos commoveat, ut in hoc loco maxime & in
hoc tempore me voluit & tuæ Sublimitati gratias agere & sibi suæque
fœlicitati gratulari.   Nam & longe nimis intervallo sumus ab hoc loco
disjuncti, & nihil videmur commune habere cum hiis muris & turribus,
cum hac arce, cum hoc tremendo Martis domicilio.   Qui enim Musis
cum Marte conveniat?   Aut quæ poterit esse conjunctio pacis &
literarum studiosis, cum munitissimis hujusmodi belli propugnaculis?
Hujus igitur & facti & consilii nostri rationem, quæsimus ut & tua
Regalis Majestas pro solita clementia benigne audiat, & alii, si qui sint
qui dubitent, pro sua dignitate gratis & amicis animis accipiant.

Cum superioribus hisce proxime mensibus levi quodam, & incerto
rumore ad nos delatum esset futurum ut hoc anno tua Majestas
nostram Academiam inviseret, vix profecto credi potest, quam diffi-
culter potuerimus exultantem in animis nostris lætitiam cohibere, quo
minus erumperet quopiam indicio seipsam proderet, tum apud alios
cives nostros, tum apud tuam inprimis Celsitudinem.   Sed postquam
nobis denunciatum est hanc profectionem certo tibi statutam &
decretam esse, non jam effervescentis animi effectus modo, sed officii
nostri & honesta & justa & necessaria recordatio coegit, ut quacunque
ratione significaremus hoc tuo consilio, nec a te quicquam cogitari
potuisse humanius, benignius, clementius, nec nobis contingere gratius, optatius, jucundius.   Quamvis autem ad hanc officii nostri &

[1] Of him see Wood, Ath. Ox. I. 265-267. [v. s. p. 182.]

lætæ mentis significationem omnis mora longa nimis videretur, in hoc
tamen tempus certo consilio distulimus, & hunc locum ut huic rei
maxime idoneum delegimus. Nam & nunc, jam (Serenissima Regina)
videris in Oxoniensis Academiæ fines ingressa, cum ad eum accesseris
virum clarissimum, cujus patrocinio Scholæ nostræ dignitas hoc tempore maxime & vigeat & floreat. Quis enim non existimabit eum
corpus alicujus contingere, qui caput contrectet? arborem nutrire,
qui radicem foveat? homini prodesse, qui animum exhilaret? In hiis
autem ædibus, & in hac arce, & caput est & radix & anima & vita
nostræ Academiæ. Cujus dignitatem quacunque tua Celsitudo complexa fuerit benignitate, eadem et nostras metas affici necesse est, qui
spiritum ab illo & vitam trahamus. Quamobrem cum augustissima
tuæ Majestatis presentia in has ejus ædes singularem & pene incredibilem letitiam intulerit, qui fieri potest ut non ejusdem sensus ad nos
etiam perveniat quantumvis magno locorum intervallo disjunctos? Nos
ergo nostri officii memores & quas debemus eas habemus tuæ Sublimitati gratias & hujus dignitati nostræque fortunæ mirifice gratula-
mur. Multa scio patronum hunc nostrum pro singulari sua fœlicitate
vidisse tempora in quibus antehac maxima fuerit affectus animi voluptate ; sed nullus unquam illuxit dies qui tanto gratus, quam jucundus,
tuus hic adventus sit. Si quisquam tam alieno fuerit animo ut de
eo dubitare possit, vel hinc satis omnibus perspicuum fiat, quod
quicquid habeat vir amplissimus ingenii, quicquid opum & divitiarum,
quicquid splendoris & magnifici apparatus, id totum videatur ad tuum
adventum condecorandum deprompsisse. De conviviorum, ludorum,
spectaculorum aliorumque munerum magnificentia nihil mihi nunc
dicendum arbitror. Ipsi profecto parietes hujus arcis, post diuturnum
squalorem, novo quodam splendore illustres, palam loquuntur & præ-
dicant, quam mirabilem jucunditatem in hoc tempore Regalis tuæ
Majestatis aspectus concitarit. Quod si lapides isti sensu quodam
voluptatis moveantur, quomodo credis generosum illud pectus affectus [1]
affici, quo nihil unquam natura finxit vel gratius vel humanius vel
benignius. Sed non sequar quo me rapit affectus. Hoc quicquid
est officii, dignitatis, honoris, quod in tuam sublimitatem vir amplissimus hodie confert, non ea causa facit modo quod Regalis tua
clementia maxima semper humanitate ipsum seperatim complexa sit,
sed multo magis quod ejus prudentia videat & se & omnes hujus
regni cives tuos communi quodam officio devinctos esse, ut non opes
modo & facultates, sed operam, diligentiam, industriam omnem, atque
adeo vitam ipsam ad amplitudinem tuam illustrandam convertant.

[1] Sic. ? om.

Quibusvis principibus etiam malis honos debetur & obedientia : Præ-
claros vero, præstantes, & excellentes, non obedientia modo, sed
pietate, sed veneratione, sed admiratione prosequuntur. Mirificus
enim est & incredibilis bonorum civium amor in Principem bonum.
Nusquam major pietas, nusquam major charitas se prodit. Non
uxoris vehementior est in conjugem, non filii in parentem, non civis
in patriam. Omnes omnium charitates unus amor Principis complec-
titur. Nec enim viri conjugibus, nec filii parentibus, nec cives patria
frui possent, si non accederet boni Principis industria. Maxime
igitur secundum Deum, Principem veneramur, quem & in pace recto-
rem, & in periculis custodem nobis constituit. Quo plura vero &
majora cujusque extiterint in suos merita, eo majori vicissim ac
ardentiori benevolentia ipsum & semper complecti solent & jure complecti debent. Ego vero cum respicio ad spatium præteriti temporis
& vetustatis memoriam recordor ultimam, multos video fuisse in hac
regione clarissimæ memoriæ reges, sed nullum per quem Deus hanc
gentem vel pluribus vel majoribus vel præstantioribus beneficiis cumu-
laverit, quam per tuam Celsitudinem. Deus bone, quam vastum nunc
ego mihi pelagus laudum tuarum propositum sentio ? Ingressum
video, sed quomodo inde expediam non intelligo. Vereor profecto
ne tenuitatem meam temere præcipitem in eam profunditatem, unde
me nulla vis ingenii, nulla facultas orationis vindicare possit. Sistam
itaque gradum, & extrema tantum ita cursu orationis meæ perstrin-
gam, ut me leniter potius laudes tuas attigisse, quam in tantam
rerum multitudinem ingressum esse merito existimes. Quid hic com-
memorem, in ipso regalis tuæ potestatis aditu confractum & rejectum
papisticæ tyrannidis jugum, quo multis annis misere gens Anglica
pressa & gravata fuit ? Quid verum Numinis cultum, quem scelerate
ab adversariis deformatum, ab omnibus antichristianæ perfidiæ sordibus repurgasti ? Quid publicam pacem & tranquillitatem tantam,
quantam tot simul annis nulla unquam vetustas viderit ? Quid omnium rerum affluentiam tam abundantem, ut magis nobis sit metuen-
dum, ne copia lascivere quam inopia gravari videamur. Quid
numisma nostrum, cum non exiguo gentis hujus dedecore corruptum
& adulteratum, a tua tamen magnificentia in pristinam æstimationem
ac puritatem restitutum ? Sed nullus est enumerandi finis, si omnia
vellem persequi quæ per hoc fælicissimum imperium tuum mirifica
Dei bonitas in tuos cives contulit. De illis autem ornamentis & animi
& corporis quibus illius benignitas Regalem tuam Majestatem mirabiliter decoravit & illustravit, si nunc orationem instituerem, vereor ne
fortunæ & amplitudini tuæ assentari magis, quam præstantissimis

virtutibus meritas tribuere laudes existimer. Illas tamen divinas &
præclaras animi dotes, quæ ad morum suavitatem & facilitatem pertinent, quod iisdem nos incredibili voluptate fruamur, sine scelere
& ingratæ mentis suspicione silentio præterire non possum. Quis
igitur unquam in summo potestatis fastigio majorem audivit mansue-
tudinem atque clementiam? Quis multis jam annis vel insontem
injusta pœna, vel nocentem crudeli supplicio vidit affectum? Quis
in hoc toto clementissimo tuæ Celsitudinis imperio vel minimum
crudelitatis vestigium conspexit; vel in ipsos papisticæ tyrannidis
patronos, quam præter omnium expectationem clemens & misericors
fuisti? Quamdiu strictam in illos legum aciem incredibili levitate
cohibuisti! Novit enim regalis tua pietas nihil minus Christianam
principem decere quam diffluere suorum civium sanguine. Quamobrem exemplo Cæsaris experiri voluisti, num adversus pertinentes
& præfractos cives plus valeret ignoscentiæ lenitas quam severitas
animadversionis. Quod si hac tua mansuetudine & misericordia
abutantur, meminerit proculdubio tua prudentia, ita laudanda in principe lenitatem ut interdum reipublicæ causa adhibeatur severitas.
Nulla enim re scelerati in perniciem deducuntur magis quam spe
impunitatis & ignoscentiæ. Itaque summa in te clementia cum
severitate sic est conjungenda, ut neque indulgentia malos ad flagitia
excitare neque crudelitas bonos a libertate deterrere possit. Quid
dicam de eximia & inaudita comitate tua, ad cujus Majestatem tam
faciles sunt accessus, etiam privatorum, tam liberæ querelæ de aliorum
injuriis, ut nemo jure queri possit præclusam sibi viam esse ad
æquitatem obtinendam. Neque tamen aures ita patentes habes ut
eorum temere calumnias admittere velis qui studio & voluntate in
aliorum infamias & criminationem incumbunt, qui laudem sibi &
gratiam quærunt ex obtrectatione alienæ virtutis, qui importunissimis
contumeliis & injustissimis calumniis optimorum civium dignitatem
operire ac opprimere conantur. Has tu labes Reipublicæ tuæ
(Regina splendidissima), has pestes, has furias, non ab auribus modo
tuis, sed a conspectu & oculis, ut nocentissimas bestias procul abigis.
Satis enim videt tua prudentia duas deterrimas & nocentissimas
bestias Calumniam & Assentationem plerunque in illustrium principum aulis magno cum multorum exitio versari. Quarum alterum
in vitæ innocentiam suam rabiem furiose exercens, bonos cives in
scelerum & flagitiorum suspicionem inducit. Altera blanditiis &
assentationibus ita principi omnem æquitatis & officii cogitationem
excantat, ut nihil sibi licere non putet quod vel libido suadeat, vel
voluptas expectet vel affectus poscat. Nulla res alia Commodum

Imperatorem ab honesta vitæ ratione a sanctissimis majorum institutis, a jure, a legibus, ad turpissima quæque flagitia, ad libidinem, avaritiam, crudelitatem abduxit, quam quod se adulari passus sit, & aures perditissimorum hominum assentationibus patefecerit. Quamobrem hæc tua laus (illustrissima Princeps) quod hoc genus hominum tam diligenter averseris, & cum immortali tui nominis gloria & cum incredibili nostræ reipublicæ commodo conjuncta est. Sed quo me rapuit impetus orationis meæ? Quousque provexit admiratio virtutis tuæ? Hoc erat quod modo querebar, ingressum esse facilem, exitum supra modum difficilem. Abrumpam itaque in medio cursu orationem meam, & hoc totum negotium in aliud tempus differam. Erit enim propidie, erit spero dies (clementissima Regina) cum ista si non pro tua dignitate, certe pro benevolentia[1] civium facultate illustri prædicatione omnium & oculis & auribus exponentur. Ergo in id tantum hoc tempore incumbam, ut potius necessariam officii nostri rationem explicandam, quam justam tuarum laudum excellentiam prædicandam suscepisse videar. Sic igitur apud animos nostros & de immensa Dei in nos bonitate & nostro in te officio cogitare solemus: Cum in maximis olim & gravissimis nostris temporibus admiranda Numinis providentia tuam Majestatem ex custodia, ex carcere, ex vinculis, ex ipsius pene mortis faucibus liberarit, ut aliquando sedens ad gubernacula istius imperii, nos, parentes, liberos, hanc communem patriam nostram, divinis & immortalibus afficeres beneficiis: vehementer nos ingratos, improbos, sceleratos futuros, si non omnibus modis contenderimus, ut auspicatissimam tuam felicitatem officiis colamus, fide conservemus, virtute defendamus. In malum principem sceleratum se gerere nefarium puto; piam vero & præclare de nobis meritam debita veneratione non colere, impium, nefarium, beluinum existimo. Canes etiam cæci heris suis blandiuntur. Elephantes vasti & crudeles rectores tamen venerantur. Ursi & leones custodes diligunt & tuentur. Homo vero canibus ferocior, elephantis immanior, ursis & leonibus truculentior, principem, reipublicæ custodem, patriæ parentem, non diliget, non suspiciet, non admirabitur? Qui sic affecti sint, non jam illi mali cives, sed nec cives nec homines existimandi; immo ut belluæ immanes ex finibus humanæ naturæ exterminandi. Nos vero (Princeps præstantissima) Dei beneficio melius instituti, pro eo atque debemus, etsi forte non quantum debemus, propter tuorum magnitudinem meritorum, tamen pro humana parte quanta maxima possumus veneratione, tuam Majestatem prosequimur, ardentissimis votis omnia læta comprecamur, aspectu lætamur, præsentiam optamus,

---

[1] Sic. ? benevolentium.

speramus, expectamus. Quam si Regalis tua clementia nobis ad tempus constitutum exhibere conetur, ut & nostræ mentes eadem tanquam fausto sydere exhilarentur, alii fortasse pro suis opibus, & pro tua amplitudine majore apparatu, splendore, magnificentia, sed nulli unquam magis fidis, gratis & benignis animis exceperint. Si forte (quod vehementer deprecamur) casus aliquis, tibi necessarius, nobis infestus, utrisque ingratus, hoc tuum consilium mutaverit, & tam speratam hanc optatam lætitiam interverterit, nos sane pro rei magnitudine, summo conficiemur dolore; sin quod certissime speramus, quam suscepisti in nos propensionem voluntatis, eam tua ad nostram Academiam accessione confirmaris & absolveris, cum referendi muneris facultas desit, quod solum possumus, gratias & agimus maximas & habemus sempiternas.

Orator Publicus KINSMILLUS[1].

Etsi non sum nescius quam incredibile videri possit ut qui fruatur lætitia, non careat metu, quia lætitia est cum securitate, metus non est sine dolore: equidem tamen, serenissime Princeps, sic afficior ut me nec lætari nimis, nec timere satis posse in hoc tempore intelligam. Cum vero primum in suspiciendam Majestatem tuam, quam religiosa sane veneratione, sicuti æquum est revereor: deinde vero in tam illustrem tot præclarissimorum virorum frequentiam quorum auctoritatem non debeo aspernari: postremo etiam in hujus celeberrimæ Academiæ aliquam existimationem intuear, cujus habenda est mihi ratio diligenter: nec me præ nimia verecundia tam hæsitantem esse decet ut sine magna voluptate, nec præ immoderata lætitia tam exultantem, tamen ut sine magna fortitudine in hanc tantam & tam insignem celebritatem præsiliisse videar. Quanquam in hac quidem ipsa celeberitate si mihi pro me esset modo dicendum, esse hoc tantopere querendum non videretur: nunc vero cum mea vox non mea sed hujusce literatissimi cœtus esse debeat, tantum abest ut non timeam, ut me timere etiam oportere existimem. Neque tamen ego non video mea quid intersit. Prorsus vero ut Cæsar tanta facilitate fuisse fertur, ut Marius non semel dixerit, 'Qui apud te audent dicere,

---

[1] Thomas Kingsmill, born at Sidmanton, in Hampshire, was a stndent of this University about 1555; A. B. and Fellow of Magdalen College, 1560; elected Public Orator, and in 1569 Hebrew Professor; and in 1572 was candidate for a doctor's degree. Too mnch study having disordered his brain, the famous Richard Hooker supplied his place as professor. He recovered his senses, and was living in 1605. Ath. Ox. I. 329. [Boase, pp. 226, 241.]

o Cæsar, magnitudinem tuam ignorant; qui non audent, humanitatem:' id de te, o Regina, facilius & verius dixerim, videri me scilicet dicendo tuam non satis vereri celsitudinem, tacendo tuam non satis fateri clementiam. In hac autem mea cura tam ancipiti & dubia, dum illinc regia Majestas terreat, hinc singularis humanitas alliciat, utra tandem vicerit non potest esse obscurum cum pateat quid fecerim. Illa vero, illa inquam suavi tua ac singulari mansuetudine, quæ tibi nunquam nocuit, multis sæpe profuit, nulli unquam defuit, sic me erigi, sic refici video, ut non possim sane perinde tuam reformidare magnitudinem, quam admirari lenitatem. Cum itaque album mihi velum facilitatis tuæ jam erigi videam, quid est quod præterea in dicendo impediat, nisi quod honorificentissimus & suavissimus amplitudinis tuæ aspectus tantam animis nostris alacritatem instillaverit, ut eam nulla ingenii acies pertingere satis acute, nullum orationis filum perstringere satis expedite, nullum denique verborum flumen effundere satis largiter & copiose possit. Nam ut qui in mare ingrediuntur, quo progrediuntur longius, eo in majorem undarum altitudinem prolabuntur periculosius, & impingunt facilius: ita sane quo tam immensam hanc omnium ordinum et hominum voluptatem emetiri cupio magis, eo magis crescere mihi video copiam orationis meæ, nec ullum aut finem aut modum sortiri. Nequeo satis respicere quid majoribus nostris priscis illis temporibus bene feliciterque acciderit: nostra sane memoria nulla res vel tam diuturnam attulit lœtitiam, vel tantam. Solet nimirum hæc terra, o Princeps, quæ vacua & ante gratam expectationem adventûs fuit solitaria, nunc autem quanta hominum multitudo subito convenerit vides: horum omnium ora, oculos, vultus, motus, nutus, in te unam conjectos esse sentis. Perinde vero ut Miltiadis trophæum sæpe e somno Themistoclem; sic nos sane conspectus Majestatis tuæ non dicam e somno, ut illum quem modo nominavi Themistoclem, sed ab omni rerum nostrarum sollicitudine atque adeo cogitatione avocavit. Quod usque adeo mihi ego presentiscere videor, ut hodie mihi & senes repuerascere, & ægri convalescere, & semimortui reviviscere videantur. An vero ullam aquilam tam ætate ingravescentem arbitramur, cujus ætatem hic dies non renovet? An ullam tam intermortuam aut consepultam phœnicem cujus cineres hæc lux non exsuscitet? Nolite vero putare, ornatissimi Viri, reviviscere illam nescio quam Lacænam fœminam, quam quia Regis filia, regis uxor, regis mater fuit, beatissimam nimirum censuit antiquitas: sed esse auspicatissimam hujus Academiæ & universæ Reipublicæ Anglicanæ Reginam & Principem, cui Rex pater, Rex frater, Regina soror, cujus prima, media,

omnis ætas, vel erudita literis, vel edocta literis [1], vel edocta periculis,
vel adornata honoribus, jam ad gubernacula Reipublicæ ipsa sedet,
hanc bonis legibus ac institutis temperavit, hinc gravissimas commu-
nium temporum procellas densissimas errorum tenebras dispulit,
discussit, plumbeum & æreum non dico nummum, quod tamen vere
dici potest & sæpe dici debet, sed id quod multo est præstabilius,
purum Dei cultum, qui in exulceratissimis illis temporibus in plumbum, in æs, in scoriam erat adulteratus, repurgavit, restituit; quæ
denique duas res præstantissimas præclarissimasque invexit, tranquillitatem pacis Reipublicæ, lucem veritatis Ecclesiæ. Satis opinor
hoc esse laudis, atque ita reputo ut id jam intelligatur, hæc a me
de auspicatissima Celsitudine tua sic dicta esse, ut eadem de alio
principe dici non possint. Quid vero agitis, ornatissimi Viri? quid
cogitatis? quid putatis? Parvæne vobis multa fecisse videri potest,
quæ duas res, ut dixi præstantissimas præclarissimasque invexit
pacem reipublicæ lucem Ecclesiæ. Quid igitur exterarum quæso
rerum publicarum calamitatem ac infortunium mecum aliquandiu
recognoscite, perlustrate animis, omnes exteras gentes præcipue
autem eas quæ propinquæ & vicinæ sunt. Intuemini Scotiam,
Galliam, Hispaniam; quas licet respublicas alioqui potentes & florentes esse non diffitemur: videte tamen, videte inquam per Deum
immortalem num similiter vel in istis rebus publicis tranquillitas vel
in ecclesiis veritas constituta & patefacta videatur. Atque hæ sunt
illæ scilicet Virtutes divinæ & tuæ, o Sacratissima Regina, quarum
non modo Anglia & Hibernia, sed etiam ipsa illa Scotia & Gallia,
non dico laudem & famam, sed certe utilitatem & fructum perce-
perint. Quæ licet tam late pateat, sintque nobis cum reliquis com-
munes, a me tamen penitus in dicendo pretereundæ non fuerint.
Nunc autem ad illa venio quæ nos nostramque Academiam proprie
attingunt. Dum ergo sane perspicue attingo quæ beneficia Majestas
tua, quæ omni posteritatis memoria celebrandi majores tui in hanc
Academiam contulerint, ab eximia tua facilitate peto, ut digneris
aliquantisper attendere. Sexcenti jam sunt anni cum clarissimus Rex
Alphredus hanc Academiam tum collapsam restauravit, & non modo
in pristinam dignitatem restituit, sed aliquot publicis Scholis ampliorem fecit. Ex quo tempore ita paucis annis crevit ut plurimos
haberet alumnos, non literarum modo fama celebres, sed monumen-
torum etiam numero & dignitate claros. Nolo in presentia commemorare Patricium Armachanum, Bachonos, Banchothorpum, Nicolaum
Lyrensem, Wiclefum, aliosque tam multos & tam celebres, ut prop-

---

[1] Sic. ? om. *vel edocta literis.*

terea factum esse putem, ut Oxoniensem Academiam & exterarum gentium scriptores, cum studiosorum celebritate, tum auctoritatis amplitudine, semper nobilissimam præstantissimamque prodiderint, & hanc eandem multi ipsi principes plurimis maximisque beneficiis cumulaverunt. Hanc vero Edwardus III. Richardus III. Henricus IV. Henricus VII. partim donis amplissimis partim honestissimis privilegiis auxerunt. Edwardus II. collegium condidit a Regio titulo Regale dictum. Joannes Baliol non incellebris Scotorum Rex ab ipsius nomine Baliolense gymnasium. Philippa uxor Edwardi IV. femina clarissima a sua dignitate appellatur Reginæ collegium. Celeberrimæ & clarissimæ memoriæ princeps Henricus VIII. tuæ Majestatis dilectissimus pater & hoc illustre gymnasium, quod a Christo nomen habet, magna studiosorum frequentia auxit, & prælectiones illas publicas in Theologia, in Jure Civili, in Medicina, & Græcis & Hebraicis, ad perennem ac prope immortalem totius Orbis Christiani utilitatem instituit. Edwardus VI. suavissimus frater tuus, de cujus laude neque hic locus ut multa dicantur neque nimis tamen multa dici possunt, quam singulari benignitate vel hanc Academiam vel Cantabrigiam complexus est, tum ostendit, cum Petrum Martyrem & Martinum Bucerum pios sane & doctos patres huc ex ultimis Germaniæ partibus evocavit. Quorum multo[1] sane filios tua, o Sacratissima Regina, bonitas ex eadem illa Germania collegit, & P. Martyris selectiss. auditorem P. Martyris meritiss. hæredem fecisti patri certe suo sola ætate inferiorem. Sed quousque tandem orationem meam quædam quasi lenta enumeratio factorum, ne ad id quod præcipuum & optimum est perveniret, detinuit. Est vero hæc ipsa Augustissimæ Majestatis tuæ presentia beneficium scilicet tale & tantum, quale & quantum nec ab omnibus oratoribus una hora, nec omnibus horis ab uno oratore dici potest. Quid esse aliquam in terris principem, atque eam natam esse fœminam, quam nulla regio, nulla urbs tam delectet quam Academia, quæ et ipsa literatissima est, & cui deliciæ sunt literæ. Ergone ulla res ab immortali Deo mortalibus hominibus dari potest aut tam sancta aut tam suavis quam nobilissimi Monarchæ & Principes qui eruditioni ac pietati favent. Quorum ipsorum ad homines in pietatis ac eruditionis studio vigilantes accessione dici non potest quanta ipsi eruditioni ac pietati fiat accessio. Quod ipsum a tua Regia bonitate fit tam insigniter, ut vetera illa majorum tuorum beneficia vel si fuerunt nimis antiqua renovet, vel si fere oblivione sepulta resuscitet, vel si adhuc inchoata consummet. Cum itaque ad cætera illa ut dixi magna ac prope divina in nos merita hæc etiam

---

[1] Sic. ? multos.

accessio tua tanquam cumulus accesserit : quid est cur Academia vel
Celsitudini tuæ vel felicitati suæ non serio tandem ac mirifice gratu-
letur.   Nam quantum boni vel Academia vel Respublica vel certe
ecclesia ex auspicatissimo Majestatis tuæ adventu consecuta sit, si
cæcum ac imperitum hominum genus non intelligat: ergone hæc
literatissima sedes quam ipsius hujusce reipublicæ & Ecclesiæ Anglicanæ lumen, linguam, mentem, dicimus, aut tam cæca erit ut non
videre, aut tam muta ut non eloqui, aut tam ingrata ut non fateri
velit.   Quin imo suum florem, o præstantissime Princeps, educet, ut
quemadmodum Nestor ille ut est apud Homerum, decem sibi ora,
decem linguas optarit ; sic hæc sedes multorum sane claras & suaves
voces, acuta & penetrantia ingenia evocabit, quæ quantumvis in variis
ac multiplicibus vel artibus vel rebus versentur, spectent tamen unum
atque idem, ut quam scilicet hoc tempore lætitiam & voluptatem
animis imbiberint, hauserint, eam aliquousque Celsitudini tuæ aperiant, impertiant.   Est hæc, Deus bone, hujus Academiæ singularis
& rara felicitas, quæ quoniam hujusmodi est ut diuturna esse non
possit, si quidem huic lætitiæ mœror, ut serenitati tempestas imminet,
propterea nobis quod possumus cura videndum est ut summam hanc
voluptatem modica quædam mœstitia tanquam salutare quoddam con-
dimentum ac non extremus dolor excipiat.   Sic vero mea oratio
optabilissimum, ut mihi persuadeo finem sortietur si perinde ut Camil-
lus devictis Veiis precatus esse dicitur ut si cui deorum hominumque
nimia sua fortuna populique Romani videretur, ut eam expiare quam
minimo suo privato incommodo, publicoque Populo Romano liceret :
Itidem ego religiose, sane, ac ardentissimis precibus contenderim, ut
hanc tam illustre & tam insigne, cum hujus Academiæ, tum hujus
civitatis fortunam, quam minimo dolore levire ac levare velit ; ita sane
fiet quod tamen vix optandum videtur, ut patefacta veritate in ecclesia,
constituta pace in Republica, exsuscitata eruditione in Academia, nos
scilicet cœlesti quadam animorum voluptate sine omni calamitate, aut
calamitatis metu perfrui possimus.

HENRICUS BUSTUS[1] in adventum Regiæ Majestatis
in Magdalenenses.

Quoniam Magdalenei tui te antea desideravimus quam expecta-
vimus ; & amavimus, quam cognovimus, serenissime Princeps, minime
mirari debet Celsitudo tua, si cum te hodie præsentem intueamur,

[1] v. s. p. 175, n. 25.

gestientes animorum affectus comprimere silentio nequeamus. Quamvis etenim ea sit virtutis præstantia, ut propter ipsam eos sæpe diligamus, quos nunquam vidimus: oculi tamen nescio quomodo efficiunt, ut quamvis benevolentia prius cumulata etiam fuerit, nunc tamen aucta esse quodammodo videatur. Neque vero satis adhuc factum desiderio nostro putavimus, lectissima Regina, quod te nuper adventantem universi vidimus, quod semel adeoque etiam simul te salutavimus. Imo plurimum etiam pietatis nostræ interesse videbatur, cum in te semper fuerit singularis ut etiam te singuli & seorsim & sæpe & sæpius & sæpissime, si fieri posset, cerneremus. Cum vero quas urbes adieris, quos homines viseris, quibus locis permanseris, apud eosdem tanta clementiæ tuæ vestigia reliqueris, ut longissime te abire nolint, citissime te redire velint. Equidem & Magdalena nostra, vel potius tua, etsi aliarum forte civitatum magnitudine, populorum multitudine, locorum splendore, facillime superetur, at certe officio, benevolentia, fide, nulli unquam concedet, ut in te sit quam est ipsa firmior. Quæ omnes jam excussisse lachrimulas ipsoque triumphare gaudio videtur qui te quam necesse fuit colere qualiscunque esses talem habeat ut libenter etiam amplecti velit. Est vero rara sed certe chara in summa potestate tanta erga literatos indulgentia ut cum in eos plus officii contuleris quam in cæteros (sicut filiolos suos e schola redeuntes Gracchorum mater) sic facile omnes intelligunt quænam esse putes ornamenta tua. Cum etiam & Alexandrum quoque illum magnum ad Diogenem se contulisse legimus, sed tantum legimus. Et Pompeium ex Syria Rhodum contendisse ad Possidonium audivimus. Cum vero & nobis apud te officii testificandi locum dederis, tuus aspectus multo certe jucundissimus utrum nobis plus dignitatis in perpetuum, an delectationis quotidie sit allaturus, haud facile quidem dixerim. Quo igitur majore te lætitia excipimus, illustrissime Princeps, eo majore a te dolore divellimur, ut plane verear ne Magdalena discessu tuo veteres statim renovandi fletus occasionem inveniat. Quamobrem, Nobilissima Regina, sicut voluntas nostra te quam primum huc venire, sic pietas quam diutissime hic manere desiderat. Venienti obviam tibi non sine lætitia processit, abeuntem vero etiam cum lachrymis prosequetur; præsentem humiliter colet, absentem ex animo diliget. Voluntatis vero tantam tibi tribuere possumus, quantum ipsa cupis, officii tantum præstare cupimus quantum certe ipsi possumus. Quare & a Deo ardentissime precibus contendo, ut te nobis Principem semper conservet, & a te supplex peto, ut quos semel intueri vis, eosdem semper tueri velis.

In adventum illustrissimi Comitis Leicestrensis & clarissimi viri G. Cecilii Regiæ Majestatis Secretarii utriusque Academiæ Cancellariorum Gratulatio.

Felix, aiunt, est occursus bonorum, bonorum autem nobilium felicior, doctorum vero & doctrinæ fautorum longe felicissimus. Cum ergo vos & virtute præditos, & honore illustres & literis præstantes Oxoniam invisatis, adventum vestrum nobis & Academiæ universæ gratissimum esse ut libenter nos confitemur, ita vos certo de nobis polliceri debetis. Adestis duo Scholarchæ, adestis Academiarum defensores, tutores, præsides. Pergite literas colere, conservare, literatos diligere, fovere. Non ignoratis illam auream vocem Imperatoris Augusti, 'Romam lateritiam accepi, marmoream relinquo.' Facite similiter vos, & efficite, autoritate, prudentia, ut Academias ex parvis maximas, ex mediocribus florentissimas habeamus. Ita nobis & Academiæ gratissimi semper advenietis: ita Christus summus Cancellarius vestrum iter fortunabit, ita operam Deo acceptam, scholis jucundam, toti Reipublicæ utilem navabitis.

J OANNES R USSELLUS.

In adventum Regiæ Majestatis ad Magdalanenses Oratio.

'Ανέγνωμεν Καίσαρα Σεβαστὸν πράγματός τε τέρατι καὶ ἀνθρώπου φρονήματι ἡδόμενον πένητά τινα εὐεργετῆσαι διδόντα δαρεικοὺς δισμυρίους, ὅτι δίδαξας ἔτυχεν τὸν κόρακα λέγειν, Χαῖρε Καῖσαρ. Σὺ δὲ εὐδοκιμώτατη βασίλισσα, ἐπείδη τῷ ἐλθεῖν πρὸς ἡμᾶς, τὴν τοῦ Καίσαρος εὐεργεσίαν ἐπιτηδεύῃς, ἐπίτρεψον ἡμῖν καὶ ταύτῃ τῇ φωνῇ σὲ ἀσπάσεσθαι μόνον λέγουσι, Χαῖρε Βασίλισσα. 'Εν τούτοις γὰρ ἔπεσι δυσὶν ἅπαντα συμπλέκομαι ἅ τε δύναμαι καὶ βούλομαι, καὶ ἃ χρὴ λέγειν. πολλὰ γὰρ ἂν δυναίμην, πλείω δὲ βουλοίμην, πάντα δὲ ἂν πρέποι φάναι, ἃ συνέχει σοῦ τὰ ἐγκώμια, καὶ τὰ καθήκοντα ἐμοί. ἀλλὰ, εἰ μὴ ἔδοξαν ἄλλοι λογοποιοὶ κατὰ τὴν τοῦ πράγματος ἀξίαν ἱκανὰ εἰρηκέναι, ὅμως σὲ κατὰ τὴν σὴν σωφροσύνην ἱκανὰ ἀκηκοέναι ἰσχυρῶς ἂν ὁμολογήσαιμι. διηγοῦνταί τινα τῷ ὀνύματι Ψάφονα θεοποιεῖσθαι βουλόμενον, παμπόλλὰς ἐμφώνους, καὶ ἀνθρωπογλώττους ὄρνιθας πρὸς τὰς ὕλας καὶ τὰ ὄρη ὑπέκπεμψαι ἐνάρθρως λαλεῖν ταύτας διδάξαντα, τὸ, μέγας θεὸς Ψάφων. 'Εγὼ δὲ εἰ τοσοῦτον σὲ κολακεύσαιμι, ὅσον ἑαυτὸν ὁ Ψάφων, ἀνυποκρίτως πάντων τῶν ὀρνίθων μεγαλοφωνότερος ἂν εἴην, πάλιν καὶ συχνῶς ἀναβοῶν καὶ ἐπανακυκλῶν, μεγάλη, ὦ μεγάλη, ὦ μεγίστη, ὦ εὐσεβεστάτη, σοφωτάτη, καὶ σωφρονεστάτη βασίλισσα. 'Εστὶ γὰρ ἡ μὲν εὐσέβεια, ᾗ εὐσεβεῖς πρὸς τὸν Θεὸν ἱερωτάτη, ἡ δὲ σοφία, ᾗ ἄρχεις ἡμῶν θαυμαστὴ, ἡ σωφροσύνη ᾗ σωφρονίζεις ἑαυτὴν, θεοφιλευτάτη.

ὅμως βουλοίμην ἂν ἐγὼ μᾶλλον πένητος ἐκείνου ἢ Ψάφωνος ὄρνιθας μιμεῖσθαι.
εὐδοκίμως γὰρ κυνικὸς αὐτός, κρεῖττον εἶναι ἐς κόρακας ἀπελθεῖν, ἢ ἐς κόλακας.
οὕτως ἔγωγε μᾶλλον κόρακος, ἢ κόλακος τὴν φωνὴν ὑποκρινόμενος, ἀπολείψω
πάντα κόσμον, πᾶσαν λαμπρότητα τοῦ λόγου, ἵνα πολλὴν ὑπακοὴν, εὔνοιαν
μεγίστην, καὶ ἄπειρον χαρὰν βραχίστοις λόγοις συντελῶ, Χαῖρε Βασίλισσα.

NICOLAUS BALGAY[1].

LAURENTII HUMFREDI S. Theologiæ Doctoris pro Regia Majestate ad Deum precatio.

O deus altitonans, mundi supreme Monarcha,
    Qui superos, terras, infera quæque regis:
Prospice de cœlo, vitem spectato Britannam,
    Labentem digito surrige quæso tuo.
Serva Reginam, serva, mitissime Christe,
    Ut tua sit semper: sit quoque nostra diu.
Fœmineum regnum dextra fulcito potente,
    Ne quasset gentem dura ruina tuam.
Spesque metusque jubent, me sic, O Christe, precari,
    Nam sic confligunt spesque metusque simul.
Speramus timidi, mox sperantesque timemus:
    Spes, metus, huc, illuc, hæc vocat, ille trahit.
Quod clemens Pater es, speramus: deinde timemus,
    Quod justus Judex, atque severus eris.
Per te Reginam nunc possidet Anglica tellus,
    Et per Reginam commoda multa metit.
Ampla tua est bonitas; major maledictio nostra.
    Quo magis es clemens, hoc magis horror adest;
Nam per Reginam, divinum Manna dedisti,
    Spes est: at causa est nausea nostra metus.
Floret religio: spes est, sed manet in horas,
    Est metus: hanc solam labra librique sonant.
Est spes, quandoquidem regnat lectissima Princeps,
    At quia mortalis, jam subit ecce metus,
Oxoniæ morbus tetigit timor inde subortus;
    At quia mors parcit, spes renovata venit.
Orba viro est, timeo. Sed non est viribus orba,
    Spero, sed prudens imperat, at Mulier.
O virgo Elizabet, phœnix & gemma regentûm,
    O flos, o patrii stella decusque soli.

[1] [Boase, p. 242.]

Si vives, magni Jovæ clementia sola est;
   Si moreris, nostrum est promeritum atque malum.
En fuit, en non est Babylon, non Persica pompa,
   Non Græcum imperium, non Latialis honor.
Spes est, quod fuerint; sed nunc non esse, timendum;
   Spes est, esse quidem, porro fuisse malum.
Quod præsis populo, quod sis, confido; sed oro,
   Ut semper possis esse, vel esse diu.
O utinam vivas, vivas ut post moriare;
   Mortua post vivas, ne moriaris.   Amen.

D. Edowardus Russellus[1], ornatissimus Comitis Bedfordii Filius.

Oxonium merito lætare, simulque triumpha,
   Abjice mœstitias, lætitiamque cape.
Nam venit huc Princeps, te, te, Regina salutat
   Princeps sola salus, præsidiumque tuum.
Nunc omnes rugas tetricæ dispellito frontis,
   Oxonium nebulas abjice, quæso, tuas.
Nunc quorsum nubes, quorsum frons mœsta dolorque?
   Lætum tempus adest, atque serena dies.
Cur exultemus cuncti, justissima causa est:
   Quam paucis verbis dicere constitui.

R   Reginam venisse bonam, venisse monarcham
E   Et quod eam videant, maxima lætitia est.
G   Græcam rite tenet linguam simul atque Latinam
I   Insignis Princeps ancora sacra piis.
N   Non etenim hæc solum doctrinæ munere claret,
A   At virtute nitet, relligione, fide.
V   Virgo prælustris, princeps & fœmina docta,
I   Ingenio raro, & pietate bona.
R   Rex pater & frater, mater Regina sororque,
GO   Gothos atque rudes subjicit illa sibi.
P   Princeps permagno flagrat pietatis amore,
I   Integritas vitæ est concelebranda suæ.

[1] Edward Lord Russell was eldest son of Francis second Earl of Bedford.   He married Jane Sibilla, daughter of Sir Richard Morison ; died without issue, in his father's life ; and is buried at Cheneys.   Peerage, 1779. I. 252.   [Boase, p. 263.]

A   Audacter possunt meritoque hoc dicere cuncti,
D   Docta venit nobis & bene culta venit.
O   Omnibus eximiis imbuta est dotibus ipsa,
C   Clarum Pieridum diligit illa chorum.
T   Tanta est ingenii bonitas, prudentia tanta,
A   Artibus illa valet, cognitione nitet,
CL Clemens hæc multum est, ac multis magna remittit;
E   Est pacata cito, mitis & ipsa manet.
M   Multos ac miseros a pœna liberat ipsa,
E   Est firmum miseris undique præsidium.
N   Nulli crudelis, sed grata est omnibus horis;
S   Semper fama viget, lausque perennis erit.
    In mundo regnes, ut post hæc secula regnes,
      Et regnum cœli tu retinere queas.
    Optamus vitam toto nos pectore longam,
      Optamusque annos vivere Nestoreos.
    Vivas ut regno Christi potiare perenni,
      Quod semper durat perpetuoque manet.
    Sic valeas felix, sic omnia secula vivas;
      Sicque pie vivas, sic moriare pie.
    Hæc Deus omnipotens concedat singula vota
      Ut loca cum divis cœlica possideas.

JOANNES RUSSELLUS[1], frater.

    Principio votis summis vos invoco Musæ,
      Pierides omnes obsecro adeste mihi.
    Pangere versiculos certum est & carmina quædam,
      Pingere & egregiam deliniare ducem.
    Nomen Reginæ Musæ mihi dicite quæso,
      Nobilis & præstans dicitur Elizabeth.
    Natales quinam fuerant? a Regibus orta est,
      Nam pater Henricus, mater & Anna fuit.
    Fortunæ quibus aucta bonis, dic oro Thalia,
      Felix imperium lautaque regna tenet.
    Florens qui status? species quæ corporis? effer.
      Formam vel sensus indicat ipse tuus.

---

[1] John Lord Russell, brother of the preceding, married Elizabeth daughter of Sir Anthony Cook, of Giddy-hall, Essex, and widow of Sir Thomas Hobby, of Bisham, in the county of Berks; by whom he had two daughters; and dying 1589, in his father's lifetime, was buried in Westminster Abbey. Peerage, 1779, I. 252.

Dotibus ingenii quibus est dic, prædita, claris?
  Doctrina, verbi cognitione sacri.
Dissimilis non est nostris majoribus olim
  Divinas dotes dicere nemo potest.
Non igitur vastum pelagus mea cymbula findet,
  At cœpti cursus contraho vela mei.
Vive diu felix, Princeps clarissima, vive,
  Et vitæ stamen protrahe. Vive. Vale.

IDEM.

Si centum linguæ mihi adessent, oraque centum,
  Si fons Rhetoricæ Tullius efficerer:
Si modo nunc essem præclarus Naso poeta,
  Omnem lætitiam non tamen exprimerem.
Iste dies felix simul & faustissimus extat,
  Et saxis albis iste notandus erit;
Nam Regina venit: Cives lætentur oventque;
  Princeps docta venit, gaudeat ergo schola.
Hæc schola te salvam, Regina, videre triumphat,
  Nam caput es nostrum, præcipuumque decus.
Omnes lætantur simul ac Ecclesia tota,
  Hujus enim nutrix & bona mater adest.
Per te nunc Domini verbum florescit ubique;
  Per te Papa ruit, fictaque Relligio.
Per te deleta est penitus nunc impia Missa,
  Successitque ejus cœna sacrata loco.
Per te fit tandem Romanus Episcopus exul;
  Per te jamque suum perdidit imperium.
Tu regnas Princeps prudens & relligiosa;
  Tu nostri regni regia sceptra tenes.
Per te Romanæ Bullæ sunt obliteratæ;
  Per te nunc plumbum desiit Italicum.
Per te sublatus nunc est Papisticus ignis;
  Per te nunc Christus regnat & imperitat.
Jamque sumus docti meritis diffidere nostris,
  Nec jam laudabit quis benefacta sua.
Per Christum culpas deletas cernimus esse,
  Ac omnes solam ducere ad astra fidem.
Has vivas undas populo, Regina, propinas,
  Hæc nunc casta fides relligioque viget.

Sic per te vere est felix ecclesia tota,
   Per te nos omnes. Sic Deus ipse beat.
Est igitur Domino summo laus attribuenda,
   Atque diu vivas secula longa precor.

GULIELMUS LANUS[1].

Excipiunt plausu, Princeps, te cuncta, sorores
   Lætantur Musæ Pieridumque chorus.
Infima lætantur, sic gaudent maxima quæque,
   Saltat more suo bellua quæque ferox.
Almis sic vincis naturæ dotibus omnes,
   Bellæ & Reginæ nomine digna sies.
Extollunt, Princeps, te summis laudibus omnes,
   Tam vita sanctam, quam probitate piam.
Haud certe immerito: nam per te prælia cedunt.
   Arma nihil possunt, horrida bella jacent.
Regnat sancta quies demum pax candida floret,
   Et cedunt doctis arma cruenta togis.
Gaudia jam regnant, luctusque depellitur omnis;
   Impia jam cessit fictaque Relligio.
Nil edicta valent per te Papistica prava,
   Abjectum Papæ nil diadema valet.

Ejusdem Thesis. *Fœminam posse imperare.*

Quæstio longa fuit sed nunc est quæstio nulla,
   Num possit mulier jure præesse viris.
Euome quicquid habes, quæ possis funde maligne
   Utrum obstet quicquam, quo minus illa regat.
Major.   Nil valet hic sexus, regem sapientia reddit,
   Et sane merito, qui valet arte, regit.
Minor.   Principis at nostræ mens est ornata Camœnis;
Conclusio.   Civibus ergo suis, illa præesse potest.
Major.   Et quæ majorum semper documenta probarunt,
   Temporibus nostris sunt retinenda pie.
Minor.   Ast illis semper muliebria regna placebant,
Conclusio.   Nunc ergo imperium fœmina jure tenet.

---

[1] Of him I find no account in Wood. [Boase, p. 267.]

Probatio. Ast placuisse olim priscis, exempla docebant,
Minoris.   Cujus nunc videas hic monumenta rei.
Exempla. Vicit Olophernem lectissima fœmina Judith,
           Et populi judex Debbora sancta fuit.
       Non ego Corneliam verbis ornabo peritam,
           Quæ fertur Gracchos instituisse suos.
       Itala laudatur prælustris Olympia passim,
           Græcis & Latiis, prædita litterulis.
       Quid multis opus est? quid pergo dicere plura?
           Exemplo nobis Elisabetha siet.
       Namque fovet doctos, Musas defendit amœnas,
           Virtutes ornat, pascit alitque pios.
       Annon Reginam mulierem Gallia fecit?
           Annon præficitur fœmina clara Scotis?
Objectio. Ast vires dices, animumque deesse virilem,
           Nil tenerum corpus fœmineumque valet.
Solutio.   Ast istuc præstare viri, præstare feroces,
           Possunt & Martis mittere tela duces,
       Ergo exempla docent quod fœmina jure gubernat,
           Sic dicunt docti, sic ratioque docet.
       Quare nobiscum vivas, clarissima Princeps,
           Incultis præsis fœmina culta viris.
       Ulterius caveat jam carpere Zoilus audax,
           Et cesset Momus fundere stulta loquax.

Ejusdem Sapphicum.

       Induunt frontem placidam atque lætam,
       Dona dant omnes animi benigni,
       Signa, quod te jam videant adesse,
                        Splendida Princeps.

       Te colunt Musæ simul atque laudant,
       Te mali vitant metuuntque pravi,
       Diligunt docti, manibusque plaudunt,
                        Splendida Princeps.

       Nam faves Musis, merito ac adoras,
       Atque pravorum malefacta punis,
       Ac amas omnes probitate claros,
                        Splendida Princeps.

Arma nunc cessant violenta Martis,
Nunc jacent prorsus truculenta tela,
Sanguis ac cædes miseranda cedunt,
           Splendida Princeps.

Castra tu castæ sequeris Minervæ,
Et quies per te venit huc sacrata,
Pax viget tandem nivea atque sancta,
           Splendida Princeps.

Ergo sint frontes animique sereni,
Et graves prorsus valeant dolores,
Nam præest nobis (homines Britanni)
           Splendida Princeps.

Ut diu vivat Dominum precamur,
Ut diu præsit populo rogamus,
Utque post vitam hanc habeat perennem,
           Splendida Princeps.

EDWARDUS WOTTONUS[1].

Omnia lætantur, rident, ac omnia gaudent,
  Quippe quod Oxoniam Regia Virgo venit.
Gaudet doctorum clarissima turba Sophorum
  Gaudet & urbs quoniam Regia Virgo venit.
Gaudent indocti, docti, juvenesque senesque,
  Adventu exultant (Regia Virgo) tuo.
Gaudia si possent sua, vel durissima saxa
  Exprimerent; scopuli lætitiamque suam
Proferrent; vasti colles montesque moverent,
  Si fas, si facile hoc, si licitumque foret.
Et quare? Phœnix avis huc rarissima venit,
  Visit quippe Scholas Elizabetha suas.

---

[1] Eldest son of Thomas Wotton, of Bocton Malherbe in Kent, who entertained the Queen on her Progress into that county, and brother to Sir Henry Wotton, Provost of Eton. He was knighted by the Queen 1592, was employed as her Embassador to Portugal and Scotland, and created Lord Wotton and Baron of Morley, in Kent, and made Comptroller of the Houshold and of the Privy Council, and Comptroller of the Houshold to her successor, a. r. 14, and seems to have died the year after, having married, 1. Hester daughter and heir of Sir William Pickering, bart. and, 2. Margaret daughter of Philip Lord Wharton. Hasted, II. 429.

Visu Reginæ privata & publica gaudent,
   Ac omnes hilares Elizabetha facit.
Grata venis clamat tota hæc Academica turba,
   Hæc vox auditur publica, grata venis.
Et quare? quod sis Musis charissima nutrix,
   Tutatrix quod sis Pieridumque choro.

Ejusdem Sapphicum.

Livor hinc cedat, dolor et malignus,
Ecce nunc venit reverenda Princeps,
Ecce nunc omnes quasi vos salutat,
        Elisabetha.

Vosque nunc lætæ canite, o Sorores,
Tu nunc, o Pallas, Charitesque Sacræ,
Namque Doctrinæ venit ipsa fautrix
        Elisabetha.

Divites omnes inopesque rident,
Et rudes cuncti simul eruditi,
Quod suam salvam videant salutem
        Elisabetham.

Sola tu nobis decus atque spes es,
Esque doctrinæ quoque mater ipsa,
Tu bonas artes alis ac tueris,
        Elisabetha.

Tu Deum vere colis ac honoras,
Tuque Papistas aboles superbos,
Tu viros cunctos adamas honestos,
        Elisabetha.

Ista sed mitto, memorare nolo
Trita sunt sane patuere multis.
De tribus dicam propriis beatæ
        Elisabethæ.

Nam quod est mirum, populum potentem
Non Vir, at Virgo pia sola & una
Dirigit, clavum placide gubernans,
        Elisabetha.

Non labris summis, leviterque Musas,
Imbibit, plenis quasi devoravit
Faucibus libros, bene perpolita
      Elizabetha.

Tertio Reges pietate vincit
Et fidem veram populo propinat,
Hic tribus sola est decorata Princeps
      Elizabetha.

Prosopopœia Academiæ.

Ergone chara venit Princeps? ergone penates
 Elizabetha petit Regia Virgo meos?
O felix & fausta dies! quæ munera tanta
 Principe digna dabo? quæ pretiosa satis?
Aurea porrecta num fundam zenia dextra?
 Talia sunt vulgi vilia dona levis.
Gemmea mox dedero. sunt, o sunt, inclyta Princeps,
 Aurea parva nimis; & aurea parva nimis.
O me felicem, qui te quam sæpius opto,
 Nunc spero in tectis posse videre meis.
Cambria nostra soror lætis te acceperat ulnis,
 Principis hospitio Cambria læta suæ;
Ast ego quæ natu major, tui amantior, atque
 Cura tuis a torvis, semper, avisque fine[1].
Qua te lætitia, quibus excipiamus triumphis?
 Quo studio, officio, qua pietate, fide?
Scilicet ut proles patrem, pauperque patronum,
 Tu mihi namque parens: tuque patrona simul.
Multa equidem Regum benefacta illustria sensi,
 En monumenta patris: ecce sororis opus.
Rex mihi fautor erat, Rex est mihi primus & author;
 Regibus orta fui, Regibus aucta fui.
Sed tua clara magis, me me præsentia honestat,
 Quam poterant Regum, quæ[2] benefacta Ducum.
Principio nomen mihi Fridisvida perenne,
 Huc fugiens hostem Regia Virgo dedit.
Regia Virgo dedit: quæ quod bovæ per vada vecta est,
 Inde boum vada sunt postea dicta loca.

[1] Sic.   [2] Sic. ? quam.

Illa dedit nomen: tu das mihi nominis omen,
    Dum venis auspiciis, Elisabetha, bonis.
Hinc venit Alfridus, Rex illustrissimus olim,
    Alfridus generis spesque, decusque sui.
Hic in me Musis, hic castis castra Camœnis
    Præparat, & magnæ semina prima scholæ,
Edificatque domum media quæ consita in urbe
    Communi mecum nomine dicta viget.
Hic me fundavit, tu firmas; ille paravit,
    Tu reparas miris Elizabetha modis.
Sed nec adhuc Regum mihi munificentia clausa est;
    Principibus semper maxima cura fui.
Hic domus ostendit Reginæ nomine felix
    Parva, sed ingenuis artibus apta domus.
Hanc Regina dedit, sed tu Regina tueris,
    Scilicet exornas inclyta facta patrum.
Sed quid cuncta sequor? quid demens singula pando?
    Altius & repetens secula prima sequor?
Tempora temporibus dum confero postera primis
    Materiæ tribuunt tempora nostra nimis.
Nam quæ prima subis, sunt en monumenta parentis
    Henrici Octavi, nobile Regis opus.
Hæc quia patris erant fundata laboribus ipsa
    Sunt in tutelis, Elisabetha, tuis.
Deinde Scholæ medio stant augustissima in urbe
    Quas soror extruxit chara Maria tua.
Illa nonne Musis totidem Musea locavit,
    Artibus & sacris tecta sacrata Deis?
Illic Caliope, Clio, dulcisque Thalia,
    Melpomene, Euterpe, Terpsichoreque sedent.
Hic Erato, necnon Polymnia casta refulget,
    Cumque Deis reliquis Urania ipsa sedes.
Hæc tua casta soror sacrarum castra sororum
    Fecerat, hæc cernas tu quoque, & ipsa soror.
Virgo construxit, tu, Regia Virgo, fovebas.
    Scilicet es Virgo, virginibusque faves.
Hiis ego nominibus sum devinctissima multis
    Regibus antiquis principibusque viris.
Sed quod me caulam, potius quam principis aulam
    Hospitio illustras, Elisabetha, tuo,

Sum tibi quam reliquis facile devinctior ullis,
    Angligeni o Princeps flosque decusque soli.
Quod venis ad cives facis illud more recepto,
    Quod venis ad doctos illud amore facis.
Quin quod adesse velis facile clementia summa est
    Posse præesse tamen, splendor, honosque fuit.
Vive, vale, Princeps, gentis spes sola Britannæ;
    Musarum fautrix, vive valeque diu.

ED. LILYE[1].

Ad Serenissimam Reginam Carmen Gratulatorium.

Grata venis, quocunque venis, gratissima Princeps;
    Nilque tuis quam tu, gratius esse potest.
Non tamen ex æquo conspectæ quælibet urbes
    Adventu plaudunt, Elisabeta, tuo:
Crede mihi, magnas Oxonia vicerit arces;
    Parvula sed magno grandis amore tamen.
Non tamen ex æquo studiis lætantur eisdem
    Oxoniæ Cives, Oxoniæque Scholæ:
Crede mihi vincit reliquas Achademia partes,
    Et resonat variis gaudia plura locis.
Non tamen ex æquo Gymnasia quæque triumphant
    Quod superet reliquos Gymnosophista viros:
Crede mihi reliquas ut Magdalena sorores
    Excedit forma, sic & amore magis.
Non tamen ex æquo, turba lætamur in ista,
    Nec cuncti similes in pietate sumus:
Crede mihi non est Busti qui gaudia vincat
    Aut locus, aut sacræ qui sit in urbe Deæ.
Ergo grata venis: quid ingratissima dicam,
    Cum sint hæc animo verba minora meo.

HENRICUS BUST[2].

---

[1] He was a Lincolnshire man, admitted first at Magdalen, and about 1580 Master of Baliol College, archdeacon of Wilts 1591, an excellent divine; and dying 1609, was buried in St. Mary's church, at Oxford. Wood, Fasti Ox. I. 120. [Boase, p. 253.]

[2] v. s. p. 175, n. 25.

Ejusdem in Adventum Reginæ.

Juno, Venus, Pallas, nemorosæ vallibus Idæ
   Discrimen formæ cum subiere suæ,
Inter formosas si tu Dea quarta fuisses,
   Vicisses reliquas (O Dea quarta) Deas.
Quam Juno jejuna foret? quam pallida Pallas?
   Quam Dea vana Venus, quam Dea sola fores.
Juno jactat opes: quidni prudentior illa
   Est Pallas prudens, non opulenta tamen.
Sic Venus (alma Venus) regni virtutis egena est;
   Omnia sunt tua, tu Juno, Minerva, Venus.

Magnanimus veluti diffundit gaudia victor
   Cum bello valido grata trophæa tulit:
Omnes adventum sic nos lætamur ad unum,
   Gratius adventu nil queat esse tuo.
Grata venis, semper remanet tua gloria, noctu
   Ignea dum fulgent sydera, grata venis.
Grata venis nummum quibus astat copia, dicunt
   Alta permiseri voceque grata venis.
Grata venis, cui non vestra est præsentia læta?
   Urbs hæc te gaudet cernere, grata venis.
Grata venis clamat non parva voce juventus,
   Grandævus clamat ter mage grata venis.
Grata venis merito doctis es grata scholarchis,
   Quantum quisque potest dicere, grata venis.
Grata venis liquido prius unda humore carebit
   Quam tua deliteat gloria, grata venis.
Dotibus ingenii complures vincis & armis,
   Et vera nutris cum pietate fidem.
Et sicut patriæ renovas virtutis honorem
   Armis, consilio, religione, fide;
Sic etiam studiis patriam melioribus ornas,
   Nominis est vere gloria summa tui.
Libera fit tua mens affectibus alta per astra
   Scandens, huic remanet gloria lausque tua.
Friv la contemnis temnens[1] velut ignis in altum
   Tendis, & hæc tua laus sydera summa ferit.

[1] Sic. ? tendens.

Iram compescis, quoniam parit ira furorem,
    Quod pariat demens vulnera magna furor:
Maxima quod pariant permœstum vulnera lœthum
    Non vis elatos, vis humilesque viros.
Invidiam refugis cum sit sævissima pestis,
    Te quivis adamant cum pietate tua.
Virtutem laudas, laudas benefacta piorum,
    Quorum laus nullo est interitura die.
Non quicquam tribuis tranquilla per ocia laudis
    Degenti, ignavam desidiamque fugis.
Ingluviem refugis, recte refugisque ciborum,
    Qui caput & cerebrum, qui stomachumque gravant.
Virtutes adamas, es servantissima justi,
    Observare tuos singula justa facis.
Raucæ dum viridi cantant sub fronde cicadæ,
    Non ulla est malans[1] interitura die.
Secula quot cervum quot vivere secula dicunt
    Cornicem, quot et hic secula mundus habet:
Tot quoque pro meritis, Regina beata benignis,
    Gloria vestra manet, lausque perennis erit.

SAMUEL COLUS[2].

Vere calente novo decorantur floribus arva,
    Frigida cedit hyems vere calente novo.
Vere calente comas lapsas quoque sylva reponit,
    Et viret omne solum vere calente novo.
Undique lætamur sic nos, resonantque boatu
    Valles, te quivis laudat amatque piam.
Vere calente nives recidunt de montibus altis
    Canæ, cuncta nitent vere calente novo.
Vere calente novo volucres modulamina tentant,
    Mille modisque canunt vere calente novo.
Te veniente novos vultus præbemus, & omnes
    Gaudia præbemus te veniente nova.
Vere calente suas renovat Philomela querelas
    Dulciter & volucres vere calente canunt.
Milvus hiat longos ducitque per aëra gyros,
    Et vultu læto trinsat hyrundo vaga.
Te veniente tuo vultu' lætamur abunde,
    Gaudia quæ nobis, lætitiamque moves.

---

[1] Sic.   [2] Of him we find nothing in Wood. [Boase, p. 271.]

Dum te laudamus, laudando nubila vincis,
  Claraque quæ superat sydera pinus eris.
Pinus eris constans dum sis & clarus Olympus,
  Quem multi celebrant & super astra vehunt.

Samuel Colus.

Ηρεμος ἦν πελετας [1] πόντος μετὰ λαίλαπα ναύτης
  "Οψιν ἔχειν ἀγλαὴν γηθοσύνην τε δοκεῖ.
Οὔτως 'Οξονίη βασίλισσαν ὁρῶσα ἐλεύθειν,
  Νῦν χαίρει πρότερον πολλὰ παθοῦσα κακὰ.
Σοὶ πληρεῖ δ' ἀρετῆς πλούτος, καὶ κῦδος ὀπηδεῖ,
  Αἰσχροτάτους φεύγεις καὶ μέγα σινομένους;
"Εργων ἀντ' ἀδίκων δεινήν τε ἄπασιν ἀμοιβὴν
  'Εντίθης, ἀγαθοὶ δῶρον ἔχουσι πολὺ.
Τὸ Εἶκον ὡς φεύγεις, φεύγεις ἀεσίφρονα θυμὸν
  'Αγνὸν ἔχεις, καθαρὸν, λαμπρότατόν τε βίον.
Πᾶσιν κυδίστη πάμπαν βασίλισσα φαείνεις,
  Τούς τε κακοὺς φεύγεις, τοὺς ἀγαθοὺς τε σέβῃ
Οὔ ποτε, σεμνοτάτη γύναι, παρακαίρια ῥέζεις
  Χρήματα πάμπολλος τλήμοσι πολλὰ δίδως.
Πολλὰ δὲ γήθουσιν πάντες, δῆμός τε πόλις τε.
  'Ανθρώπων πολλῶν κυδρὸν ἄριθμον ὁρᾷς.
"Ενθα καὶ ἔνθα ὁρᾷς πάντας γήθοντας ἐλεύθειν
  Σὲ δοκίμην, σοφίην πᾶσαν ἐπισταμένην.
Πλαστὸς ἔρως ἡμῶν οὐκ ἐστὶ, φιλοῦμεν ἀνακτην [1].
  Πάντες φιλετάτην οὐδὲ φιλοῦσι μάτην.

Σαμουὴλ Κῶλες.

IDEM.

Qui maris immensi sulcant vada salsa carinis
  Solliciti & vastas ingrediuntur aquas:
Atque feri venti turgent ac æquora surgunt,
  Atque procellosis fluctibus unda fremit,
Et nunc in cœlos rapiuntur & infima fluctus,
  Tartara mox, animo deficiente, labant:
Nautæ solliciti magno & mœrore repleti,
  Implorant miseri numina sancta viri:
Et cum discussa mare tempestate serenat,
  Salsaque compositis fluctibus unda silet;
Exultant nautæ quod murmura rauca quierint,
  Quod ventos faciles tuta phaselus habet:

[1] Sic.

Sic nos gaudemus cum te videamus adesse,
  Quæ quasi desertis dulce levamen ades.
Dulce levamen ades, dum cogis pellere curas
  Nos et dum recreas dulce levamen ades.
Frena voluptati durissima ponis, & omnes
  Illecebras dulces corporis ista fugis.
Diceris & merito vivendi regula pura,
  Virtutes sequitur lausque decusque tuas.
Si numero certo vestras comprendere coner
  Virtutes, omnis cedet arena maris.
Non astricta manus vestra est quæ largiter omni
  Plurima dat prompta quisquis egebit ope.
Laudibus & facilem te quivis perque benignam
  Extollet sua dum vita superstes erit.
O tua stelliferum bonitas transcendit Olympum
  Quis poterit laudis non memor esse tuæ?
Nostra tibi laudem nunquam non ora loquentur,
  Et tibi nonnunquam lingua jacebit iners.
Queis fortuna parum fausta est, te sæpe benignam
  Præbes paupertas invida quosque premit.
Sic valeas multos vivas longæva per annos
  Enumeres vitæ tempora multa tuæ.
Vive diu felix ævi prudentia nostri,
  Vive diu dulces Nestoriosque dies.

Ad Oxoniam.

R	Regia Virgo venit, lætos celebrate triumphos,
E	Exuperans Reges Regia Virgo venit.
G	Grata peregit iter cum primum visa veniret,
I	Invisit cum te grata peregit iter.
A	Accipis ecce tuam Reginam, Oxonia felix,
V	Vincentemque viros accipis ecce tuam.
I	Incipias hilares, hilaris celebrare triumphos,
R	Regia Virgo tibi grata peregit iter.
G	Gaudia summa dedit veniensque videndaque visa
O	O certe plusquam gaudia summa dedit:
T	Tu properare jube lætantes carmine vates,
I	Ingenium prodant tu properare jube.
B	Blateret ipse suos versus, recitetque Cherillus,
I	Ignarus quamvis blateret ipse suos.

G   Gaudeat & Faunus cum Phœbo, & quisque triumphet,
R   Regia Virgo tibi grata peregit iter.
A   Accipiantque sonos mirantia rura canoros
T   Te lætam noscant, accipiantque sonos.
A   Adjuvet atque tuas voces campana cadentes,
P   Perstringatque aures adjuvet atque tuas.
E   Ex quocunque modo poteris celebrato triumphos
R   Regia Virgo tibi grata peregit iter.
E   Ergo triumphus eat? sed non satis istud at isto
G   Grandius haud possis, ergo triumphus eat.
I   I cito cuncta para, Regina (Oxonia) tecum est,
T   Tarda quid hic cessas? I cito cuncta para.
I   I cito parva para, nam sedula pauca parare,
T   Tanta digna nequis, I cito parva para.
E   Et tamen illa licet sint parva & pauca triumpha,
R   Regia Virgo tibi grata peregit iter.

G. LUDFORD[1].

ROB. TEMPLE[2].

Ter felix hæc clara dies, ter gaudia nostra
    Conduplicat, curas, tristitiamque fugans;
Tristia cuncta fugans tua nos præsentia lætos
    Efficit, & curas concoquit illa graves.
Lætamur salvam nobis jam nobilem adesse
    Reginam, insolita quæ pietate viget.
Scilicet ut vitam cupimus, veramque salutem
    Sic nihil adventu gratius esse queat.
Ergo jam curas animi secludimus omnes,
    Plaudimus optantes prospera cuncta tibi.

Ejusdem.

Ite triumphantes, hilares incedite Musæ,
    Dulcia nunc Dominæ vota referte piæ.
Fausta venit nobis etenim Regina, perenni
    Fons bona cuncta ferens & quasi stella micans.

---

[1] Of him no notice is taken by Wood. [Boase, p. 266.]
[2] A native of Oxfordshire, of Magdalen College, B.D. 1588. Chaplain to Aylmer bishop of London, and preached one sermon, which is all Wood knew of him. Fasti Ox. I. 135. [Boase, p. 279.]

Hæc lux, hæc lumen gentis quoque gemma Britannæ
  Mater et est patriæ vita salusque suæ.
Formosæ sacro nutrita est lacte Minervæ,
  Ingenuas magnas antcit arte Deas.
Versibus hanc igitur nunc omnis tollat in altum
  Sydera quæ superat laudibus ipsa suis.

ROGERI MARBECCI[1] Oratio, quâ gratulatur adventum
Serenissimæ Reginæ ELISABETHÆ, remotioribus
Oxoniæ finibus habita.

From Harl. MS. 129. fol. 102.

Multa sunt divinæ erga nos bonitatis testimonia, quocunque nos
vertimus (potentissima Princeps); & illa quidem numero infinita,
magnitudine immensa, dignitate excellentia: sed tamen hoc uno
beneficio, quo in præsenti affecti sumus & cumulati, cæteris omnibus
antegressis, nos tantum cumulum putamus accessisse ut cum antea
in felicitatis limine & quasi vestibulo poneremur, nunc certe in stabili
& firma illius possessione collocati esse videamur. Magnum profecto
est & summæ voluptatis plenum intueri vultum Principis; at vero non
modo præsentem, sed alloqui præterea: nec alloqui tantum, sed
loquentem etiam audire, & in erudita hominum frequentia sapienter
& acute perorantem videre. Hoc nos tantum opinamur, quantum
ante hanc nostram ætatem adivisse certe paucos, vidisse fortasse
multos, audire autem voluisse & audire certe cupiisse vel omnes vel
plurimos arbitramur. Nos vero fatemur incredibilem voluptatem nos
nuper cepisse cum Academia nostra suum Cancellarium (quem honoris causa nominamus) sine pompa fortassis & apparatu splendido,
summa tamen cum benevolentia excipiebat ; qui cum per tuam bonitatem non solum nostræ Academiæ caput sit præclarum & gloriosum,
sed totius etiam Angliæ proxime & secundum Majestatem tuam decus
& ornamentum; vix[2] dici potest, quanta lætitia tanti & tam nobilis viri
aspectus animos astantium perfuderit cum Academia suum decus
& gloriam, membra caput, studiosi patronum, filii parentem, pii &
religiosi solidam & expressam veræ virtutis imaginem intuerentur. Sed

---

[1] Roger Marbeck was son of John Marbeck, organist of Windsor, and the first
standing or perpetual orator of the University. He was educated at Eton, admitted
of Christ Church 1552, was canon of the first stall there, provost of Oriel, both
which places he resigned 1566 and 1567, and became chief physician to the Queen.
Wood, H. and A. Ox. II. 47. Fasti, I. 109. [Boase, p. 226.]

[2] vir MS.

hæc voluptas, quantacunque ea fuit, quæ certe maxima fuit, si tamen cum hodierna lætitia comparetur, parvam certe iudicamus.   Est enim mira virtutis vis, & bonæ literæ (ornatissima Regina) ubicunque habitant & commorantur incredibiles[1] excitant amores sui : at cum in Principe sedent & conjunguntur nescio quomodo personæ dignitate illarum splendor multo fit illustrior.   Nam ut sol in quacunque cœli parte est, formosus est ; at quo altius & sublimius escendit, eo majorem se ferre videtur dignitatem : sic virtutes & literæ cum in Principis pectore ut in loco celsissimo & illustrissima sede collocantur, propter loci præstantiam majorem laudem & ampliorem dignitatem consequuntur.   At ignoscet mihi uti spero Majestas tua, si de summis tuis virtutibus mea conticescat oratio.   Non se voluit Alexander a quovis fingi sed a Licippo, nec a quovis pingi sed ab Apelle : sic Regiæ tuæ virtutes (illustrissima Regina) non quemlibet e multis pictorem, non plebeium aliquem aut vulgarem, sed summum & perfectum artificem requirunt ; a qua perfectione cum longissime absum, malo tua cum venia reverenter tacere quam infra rei dignitatem indecenter loqui.   Cæterum cum mihi dicenti incredibilis quædam lux tuæ humanitatis exoritur, hoc unum (serenissima Regina) pace tua libere & audacter dicam ; inter eximias virtutes multiplicesque laudes divinas, quæ longe lateque per orbem terrarum pervagantur, nihil est vel ad tuam laudem illustrius vel ad populi tui & universæ multitudinis voluptatem optabilius, quam [quod] ipsa tam sis literata Regina, & civibus literatis tam unice & precipue delecteris.—Quid enim ? an illud unquam ex hominum memoriis excedere & elabi potest, quod a tua Majestate nuper factitatum sit ? an illa tua ad Cantabrigienses profectio, illa inquam gloriosa profectio, quæ non minus fuit alienis læta, quam tuis jucunda, ullis unquam vetustatis tenebris obruetur ? Hoc nimirum illud est de quo homines tantopere loquuntur, quod admirantur, quod obstupescunt, fœminam primariam, & principem totius Europæ fœminam, multas regni sui partes cum incredibili civium lætitia peragrasse, nulli labori, nullis vigiliis pepercisse, venisse ad Academiam hominum doctissimorum celebritate vigentem, linguarum varietate florentem, valentem judiciis, abundantem ingeniis, omni denique literarum genere præstantem ; ad locum inquam tam celebrem & eruditum non venisse modo, sed in publicam sæpe literarum palestram prodiisse, interfuisse libenter, assedisse, sine tædio audivisse attente ; & quod summum & maximum erat, e loco superiori ad multitudinem tam scienter & erudite locutam fuisse, ut non tam literatam Principem in terris loquentem, quam Minervam ipsam

---

[1] incredibilis MS.

e cœlo tonantem audivisse videretur. O Reginam vocem omni pos-
teritati commendandam: O Principis factum vere Principe dignum!
In nobili familia nasci & e stirpe Principis promanare honorificum
est ; sed laus generis est : in summa rerum potestate vivere, & cæteris
omnibus dignitate anteire gloriosa est ; sed beneficium fortunæ est :
habere formam egregiam & pulchritudinem corporis excellentem præclarum est ; sed donum naturæ est : valere ingenio & plurimis linguis
loqui luculenter, laudabile est, et opus laboris est : incorruptæ religionis amore flagrare, coli a tuis, metui ab alienis, amari ab omnibus,
habere pectus omni virtutis genere cumulatum & completum, primum
quiddam & insigne est ; sed perpaucorum est : at vero hæ[c] omnia
tanta & tam excellentia bona in una congregata simul possidere, ut
& propter generis splendorem nobilissima Virgo, & propter venu-
statis excellentiam præstantissima Fœmina, & propter fortunæ præstantiam, potentissima[1] Princeps, & propter literarum scientias quasi
Dea quædam cœlestis inter mortales habearis : hoc certe totum
divinum quiddam est, & tuum est. Quæ cum ita sint, quibus te
laudibus efferemus? quibus verbis publice (nobilissima Regina) nostram
lætitiam contestabimur? quo cultu & officii genere celsissimam tuam
dignitatem prosequemur? Utinam, utinam (potentissima Princeps)
quantum voluptas nostra velit, tantum facultas nostra possit : sed
cum velimus maxima, possimus autem minima, suppliciter a tua
Majestate petimus, ut non tam valentium vires, quam volentium
animos velis ponderare. Sed cum nihil habeat Academia nostra in te
nisi quod a te profectum est, quicquid Majestati tuæ dederit id omne
sperat fore gratum, cum sit tuum. Quocirca ad Amplitudinis tuæ
pedes humiliter projecta se totam committit atque tradit pietati tuæ,
idque facit hoc ipso loco, ad quem privilegia nostra, a majoribus tuis
profecta, a nobilissimo patre aucta, a suavissimo fratre continuata,
a clarissima sorore confirmata, ab excellenti Majestate tua conservata
ad hodiernum usque diem excurrunt & propagantur : quæ quidem
privilegia etsi ea sit animi tui in bonas literas pietas, quidenim dicemus
benevolentia : ut exiguum beneficium existimes prout quæ augus-
tissimus tuus animus ad immortalem tui nominis memoriam dare
fortasse in posterum cogitat, non tamen illa tanti existimamus ut non
solum putamus esse bonitatis tuæ testimonia, sed etiam totius Academiæ si quæ sunt dignitatis tuæ fundamenta, ergo ut in eodem,
unde exorsa est terminetur oratio nostra, & de adventu tuo tam
salutari & glorioso. Et vere lætamur & triumphamus : & de singulari
tua cum in bonos omnes, tum in nostram Academiam pietate gratias

[1] patentissima MS.

agimus immortales; suppliciter & immortali Deo petentes ut quamdiu
cupiat tamdiu vivat Majestas tua; quamdiu nos velimus, tamdiu tua
Celsitudo floreat.   Sic, opinor, vives diutissime, sic certe florebis
semper: quorum utrumque ut fiat, nos omnes Academici tui ardenter
a Deo Optimo Maximo comprecamur, ut nihil a quoquam ardentius
peti posse videatur.   Dixi.

OXONIENSIS ACADEMIÆ totius orbis celeberrimæ 'Εγκώμιον.

Grandia pyramidum jactat miracula Memphis,
Atque superba suos latos Babylonia muros,
Caria magnifico Mausoli clara sepulchro est,
Atque Pharos celsis obstructam mœnibus arcem,
Per mare nocturnos quæ præbet euntibus ignes.
Sic Ephesus decorata tuo est Latonia templo,
Et Rhodon illustrat sublimis statua solis.
Ætas multorum prior hæc monumenta dierum,
Fatua proposuit stulto spectacula mundo.
Nam reges veriti, ne laus ingesta sepulchro,
Gloriaque ipsa specus squalore absorpta jaceret,
Aëreas turres, et templa minantia cœlo
Struxerunt, superet queis funera fama superstes.
At qui sinceræ caluere cupidine laudis,
Cautius ad veri præfulgens culmen honoris
Substravere viam, non huc, illucve petulci
Passibus obliquis, tortisve anfractibus errant.
Hinc (quibus incubuit rerum tutela) Dynastis
Cura fuit doctis collegia condere Musis,
Unde cohors hominum qui barbara castra fatigent
Prodiit: armatos ceu quondam magnus Epæi
Fudit equus Danaos ad tristia funera Trojæ.

Julius Cæsar Romam viris literatis ornavit.

   Cæsar ab excelsa qui cœli prospicit æde
Sydereum factus jubar, et qui providus urbis
Romanæ tutatur opes, dotasse poetas,
Rhetoras, et medicos ingenti munere fertur;
Fecit municipes et libertate beavit.

Carolus Magnus Gymnasium Parisiense et Papiense posuit.

   Cujus virtutis vestigia certa secutus
Carolus a rebus gestis cognomine Magnus,
Quo nemo rigidis aut fortior extitit armis,
Aut coluit doctas magis indulgentius artes:
Is ratus imperii geminas posuisse columnas

Et sibi, Gymnasium cum te Papiense locaret:
Quasque capit celebres populosa Lutetia sedes,
Tectaque Musarum Sequanæ contermina ripis.

Inclyta Parthenope te, Ferdinande, loquetur,
Fautoremque canet, quoties æraria nummis
Hausta videt, quoties deprompta salaria fisco
Conspicit, ut doctos homines regaliter ornes.

Æmulus inde tuæ virtutis filius hæres,
Prytaneum struxit Vitebergæ, φωσφόρον ὄμμα
Τεχνάων σοφίας τε, καὶ Ἀιετὸν ἐν νεφέλῃσι.

Nec minor est laudum cumulus, Sigeberte, tuarum,
Cujus ab interitu pia Cantabrigia nomen
Asseret, et famam longum diffundet in ævum.

Oxoniam (veteres quam olim dixere Calænam)
Struxit Aluredus, eui duri Saxones armis
Exhibuere fidem, cum quo Danique subacti
Pacem per multos coluere fideliter annos.
Ille bonas artes errorum fæce sepultas
Eruit in lucem, magna mercede disertos
Undique conscivit, queis præmia magna laborum
Contulit, et doctis amplos decrevit honores.
Hinc nova cœpta bonis Academia crevit eisdem
Auspiciis felix, regio qua nulla priorem,
Non habet ulla parem: Quicquid sua rostra Lycæum,
Aut Stoa miretur subsellia docta Zenonis.
Roma caput mundi, quondam celeberrima nutrix
Musarum, quondam sanctæ pietatis asylum,
Nunc fovet ignavum fucos pecus, atque locustas
Suscipit hospitio fruges consumere natas.
Sic olim doctas et dictas Ἑλλάδος Ἑλλάς,
Turcica barbaries fæde populatur Athenas.
Anglia nostra diu sterilis, velut orba marito,
Cum dudum jacuisset iners, et segnis ad omnes
Ingenii fœtus, tandem gravidata tumenti
Parturiens utero, est binas enixa sorores
Fautrices studiis et Apollinis artibus, unde
Serius occiduo magis inclarescere mundo
Cœpit, et elato contingere vertice cœlum.
Nam Gothus et Latii premeret cum Vandalus oras,
Cumque vorax dites vastaret flamma Mycenas:
Aonidum, Charitumque cohors, et turba novena

Ferdinandus Neapoli Academiam instituit.

Imperator Maximilianus Wittenberg.

Rex Sigbertus Academiam Cantabrigiensem locavit.

Rex Aluredus Oxoniensem Academiam inchoavit.

Pulchra Jovi soboles, luteas exosa tabernas
Huc molitur iter, terræque appulsa Brytannæ,
Incoluit sedes quas præbuit hospita tellus.
Bis sex Oxoniæ speciosa palatia cernes,
Auspicibus dicata suis, quibus adde quaternas
Marmoreas ædes, numeri sic feceris orbem.

Colleg. Universitatis.

Alphridus primum posuit, cui nomen acuto
Indidit augurio foret ut caput urbis, et omen,
Spesque scholæ fieret basis et columella futuræ.

Colleg. Bayliolense.

Hunc sequitur princeps Scotorum Bayliol, ille
Fertur Musæum pulchre statuisse secundum.

Colleg. Orial.

Rex Edouardus onus regno populoque Secundus,
Quem plebs, quem proceres infestavere duello:
Gymnasium struxit quod nunc Orialle vocamus.

Colleg. Exoniense.

Cujus temporibus Stapletonus Episcopus altum
Musæum posuit, quem præceps turba furore
Obtruncat gladio capite a cervice revulso.

Colleg. Reginea.

Tertius Edvardus nobis immunibus omni
Esse dedit censu, nos privis legibus armat.
Illius insigni bonitate, piæque Philippæ
Conjugis impensis Reginea tecta steterunt.

Colleg. Omnium Animarum.

Musæum sanctis animabus rite sacratum
Condidit Henricus Chichleius Episcopus, amplos
Cui Rex Henricus Sextus largitus honores,
Fecerat Anglorum Primatem : Papa solenni
More pedum, pallamque dedit, sacramque tyaram.

Colleg. Magdelanense.

Magdalenense bonis avibus, votisque secundis,
Nobile gymnassium struxit Wainfletus, et alto
Eduxit cœlo, quo nil conspectius orbis
Ostendit, lato qua cingitur æquore tellus.
Marmora quid memorem, laqueataque tecta superne
Picturata tholo, et validis fastigia tignis
Artifici firmata manu ? Dedit insuper agros,
Prædiaque, et fundi quantum non milvus oberret.

Collegium Novum.

Wintoniensis erat Wickamus Episcopus ille,
Quem prius a docto sata fundamenta Neoto
Consolidasse ferunt, positis ex marmore muris.

Rich. Fox Colleg. Corporis Christi.

Wintoniensis erat cui Christi Corporis ædes
Debentur, castis indicta palatia Musis.

Colleg. Mertonense.

Gualterus Merton Roffensis Episcopus almæ
Condidit egregias in honorem Palladis arces.

Smythus quo quondam Lincolnia clara gavisa est
Præsule, congestis nummis atque æris acervo,
Musæum statuit ter fausto sydere, cujus
Ardua prominulo signantur limina naso.

Hunc qui præcessit Flemmingus, præsul eadem
Sede bonus, studio parili pulcherrima struxit
Atria, quæ Thomas Rotherame post latius auxit.

Sumptibus Attalicis Christi compaginat ædes
Wolseus, obscuris primum natalibus ortus,
Quem tamen evexit fortunae ludus ad altos
Splendoris titulos, rutilo quem Papa galero
Texerat, et Tyrio saturata murice palla.

Whitus Londini præses, dignatus equestri
Ordine patricio, Divo monumenta Johanni
Nuncupat. Hunc sequitur generoso stemmate clarus
Popus eques, Sanctæ Triadi qui divite dextra
Tecta struit, lautis et vectigalibus ornat.

Struxit ugo Pricius tibi clara palatia, Jesu,
Gens ubi Cambrorum, studiis insomnibus usa,
Excolit ingenium seris operata lucernis.

En tibi nostra suis Academia fulta patronis,
Quam Pallas facunda scholis magis omnibus unam
Moribus et studiis fœcundat, perpolit, ornat.
Huc coëunt juvenes: hic Dædala castra Minervæ
Turba frequens stipat vegetas, hic miles ephæbus
Ingenii vires alternis litibus auget.
Crevit in hoc agro doctorum nempe virorum
Læta seges, calidi quos pectoris entheus ardor
Impulit hæreticas pessundare fortiter artes.
Hi sua procudunt infenso dogmata mundo,
Unde tenebrarum, ac errorum densior umbra,
Quæ prius incubuit terris vanescere cæpit,
Et novus extremus effulsit splendor ad oras:
Sicut ab aurato rutilantis corpore solis
Sparguntur radii per lucida climata cœli.

Gualterus Mapus Romæ scelerata triformis
Geryonis cum facta videt, qui dente cruento
Dissipat, et tenerum Christi deglubit ovile:
Is Papam Goliath, monachos pecus, atque profanos
Stercora pontifices arguta voce notavit.

Prosilit intrepidus pius Armachanus ad arma,

Rich.
Arma-
chanus,
Archiepi-
scopus
Hyberniæ.

Joh.
Wicklevus,
Phœnix
Anglicus.

Sincere fidei vindex, Christique satelles
Qui mendicorum numerosa examina fratrum
Divino verbo perstringit, lædit, et odit.
  Post hos eluxit Wicklevus, relligionis
Impiger assertor, pietatis nobile sydus.
Qui grave Papicolis (quos pagina sacra trucidat)
Indixit bellum, causamque viriliter egit.
Ille peregrinis fornacibus aurea nostræ
Biblia (sic perhibent) gentis transfudit in usum.
 Hunc pater Italicus Tarpeio fulminat ictu,
Pontificumque greges, et bucera turba clientum
Romanæ sedis, vitali luce fruentem
Cornibus incursat, post charo lumine cassum
Exhumat, effossi violentis ignibus ossa
Concremat, et cineres vicinas spargit in undas.
Tantæ molis erat Sanctorum perdere gentem.
Attamen ex hujus Phœnicis pulvere sicco
Crevit, et enata est sobolis numerosa propago.
Parshallus, Thorpus, Redmannus, Paynus, et Acton,
Clercus, Galfridus Chaucer, Capgravius, Onley.
Qui metamorphôsin Cœnæ, Missæque chimæram,
Furfureique dei Mauzzim portenta nefanda
Explosere suis scriptis, risere cachinnis.

G. Occa-
mus, pro
Ludovico
quarto con-
tra Papam
dimicavit.

  Vellicat Occamus dictis scriptisque cruentum
Romanum Phalarin, pedibus qui sæpe potentes
Induperatores protrivit, contudit armis.
Ille sacerdotum titulos, fastigia, fastum
Cæsaris imperio subdit, Papalia sceptro
Jura subesse probat: Gladio, Ludovice, tuere
Me precor, ait, ego te satagam defendere Verbo.

Joh.
Frithus et
C. Tyndal,
Martyres.

  Exiit hinc Frythus, Tyndallus, clarus uterque
Testis Evangelii, constantes Martyres ambo.
Qui veræ fidei doctrinam morte probatam
Sanguine consignant, quos nulla pericula terrent,
Nec resilire minæ, non vis, non vincula cogunt.
Ignibus indomiti, velut inter pocula læti
In media cecinere pyra: nec flamma vigorem
Exeruisse suum, nec ii sensisse videntur.
Sicut enim vires flammæ Salamandra retundit,
Nec potis est ignis tenues abolere Pyraustas:
Sic neque sæva dei servos incendia lædunt,

Nec rogus absumit: Nam quamvis Mulciber artus
Auferat, in cœlis victrix mens viva triumphat.

    Classibus ex nostris Anglorum gemma Juellus
Prodiit, Antistes sacrorum, præsul et exul.
Cujus fixa fides, constans patientia, virtus
Temporibus spectata malis, agitata procellis
Enituit: calida sicut fornace recoctum
Fæcibus et scoria purum secernitur aurum
Hunc Deus extorrem patria, cæcisque latentem
Sedibus, in scenam protraxit, tantaque mentis
Lumina proposuit toto spectanda theatro.
Jussit et elumbem Papam, Satyrosque bicornes
Vindicibus libris doctoque lacessere bello:
Haud secus ac Ithacus simulatum cautus Achillem
Fœmineo cultu regis Lycomedis in aula
Graias inter opes ad Dardana Pergama duxit.

    Noster erat Foxus, tersus polyhistor et amplus,
Aurea sanctorum qui tot monumenta piorum
Tot sudata dies, tanto exantlata labore,
Gratum opus Angligenis operoso stamine texit.
Hic fera Martyrii memorat tormenta, necesque,
Flagra, faces, colaphos, numellas, lora, catastas.
Nam sua Romulei peragunt cum sacra tyranni,
Ritibus explorat mystes his victima sit-ne
Digna deo: Latius quo sic Busiris ad aras,
Immolet æterno spectata holocausta Jehovæ.

    Noster erat, nostrasque scholas ornabat, amabat,
Oxoniæ decus Humfredus, præfulgidus aster
Cimmerias tenebras, errorum nubila pellens.
Qui stabulum Augiæ (studio indefessus agendi)
Sordibus oppletum mundo patefecit, et omnes
Romanæ caulæ pecudes, armenta, gregesque,
Taxavit brutæ mentis, fraudisque, dolique.
Is Jesuitarum vafræ tectoria frontis,
Et Siculas gerras fermentatamque farinam
Devitanda docet serpentum cautius ictu.
Ille per acclives gnavus gnarusque laboris
Doctrinæ calles incedit, et omnia lustrat,
Omnia libat apis, ferventi Græca, Latina
Scripta, novos veteres authores pollice versat.
Hinc ubi visus erat satis impallescere chartis,

Joh. Juellus, Episcopus Sarum.

Joh. Foxus, Martyro-logicus.

Laur. Hum-fredus, Pa-pamastix.

Grandia pervigili contexta volumina cura
Edidit, effundens fœcundi pectoris artes.
Hunc tamen abreptum funesti fossa sepulchri
Occulit, 'et regnum violentæ mortis opacat.
Quem nimis abjecte merito sine honore jacentem,
Funeris exequiis fraudatum Musa dolenti.
Singultu desiens, lachrymis mœstisque querelis
Obturbata silet, positoque hic fine quiescit.

IV

QUEEN ELIZABETH AT OXFORD

IN 1592

THE

GRAND RECEPTION

AND

ENTERTAINMENT

OF

QUEEN ELIZABETH

AT OXFORD

IN 1592

From a MS. Account originally written by

Mr. Philip Stringer

THE GRAND RECEPTION

AND

ENTERTAINMENT

OF

QUEEN ELIZABETH

AT OXFORD

IN 1592[1].

From a MS. Account, originally written by Mr. PHILIP
STRINGER, one of the two Cambridge Gentlemen[2] who
attended Sir William Cecil Lord Burghley (Chancellor of the University of Cambridge), upon that
Occasion, to Oxford. Communicated to Mr. Peck
by the Reverend Samuel Knight, S.T.P. Archdeacon of Berks.

Containing,

I.   A Relation of what passed there, on Friday
22 Sept. 1592.

1. ON Friday, 22 Sept. 1592, about three of the clock in
the afternoon, the Queen's most excellent Majestie entred into
the bounds or precincts of the University of Oxford, at a

---

[1] This was the second time of Queen Elizabeth's going to Oxford. She went
thither first in 1566. And a full account of her then reception and entertainment
there may be found in this Collection, under that year.

[2] Mr. Henry Mowtlowe, of King's College, Cambridge, was the other Cambridge gentleman who attended Sir William Cecil to Oxford. This Mr. Mowt-

place called Godstow Bridge, much about a mile from the City of Oxford ; where hir Highness was attended for by the Vicechancellor [Nicholas Bond, S. T. P. President of St. Mary Magdalen's College] and the rest of the Doctors (Heads of Colleges) with the Proctors and Beadles of the University, being all then on foot in gownes ; the Doctors in scarlet ; the rest otherwise, as was answerable to their degrees and place.

2. Upon intelligence of the Vicechancellor's being ready, with the rest, to present their dutyes unto hir Highness, hir Majestie was pleased to have the coach stayed wherein she was ; notwithstanding the foulness of the weather. Where-upon the Vicechancellor delivered up unto hir Highness the Beadles staves, which were immediately re-delivered unto him by hirself, with the signification of hir gracious pleasure to stay the hearing of a speech wherewithall they were pro-vided (as hir Highness understood) so that it were not too longe. Which being knowne, Mr. [Thomas] Savill, the Senior Proctor[1], being then upon his knees (with the rest of the company) did presently enter into a short speech. Wherein he first signified, 'what great joy the University had conceived by hir Majestie's approaching so near unto them. And then that, in the name of the whole body, for the better mani-festinge of their dutifulness, he was to yeld up unto hir Majestie the liberties, privileges, howses, colleges, temples, goods, with themselves also, and whatsoever they were by hir Majestie's goodness possessed of, with their most instant and dutiful prayers for the longe and blessed preservation of hir Highnes.'

3. This done, hir Majestie, with the Nobility, and the rest of hir royal traine, going towards the city, was, within half a

lowe was Senior Proctor of the University of Cambridge, annis 1589 and 1593. He was afterwards LL.D. and elected the First Professor of Civil Law in Gresham College.

[1] This Thomas Savile was brother of Sir Henry, and Fellow of Merton. He died in this his Proctorship 22 Jan. 1592, at London, and was after conveyed to Oxon. and buried in the choir of Merton College. Ath. Oxon. vol. I. col. 257, 258.

mile, received by the Maior of Oxford and his brethren, with
a short speech delivered by their Recorder.

4. Thence, passing by S. John's College, she was there
presented with a private speech in the behalfe of that colledge
(as unto me it seemed).

5. From whence, entring into the city, she passed thorow
the streets (the scholers standing in order on both sides of the
same) 'till her Highness came to the place which is called
Carfax, or Cator Foyse [rectius, *quatre voyes* or *voies*] where
she was pleased to hear an oration in the Greek tonge, which
was offered unto hir by Mr. [Henry Cuffe[1]], then the Greek
Reader.

6. Thence she passed along to her lodging (which was
provided for her in Christ's Church) the scholars standing on
both sydes of the street (as is already said) in their gownes,
hoods, and caps, answerable to their several degrees.

7. In Christ's-Church, going in here in [at] the end of the
minster (before hir Highnes went up to the roomes provided
for her) she was received with an oration by Mr. Smith (in the
behalf of that colledge, as I then conceived of it); [William
James, S. T. P.] the Dean thereof, and the company attending
there, for the performance of that dutye.

II.   An Account of what passed there, on Saturday
23 Sept. 1592.

1. On Satterday then next followinge, hir Majestie went to
the church of S. Maryes, betwixt two and three of the clock ;
being attended upon by hir nobility ; hirselfe being in a rich
carradge, and the nobility [riding] upon their foot-clothes.

2. Hir Majestie being there placed under hir cloth of estate,
upon a very fayre stage (which was purposely erected for hir
in the east end of the church, nere unto the quire) there was a

---

[1] Hanged at Tyburn, 30 March, 1601, for being concerned in the treason of
Robert Earl of Essex, to whom he was then secretary. Ath. Oxon. vol. I. col.
307, 308.

philosophy act provided for hir Highnes ; which was begun
upon the signification of her Highnes pleasure therein, by this
only word, ' Incipiatis ' being uttered by hirself.   Whereupon
the Proctors [Mr. Savile, and Mr. (afterwards Sir) Ralph
Winwood [1], of Magdalen] both of them together, did, after
their usual, brief and plain manner, speak unto the first Replier, ' ad incipiendum.'   Who, after three congés unto hir
Majestie, in such sort as is usual, did presently propound the
questions unto the Answerer, without any speech at all unto
her Highnes.   Hereupon the Answerer, Mr. Thomas Smith[2],
then Orator of the University (after his like three congés to
hir Highnes) repeated the questions formerly propounded ;
which were these :

> i. ' An anima [cujusvis] sit in se præstantior anima
> alterius ? '
> ii. ' An, ob mundi senectam, homines minus sint heroici
> nunc quam olim ? '

and so entred into his position, which continued almost half
an hower, hir Majestie thinking it somewhat longe (as it
seemed) for that (when hir speech was ended) the Proctors
uttering their accustomed words unto the Replier, viz. ' Pro-
cede, Magister,' her Majestie, supposing it had been spoken to
the Answerer, said, that ' He had bene already too longe.'

3. Upon these words of the Proctors, one Mr. [Matthew]
Gwin[3], the first Replier (after his like congés) uttered a pre-
meditate oration unto hir Highnes ; the first [part] being
directed unto hirself by way of excuse or supplication concerning his disability [to speak] in that honorable presence,

---

[1] Born at Ainho, in Northamptonshire, Proctor of this University in 1589.   He
was knighted 28 June, 1607, made Secretary of State in 1614, and died in Oct.
1617.   Fasti Oxon. vol. I. col. 133, 139.

[2] Afterwards Secretary to Robert Earl of Essex, Clerk of the Parliament and
Council, and knighted in 1603 ; Latin Secretary, and one of the Masters of the
Requests, to King James.   He died 28 Nov. 1609.   Ath. Oxon. vol. I. col. 352.

[3] Fellow of St. John's College, Music Professor of this University of Oxford in
1582, created Dr. of Physic 17 July, 1593.   Fasti Ox. vol. I. fol. 147.   First
Medicine Professor of Gresham College, and one of the College of Physicians.
Ath. Ox. vol. I. col. 513.

and the rest concerning the questions: wherein his wittie handlinge of the matter, and discreete behavior, seemed much to please hir Majestie.

4. His speech continued much about a quarter of an hour; after which he approved an argument in the first cause; and was then cut off by the Proctors.

5. This done, then stood up one Mr. ———— Sydney (who was placed in the lowest forme) being thereunto required by the Proctors. He forgat his congés, used no speech at all to hir Majestie, but dealt with the Answerer as though hir Majestie had not bin there. In which speech he was neither longe nor curiouse, nether for matter nor maner; who [after he had] propounded one argument in the first cause, was cut off by the Proctors, *ut ante.* .

6. This so passed over, the Proctors calling for the third Replier (whose name was Mr. ——————) willed him to oppose in the second question, which he undertooke (after he had made his congés) beginning with a speach directed to hir Majestie first, and came after to the handlinge of the question, with a speach noteing the predictions of the death and advancement of divers princes: and so ended, with one only argument in the second question.

7. The last Replier (whose name was Mr. [John] Buck-ridge[1]) was willed to dispute only in the second question; [and thereupon] did, without any speach by way of preface, frame himself thereunto, and did perform at the best purpose (as was supposed) with best likinge unto hir Majestie, as it seemed by hir Highnes gracious countenance, and requiring of him to prosecute his argument (after the Proctors had cut him off) with these hir gracious words, ‘Imo prodeat, si potest, &c.’

8. This argument ended by the last Replyer, Mr. [Henry] Savile, the Master of Martine Colledge, was willed by the Proctors to determine the questions, which he presently did,

---

[1] Fellow, and afterwards Master, of St. John's College, and at length Bishop of Rochester. Ath. Oxon. vol. I. col. 557, a.

with a very good speach, though somewhat longe; endinge that act with thanks unto hir Majestie, 'for hir great patience in hearinge, and with a longe discourse concerning such benefit as God, by hir Highnes, had bestowed upon us, and upon many forraine nations and princes, by hir Highnes means.' Which done, hir Majestie returned to hir Courte, or lodging, so attended as at hir coming out.

III.   Certain General Passages, not relating to one, but several Days.

1. It is to be remembred, that, besydes this act, there was also an English sermon especially provided for and preached in another church in the town (not far from St. Mary's) by a lerned man of special note amongst them.   Which was, in like sort, continued every morning at the same hower and place, by men of like quality, during the time of hir Majestie's remaining there with them.

2. At thes sermons we [the Cambridge men] could not be [present], by reason of [our] ordinary attendance every morning upon the Lord Treasurer, then our most worthy chancellor.

3. It is also to be remembered, that the three Esquire Beadles did give their attendance upon hir Majestie's person as oft as she went abroad in state, and had place next before the serjeants at arms, beinge in chaines of gold, and in fayre gownes, with the rest of their apparell thereunto according.

4. The entrance into St. Mary's church was kept by the guard only, standinge without the doors of the church, with their halberts in their hands, thereby to avoyde the noyse and the knocking at the dores, wherewith hir Majestie was somewhat troubled at the first.

5. Besyds that part of the stage which was new built for hir Majestie, there was a part of their ordinary stage set up on both syds of the church; but none at all in the west end: thereby to give, as I thinke, the better passage of the air unto

hir Majestie, and to avoyde the faceing of hir, as it were by an opposition, in respect of the place.

6. The Answerers had their seats and places (as we usually have) in the midst of the church beneath.   And the Disputers in every faculty had their seats in the syde of the church, somewhat lower than hir Majestie, [who] sat under hir cloth of estate.

7. There was none in the end of the stage nere hir Majestie, but such as were necessarily attendant upon hir Highnes, viz. the Lord Chamberlayne, the Lady Marquesse [of Winton] and some two or three others of the great honorable ladies.

8. The going to hir Highnes seat was an easie half paced stayre, which was of good bredth, and cast on the north side of that ende, beginning somewhat without the middle isle of the church.

IV.   An Account of what passed there, on Sunday 24 Sept. 1592.

1. On Sunday there was a sermon preached before hir Majestie, by Mr. Dr. [William] James, then Dean of Christ's Church, in the minster church of that colledge.

2. At night there was a comedy acted before hir Highnes in the hall of that colledge; and one other on Tuesday at night, being both of them but meanely performed (as we thought), and yet most graciouslye, and with great patience, heard by hir Majestie.   The one being called 'Bellum Grammaticale,' and the other intituled 'Rivales.'

V.   An Account of what passed there, on Monday 25 Sept. 1592.

1. On Monday, at eight of the clock in the morning, there was an English sermon, as is alreadie said.   And, at the same hower, their ordinary Lectures of Art were read in the Common Schooles.   And, at nine, in the Divinity School

was read a Divinity Lecture by Mr. [Dr. Thomas] Holland[1] (her Majestie's Reader in Divinity there), at which were present but a few of the nobility, and many scholars.

2. This day, the Lords of the Council dined with Mr. [Henry] Savile, at Martine Colledge, in the common hall of that house. Where, after they had dined, they heard a Disputation in Philosophy ; the Answeringe being performed by Mr. [Henry] Cuffe [abovementioned] of that house; four other of the same house replying unto him.

3. There was but one argument propounded by every one of them. Which being done, the questions were determined by Mr. [Thomas] Savile, (then the Senior Proctor) who, in the end of his determination, by reason of one of the questions, viz.

'An Dissentiones Civium sint Reipublicæ utiles?'

took thereby occasion by name to commend [Sir William Cecil] the Lord Tresurer, (who was present) in respect of his greate care in the government of this Commonwealth. And after him the Lord Chamberlain. And after him the Lord Admiral, his great worth and valiant service by sea. And, lastly, fell into commendation of the Earl of Essex, his honorable, valiant service in the Low Countryes, in Portugall, and in France : and so concluded.

4. This done, the lords went to sit in counsell. After which there was nothing shewed that day, eyther before hir Majestie publiquely, or privately before the lords of the counsell.

VI. An Account of what passed there, on Tuesday 26 Sept. 1592.

1. On Tuesday, at eight of the clock in the morning, the ordinary Lectures in Art were read as before. At nine of

---

[1] Fellow of Baliol College (which he left in 1583), Divinity Professor in 1589, and Rector of Exeter College in 1592. Ath. Oxon. vol. I. col. 377. [Boase, Reg. Coll. Exon. p. 50.]

the clock, Mr. Dr. [John] Reignolds[1] did read a Lecture in Divinity, at the which the lords of the counsell and the most of the nobility were present. At the same hower also there were, in other Common Schooles, disputations called 'Quodlibets,' by Masters of Arts and Bachelors in Art, according to their accustomed manner.

2. About thre of the clock in the afternone of the same day, hir Majestie went again to St. Maryes, accompanyed as on Saturday before; where it pleased hir Highnes to heare a Disputation in Natural Philosophy, which was answered by one Mr. [John] Spencer[2], of Corpus Christi Colledge; who was replyed upon by four Masters of Arts, *viz.* Mr. [John] Williams[3], of All Souls, Mr. [Humphrey] Pritchard, of Christ's Church, Mr. [Edward] Brearewood[4], of Brasen Nose, and Mr. ——— Buckhurst, of Magdalen.

3. This act was determined by one Mr. [Giles] Thompson[5], of All Soules, with a very learned and discreet speach, (as it was conceived by all that heard him, and the rather in respect of the Lord Treasurer's great commending thereof). He handled the questions principally, and spent no time at all in the commendation of hir Majestie, or of the nobility, 'For that (as he sayd) their vertues were greater then that they could be sufficiently recommended by him.' His speach not being above a quarter of an hower in length.

4. The Replyers were required to put forth each of them one argument without any preface; which they did accordingly: with hir Majestie's very good liking.

5. This done, and the act concluded by Mr. Thompson, (as

---

[1] John Rainolds, D.D. Fellow, and afterwards President, of Corpus Christi College. See Wood's Ath. Oxon. vol. I. col. 339.

[2] President of Corpus Christi after John Rainolds. He died 3 Apr. 1614. Le Neve.

[3] Afterwards Margaret Professor, Dean of Bangor, and Principal of Jesus College. Ath. Oxon. vol. I. col. 387.

[4] Afterwards the First Astronomy Professor in Gresham College. Ath. Oxon. vol. I. col. 390, 391.

[5] Afterwards Dean of Windsor, Bishop of Gloucester, and one of the translators of the Bible temp. Jacobi I. Ath. Oxon. vol. I. col. 721.

is already sayd) there presently succeeded a Disputation in
Physicke, which was answered by one Mr. Dr. [Thomas]
Dochin[1]; who (after his congés, as afore, and a short preface
concerning himself) greatly magnified hir Majestie 'for hir
gratious favor, in vouchsafing hir presence at this exercise,
being so excellent a Prince, and so singularly well scene even
in this very faculty, amongst many other hir virtues and
great excellency of knowledge and learning, which he wished
she might have *in*[2] use of hirself.'   And so entred into a
short exposition of one of the questions; *viz.*

> 'Quod Aere magis mutantur Corpora humana quam
>   Cibo & Potu.'

wherein he was soon cut off by the Proctors, and the Replyers
called for; who were six in number, *viz.* Dr. [Anthony]
Ailesworth[3], ——— Dalliber, [Henry] Bust[4], [Edward]
Ratcliff[5], ——— Bently, and [John] Case[6].

6. Dr. Ayleworth began with a little preface, somewhat
concerning hir Majestie's gratiousness in hearing, and hir other
virtues; and the rest concerning the questions: but was put
to an argument ere he had done.   And, the four next using
only one argument apeece, Dr. Case would have concluded
the busines with a short speach, (wherein he began to call
upon the spirits of certain honorable persons not long since of

---

[1] Thomas Dochyn, of Magdalen College, M.D. 19 Aug. 1592. Fasti Oxon.
vol. I. col. 143.   He was elected the second Lynacre Lecturer of Physic in
Merton College, 4 Nov. 1604, and died 29 Jan. following. Athenæ Oxon,
vol. I. col. 21. [Boase, p. 267.]

[2] *in* (sic).

[3] Anthony Ailesworth, alias Aylworth, of New College, M.D. Regius Professor
of Physic 29 June, 1582. Le Neve.   He was physician to Queen Elizabeth, and
died 18 April, 1619. Fasti Oxon. vol. I. col. 124. [Boase, p. 264.]

[4] v.s. p. 175, n. 25.

[5] M.D. of Cambridge, incorporated M.D. of Oxford 4 July, 1600. Fasti Oxon.
vol. I. col. 159. [Really Dr. Richard Ratcliff of Merton. v. Preface.]

[6] John Case, chorister first of New College, and then of Christ's Church, Scholar
of St. John's in 1564, Fellow, M.A.   He became M.D. in 1589, and Prebend of
North Aulton, in the church of Sarum.   He died 29 Jan. 1599, and was buried in
the chapel of St. John's College. Ath. Oxon. vol. I. col. 299, 300. [Boase,
p. 267.]

this Commonwealth) but was very soon cut off, and put to an argument in the second cause, *viz.*

'An Morbi curantur per Fascinationem & per Dæmones?'

Whereupon the Determination being called for by the Proctors, it was presently entred into and performed by Mr. Dr. ———— Jeffs, one of hir Majestie's physicians.

7. It must not be forgotten, that this day, betwene the howers of ten and eleven of the clocke in the forenone, it pleased hir Majestie to heare an oration made by the Vice-chancellor, in the Chamber of Presence, presenting hir High-nes with two Bibles (the one in Greek, and the other in Latine) in the name of the whole University.

VII. An Account of what passed there, on Wednesday 27 Sept. 1592.

1. On Wednesday, the Publique Lectures were read as before, at eight of the clock; and the Queen's Reader in Divinity [Thomas Holland [1], S. T. P.] abovementioned, read in Divinity at nine.

2. There was also, at the same time, a Lecture in Musick, with the practice thereof by instrument, in the Common Schooles.

3. At three of the clock in the afternoone, hir Majestie being again come to St. Marye's (attended, as already sayd), Mr. Dr. ———— B———— answered in Law, and four other Doctors replied.

4. The question which they most stood upon was this; *viz.*

'An Judex debet judicare secundum allegata & probata, contra Conscientiam?'

which (after the Disputation) was concluded in the affirmative by Mr. Dr. (Francis Bevans, LL.D.) Master of Jesus Colledge there, and then Chancellor of Hereford.

[1] [v. Boase, Reg. Coll. Exon. p. 50.]

5. After this act, there followed immediately a Disputation in Divinity, which was answered by the Queen's Reader (Dr. Tho. Holland), and opposed against him by the Vicechancellor (Dr. Nicholas Bond), and the Dean of Christ's Church, (Dr. William James).   Ten other Doctors being there [also] ready to undertake the same (in their scarlet gowns and silk hoods turned) which they could not do for want of time.

6. This act was concluded by Mr. Dr. [Herbert] West[phaling [1]], then Bishop of Hereford, determining this question [in the] negative ; *viz.*

'An licet in Christiana Republica dissimulare in Causa Religionis?'

7. His speech was spent, ' First, in thanks to hir Majestie for her most gratious favor unto himself in particular.   Then in proofs, whereby he inferred his conclusion of the question. Next, in petition unto hir Highnes for hir gratious pardon if any thing had unadvisedly passed, wherein they or any of the University had offended.   And lastly, in thanks unto hir Highnes, in the name of their Honorable Chancellor, of him-self, and the rest of the Doctors, and whole company of students, for hir most gratious favor in vouchsafing them again hir Highnes presence, after six and twenty years [space.] in that place, and at those exercises, &c.'   .

8. His oration was so longe that hir Majestie was somewhat wearied therewith, (as it was thought) and did therefore, with-out any speech of her owne, returne to hir lodginge.

VIII.   An Account of the Queen's Speech to the Heads of the University, and of her Departure thence, on Thursday 28 Sept. 1592.

1. On Thursday, about ten of the clock in the forenoon, hir Majestie made an oration to the Vicechancellor, the Doctors, &c. in her Highnes Chamber of Presence, in most gracious manner, delivering hir acceptance of that which they had done,

[1] [v. s. p. 174, n. 6.]

&c. as appeareth by the oration. At which we were not, beinge then in attendance upon our honorable Chancellor, at his lodging, in another part of the court.

2. Hir Highnes departed from the University this day, about eleven of the clock in the forenoon, in hir open and princely carriadge. And heard, lastly, a long tedious oration made unto hir by the Junior Proctor of the University, about a mile from the city, in the very edge of their bounds or liberties towards Shotover.

APPENDIX A[1].

D. HENRICI SAVILII, τοῦ μακαρίτου, ORATIO, habita OXONIÆ, Sept. 23, 1592, coram Reginâ ELIZABETHA[2].

THESES.

I. *Rei Militaris & Philosophiæ studia in Republicâ unâ vigere.*

II. *Astrologiam Judiciariam è Civitate benè moratâ esse exterminandam* [3].

Corpus humanum, Serenissima Princeps, nisi vis aut morbus impulerit, tribus quasi gradibus tendit ad mortem; adolescentiæ, maturitatis, & senectæ: sic respublica, non bellis externis oppressa, non civilibus ante tempus lacerata, naturali certè decursu habet incrementum, statum, & declinationem. Nam & omnia orta occidunt, & maturata defluunt, &, tempore corroborata, tempore labefactantur.

Jam artes aliæ sunt necessitatis, aliæ liberalis otii, aliæ eruditi luxûs. Necessitatis, ut, ad depellendam famem, agricultura, pecuaria; ad arcendum frigus, architectura, vestiaria; ad vim propulsandam, ars militaris, otia liberalia [4] (ut gymnastica), musica, & hæc ipsa mater artium Philosophia. Luxûs, ut pictura, statuaria, culinariæ, fucatoriæ artes, aliæque in quas magno corporum, majore animorum, damno sumus ingeniosi. Nec in omnibus reipublicæ temporibus vigent istæ omnes, nec tamen ullum est tempus in quo

---

[1] Printed from Nichols's Progresses of Queen Elizabeth, Vol. III. 1823, pp. 161 ff., collated with Bodl. MS. Tanner 461, fol. 169. (cited in the Notes as T.)

[2] Oratio Henrici Savilij, Mertonensis Collegij prepositi, coram Reg. Elizabethâ publicè habita Oxonij. A.D. 1592. Sept. 28. (Tanner MS.)

[3] Tanner omits *Theses—exterminandam.*

[4] *Otij liberalis,* T.

non aliqua. Sic enim naturâ comparatum est, ut necessitatis inventa tempore prima sint, otii media, extrema luxuriæ; sintque illa nascentis ferè crescentisque reipublicæ, vigentis altera, tertia ruentis. In constituentibus rempublicam, in bella gerentibus pro capite & salute, nasci literarum studia non solent, non possunt. Otium pacemque nactæ vel pro gloriâ tantùm dimicantis civitatis, alumna est Philosophia. Contrà, rei militaris scientia iis reipublicæ temporibus non utilis modò, sed pernecessaria. Ut enim generare naturæ nobilius eóque difficilius est opus quàm augere, quàm conservare: sic majoris animi, ingenii, artis, virtutis, imperium fundare quàm tueri; cùm novam in medio crescentem molem oderint etiam longinquæ nationes, sibi ac posteris suis metuant vicinæ. Secundum est tempus reipublicæ jam constitutæ vigentisque, in quo emicant[1] illa, quæ dixi omnia, oblectationes & otia liberalia[2], florente etiamnum rei militaris scientiâ. Quòd si idem ardor animorum maneret, idem armorum studium, labor, industria, vigilantia; nempè id in quo deos omnes frustrà votis fatigamus, jamdiu manibus teneremus, immortalem civitatem; facilè enim imperium iis artibus retinetur, quibus initio partum est. Sed nimirùm, cùm nemo jam hostis, nisi quem nos facimus[3]; nulla gens inimica, nisi propter nostras injurias; cessante necessitate, armorum, quæ necessitatis causâ primùm sumta sunt, aciem patimur hebescere. Labente dein paulatìm disciplinâ, cùm, ex superiorum temporum virtute, nihil restet præter opes virtute congestas & instrumenta luxuriæ; spreta jacet res militaris, afflicta divinæ particulâ mentis virtutis[4] imperatoria; eodemque labefactata motu concidunt literarum studia, seu præsidio militari destituta, seu commercii vitiorum voluptatumque pertæsa; ut nemini dubium esse queat, ea studia posse unà vigere, quæ non possunt nisi unà perire.

Primâ ætate à Româ conditâ usque ad Annibalem[5] Italiâ Africâque ejectum, tollitur, ut ait Ennius, è medio sapientia, vi geritur res; spernitur orator bonus, horridus miles amatur. Indè ad Augusti[6] maturitatem pono; in quâ eluxerunt illa literarum lumina, Gracchi, Scævolæ, Tuberones, Crassi, Hortensii, Cicerones, Varones[7]. Huic ætati, ingeniorum feracissimæ, debemus Livium, Salustium, Plautum, Lucretium, Virgilium; nec minùs magnos imperatores, Mummium, Marium, Syllam, Pompeium, Agrippam; & in cœlum ferendos propter summam in utroque genere præstantiam

---

[1] Eminent T. [2] Oblectōnis & Otij liberalis; T. [3] Fecimus T.
[4] Virtus T. [5] Hannibalem T. [6] Augustum T. [7] Varrones T.

M.[1] Catonem, P. Africanum[2], C. Cæsarem. Quæ tamen ætas ita rudis fuit artium ad luxum pertinentium, ita parùm intelligens Græcarum deliciarum, ut Mummius, magnus (ut dixi) imperator, captâ Corintho, cùm maximorum artificum manibus perfectas tabulas ac statuas in Italiam portandas locaret, juberet prædici conducentibus, si eas perdidissent, novas eos reddituros. Post Augustum, deflorescente jam penitùs bellicâ laude, stanteque republicâ non vi suâ, sed rerum priùs gestarum gloriâ, ex domitis nationibus peregrinis hausta infusaque in mores civitatis peregrinitas, ut eadem studia, quasi progressu quodam naturali, idem ubique exitus maneret. Ita dominante luxuriâ[3], cùm homines beati & locupletes, voluptatibus immersi, literarum studia ad Græculos servos rejicerent, dum putarent se scire quod quisquam in domo suâ sciret: à servilibus ingeniis artes liberales corruptæ, emortuam jam ante rem militarem haud longo intervallo consecutæ sunt; nisi quòd sub Trajano principe, cùm iterùm moveret lacertos imperium, redditâ quasi juventute, bonæ quoque literæ effloruerunt. Testes fero è Græcis Plutarchum, Lucianum; è nostris Plinium, Tacitum: & dubitamus adhuc eas artes posse conjungi, quæ in civitate omnium gentium principe simul floruerunt, simul perîerunt, simulque renatæ sunt? Num apud Græcos secùs? Prima ætas, usque ad Medica tempora, armis exercitatissima, literarum penè rudis. Indè ad Philippum Demetrii altera, literis armisque florens; in quâ Cimon, Alcibiades, Philippus Amyntæ, Alexander, Seleucus, Demetrius, summi imperatores; &, in omni philosophiâ principes, Socrates, Anaxagoras, Plato, Aristoteles, Chrysippus, non est necesse de singulis; nefas tamen fuerit de Pericle, Thucydide, Xenophonte Socratico, Dione Platonico, qui in utroque genere excelluerunt, silere.

Ne in nostrâ quidem republicâ factum est illud, quod plerique putant, literarum & armorum divortium; cùm iis ipsis temporibus, quibus majores tui, Augustissima Regina, terrorem nominis sui[4] in Galliam, Hispaniam, Siciliam, Cyprum, Asiam, Ægyptum[5], intulissent, elucerent domî illa hujus academiæ ornamenta, Europæ lumina, Rogerus Bacon, Walterus Burley[6], Scotus, Occhamus, Wiclevus; quos, cùm ab omnibus cùm ingenii tùm doctrinæ subsidiis fuerint instructissimi, isto orationis flore, quo nunc ferè solùm, certè nimiùm, gloriamur, æquissimo animo patior carere. Quid? quòd nè alterum quidem sine altero horum studiorum potest esse perfectum?

---

[1] Marcum T.   [2] P. Scipionem T.   [3] Luxurie T.   [4] T. omits *terrorem nominis sui.*   [5] T. adds in margin f. Arma.   [6] Burlæus T.

Literæ ab imperatore præsidium mutuantur, & tutelam, id est, spiritum & vitam: reddunt multa magnaque & adjumenta belli & ornamenta victoriæ ; historiæ veteris notitiam, id est, maximè certam brevemque, maximè multiplicem, miniméque periculosam rerum gerendarum ex gestis scientiam. Do L. Lucullum, qui, Româ profectus rei militaris rudis, rebus gestis[1] legendis in Asiam venit factus imperator; P. Africanum, qui Cyri disciplinam, à Xenophonte scriptam, nunquam solebat ponere de manibus illis gloriosis, quibus Numantia & Carthago, duæ urbes Romani æmulæ fastigii, excisæ sunt. Addo ex Philosophiâ sapientibus sententiis, gravibusque verbis, ornatam orationem ; quâ militum animos possit jacentes erigere, ferocientes reprimere, inflammatos restinguere. Addo temperamentum morum & sedationem perturbationum: nequid in bello iratè, in victoriâ superbè, in pace ultra civilem modum; neu cædibus & rapinis assueta mens immanitate efferetur.

Quid illa abstrusiora ? Astronomia, inquit Plato, imperatori futuro necessaria est ad temporum vicissitudines noscendas ; Arithmetica, ad acies instruendas ; Geometria, ad castra metanda, loca capienda, figurandos exercitus : hinc urbium muniendarum peritia; hinc bellicorum tormentorum operumque machinatrix. Ab hâc disciplinâ profectus Archimedes, legionum & classium impetum solus perlevi momento luto[2] ludificatus est. Contrà, Philippus, Demetrii scalarum brevitate, id est, ignoratione Geometriæ, à Melitæensium oppido rejectus ; Nicias, superstitione lunaris defectûs, id est, ignoratione Astronomiæ, cum exercitu cæsus in Siciliâ. Idem, cùm Sulpitius Gallus in bello cum Perseo[3] provideret, prædiceretque militibus, ne id pro portento acciperent quod, ordine naturali, statis temporibus fiat ; magnum momentum ad debellandam Macedoniam, id est, ad Romanum imperium constituendum visus est attulisse. Quare cùm his tot ac tantis adminiculis perficiatur ars imperatoria, neque aliundè sint ea quàm ex mediâ deprompta philosophiâ; concedamus sanè ea studia simul esse posse, quæ, nisi simul, non possunt esse absoluta.

Neque tamen non est aliquid, quod contra affertur, Philosophiam avocare animum à sensibus, & contemplationi tradere rerum (dii boni !) maximarum, sed ab hâc consuetudine populari abhorrentium ; quarum illecebris, quasi[4] quodam Circæo poculo delinita mens, ad rempublicam tractandam, ad res manu gerendas, nolit accedere, nè possit quidem. Nam, cùm natura, ut ait philosophus,

---

[1] T. omits *gestis*.   [2] T. omits *luto*.   [3] Persâ T.   [4] Tanquam T.

faciat unum ad unum, difficileque sit pluribus in rebus eundem
excellere; tum certè difficillimum in tam dissidentibus & naturâ
disparatis. Ex humoribus quibus constamus, aptissima ad Philosophiam melancholia, ad arma bilis, ad voluptates sanguis; quartus
ille pituita gravis ne ad mala quidem bonus. Plato tres animæ
partes ponit sedibus disclusas; rationabilem[1] in capite, irascibilem
in corde, concupiscibilem in jecore. Ad rationabilem[1] pertinet
Philosophia, ad irascibilem ars militaris, voluptuariæ ad tertium
genus. Quòd si possent illi humores ita commisceri, aut istæ sive
partes animæ, sive facultates, ita conjungi; ut altera vim alterius
non infringeret, non debilitaret; haberemus id quod quærimus, in
milite philosophum. Aut, si hoc difficile est, cùm ob alia tum quia
utriusque studii eâdem penè ætate, multo sudore, multisque vigiliis
facienda sunt tyrocinia: secernamus, si placet, à milite totum hoc
philosophari, relinquamus imperatori, ut contemplativis mediocritèr
tinctus sit; morali verò civilique philosophiâ, & politiore[2] litera-
turâ penitùs imbutus. Atque, ut demus vera esse, quæ sunt ab
ornatissimis magistris allata, tamen eam vim habent pleraque; non
ut in unâ republicâ simul esse non possint, sed ut ne in uno homine:
ne nos quidem civitatem ex philosophis constare volumus; quid
enim ad vim arcendam foret ineptius? neque ex militibus totam;
nam quid turbulentius? Respublica, nimirùm, debet esse unita, non
una; cujus dignitas salusque non unâ laude, sed uno omnium rerum laudandarum[3] temperamento, continetur.

Sequitur Astrologia, quam eventis fallacem, usu superstitiosam,
à barbaris nationibus importatam, bonis temporibus Græciæ igno-
tam, etiam malis Româ pulsam, tot senatûsconsultis, tot principum
rescriptis damnatam suffragantibus omnium ætatum philosophis
(plebeios quosdam excipio) politicisque è republicâ exterminamus:
artem, quod in arte turpissimum est, nullis textam[4] principiis,
nullâ subnixam demonstratione, nullo constantem syllogismo. Verum est cœlum in hæc inferiora luce, motu, virtute agere; ista
omnia fovere, animare; obliquum circulum causam esse ortûs & in-
teritùs; à sole & homine generari hominem; sed ab homine, ut[5]
causâ propinquâ propriâque, quæ materiam suppeditet; à sole, ut inter
efficientes coadjuvante, remotâque, & generali; qui uno & eodem
calore, & semen aconiti animat ad venenum, & brassicæ ad ali-
mentum, & rhabarbari ad medicinam; non naturam aliquam inse-
rendo, sed ea in actum, in lucem producendo, quæ priùs in

---

[1] Rõnalem T. (*bis*).   [2] Politiori T.   [3] T. omits *rerum laudandarum.*
[4] Contextam T.   [5] Ut à T.

matcriæ potentiis delitescebant. Itaque [1] sanus an morbosus sim, acutus an hebes, albus an ater, nihil ad cœlum [2] stellasque, quæ eodem lumine, eodem cœli situ, eodem momento, omnibus iisdem agentia, & ex materiâ sanè [3] dispositâ sanum producunt infantem, & ex morbosè [4] morbosum. Quid illa externa? pauper [5] an dives, honoribus clarus an secùs? quæ rerum fortuitarum temerario intercursu, nostræque [6] voluntatis libero motu, infinitis modis variata, nullum habent cum cœlo commercium. Sed de Astrologiâ [7] facilius est tacere quàm pauca dicere.

Reliquæ sunt Augustissima Regina, partes officii nostri maximis tuis immortalibusque in nos [8], in rempublicam, in orbem Christianum, meritis debitæ atque consecratæ. Patere igitur, ut id [9] unus pro omnibus dicam, quod isti omnes de tuâ Majestate taciti sentiunt. Patere tuam in obtinendo imperio fœlicitatem, in constituendo sapientiam, in tuendo fortitudinem, in administrando constantiam, cæteras virtutes tuas, quæ omnium gentium literis & linguis commemoratæ sunt, tuorum quoque, ad quos tantarum virtutum fructus propiùs pertinet, voce celebrari.

Cùm essent omnia fato quodam superiorum temporum plena suspicionum domî, forìs bellum certum, aut pax infida; cùm in oculis, in visceribus nostris hæreret, ex illo infœlici conjugio contractum, pertinax malum, Hispanorum dominatio; cùm effusum esset ærarium, imminuti fines imperii, præsidia milite, arces tormentis denudatæ; in his tot tantisque difficultatibus eluxit tua singularis, ac verè divina, sapientia, Divinissima Princeps. Gladium, in illâ rerum mutatione ac transitu, vaginâ vacuum Anglia non vidit: vidit plausus, clamores, exultationes, omnium ordinum, ætatum, hominum, nisi quibus expediret esse malum principem, hoc est, quàm dissimillimum tui. Tu Hispanos à capite, à cervicibus nostris, aut invitos depulisti, aut remisisti volentes. Tu publicam fidem, angustiis ærari vacillantem prædiorum tuorum, rerumque pretiosissimarum venditione levâsti. Tu oppida amissa, pactis conventis, quod in te fuit, recepisti; obsidum fugâ, & quorundam perfidiâ, quod præstare non poteras, perdidisti; cùmque tuæ castissimæ purissimæque menti nihil placeret fallax, nihil fucatum, tu, nummis adulterinis sublatis, commercia revocâsti, fidem restituisti. Tu religionem, majorum in curiâ collapsam, aut ipso tempore desidentem, incredibili animi fortitudine renovâsti, communemque [10] asylum omnibus genti-

---

[1] Verum T.   [2] Solem T.   [3] T. omits *sanè*.   [4] Morbosâ T.
[5] T. omits *pauper*.   [6] T. omits *nostræque*.   [7] Sed Horologia T.
[8] T. omits *in nos*.   [9] T. omits *id*.   [10] Communéque T.

bus aperuisti: neque dubitasti, nova princeps, cùm omnes propinquæ nationes propter veteres inimicitias essent infensæ, longinquarum quoque odium hâc novitate provocare.

Ab his initiis profecta, sedisti deinceps belli pacisque arbitra inter reges Christianos regina; qui, à factiosis civibus vexati, aut potentiorum injuriis per vim pulsi, in tuo consilio, armis, opibus acquiescunt. Testis Valesiorum familia, quorum infantiam consiliis tuis rexisti, ferociam mitigâsti; domumque ruentem, quantum in te fuit, sustinuisti. Testis illustrissima hæc Borboniorum, qui tuis[1] unius freti armis, nixi pecuniis, non[2] aliâ re magis quàm majestate nominis tui stantes, te parentem agnoscunt, te deam venerantur. Testis Lusitania, cujus regem extorrem ejectumque liberalissimo hospitio accepisti. [Testis hæc ipsa Scotia; quam civilibus quassatam bellis, tuaque arma implorantem situ opportunam, et quasi à corpore nostro avulsam particulam, natam ad vexandum hoc imperium, cùm victoria potuisses, et plerique tuorum non nollent, pace maluisti complecti[3].] Testis Germania, Dania, Suecia; quæ tuo nutu arma sumunt ponuntque. Quid Christianos dico? cùm ipsi Turcarum imperatores, quibus, ante hujus beatissimi sæculi lumen[4], ne nomen quidem hujus insulæ unquam fando auditum, tui reverentiâ nominis arma abjecerint, pacemque Polonis, jam ad ultima redactis, te interveniente, concesserint.

Dixi de singulis ferè partibus: nunc de universo orbe Christiano, cujus cùm maxima pars, aut hæreditate relicta, aut affinitatibus comprehensa, aut armis devicta, unius jussu regeretur; cùm Galliam per emissarios, Turciam per mercenarios, obtineret; cùm Germania partibus, Polonia bellis, distineretur; cùm omnes omnium gentium principes, proceres, aut socordiâ negligerent, aut timore abscederent, aut avaritiâ inclinarent, quà junctis[5] nuper orientis & occidentis opibus aurum præponderabat, cùm auctâ, ut fit, ex prosperis cupiditate, animus haud obscurè adjectus esset ad imperium universi, omniaque, nemine impediente, in unius sinum casura viderentur: hìc tua divina virtus enituit, hìc invictum animi robur, cum sapientiâ singulari. Quæ, oppressis primùm domesticorum insidiis, quod dii prius omen[6] in ipsum, rupto fœdere Burgundico, quod ipse, immisso in tuam provinciam latrocinio, priùs ruperat, receptis in societatem Belgis, ampliatisque imperii finibus tot urbium accessione, bellum terrâ marique, pro salute omnium susceptum, sola gessisti. Quod cujus manibus administratum sit, non quæro, cùm videam

[1] Tui T.   [2] Nullâ T.   [3] Inserted from T.   [4] Lucem T.   [5] Cunctis T.
[6] T. omits *omen.*

tuis auspiciis, tuis consiliis, provincias adjunctas, urbes captas, naves direptas, classes depressas, non hostium fines, sed urbem sedem imperii tuis signis appetitam, obsessam, oppugnatam. Tuis consiliis Indiæ, quanta terræ totius pars, quantulâ tuorum manu, quàm incredibili celeritate victoriis peragratæ! Tuis, tuis intelligo (quid dicam?) consiliis, tabulis, armisque, completa omnis hæc Oceani ora, constrata cadaveribus litora. Tuis auspiciis Hispania Anglum [1] non vidit nisi victorem, aut victoriæ immortuum; Anglia Hispanum nisi captivum. Itaque stant tuorum objectu armorum, tuorum oppositu laterum, quot sunt in Europâ regna, principatus; ipsique adeò pontifici, nominis tui infensissimo hosti, unà cum cæteris, absque tuis armis, vel serviendum fuit, vel pereundum.

Bonitatem, clementiam, justitiam, æquitatem, ista pervulgata, ac propè decantata, in tantâ principe referre, regiarum & heroicarum virtutum, quæ in Majestate tuâ elucent, injuria fuerit. Ne id quidem attingam, quæ mala, quam [2] constanti animo privata pertuleris, quæ tamen [3] & gratiorem præsentis fœlicitatis sensum attulerunt tibi, tuisque civibus certissimam salutem, principem [4] habere, quæ & semper cogitet, crebrisque sermonibus usurpet, quid aut noluerit sub alio principe, aut voluerit.

Illa commemorabo, quæ vulgo minùs nota, non minùs certè mirabilia ad laudem. Te cùm tot literis legendis, tot dictandis, tot manu tuâ scribendis, sufficias; cùm consiliariorum tuorum [5], in minimis etiam rebus, sententias dijudices; cùm privatorum precibus, principum legationibus, per te respondeas, de subditorum [6] quoque privatis controversiis sæpissimè cognoscas: in istâ tamen districtissimâ vitâ, non principum (quorum aliæ sunt nostris moribus artes), sed penè mortalium doctissimam evasisse. Te magnam diei partem in gravissimorum autorum scriptis legendis audiendisque ponere. Neminem nisi suâ linguâ tecum loqui; te cum nemine nisi ipsorum aut omnium communibus Latinâ Græcâque. Omitto plebeios philosophos, quos rarò in manus sumis: quoties divinum Platonem animadverti tuis interpretationibus diviniorem effectum! quoties Aristotelis obscuritates, principis philosophorum, à principe fœminarum evolutas atque explicatas! Dicerem liberè, nemini unquam ad sacratissimam Majestatem tuam aditum patuisse semidocto, qui non ex tuis sermonibus discesserit doctissimus, nisi meæ vehementèr me pœniteret [7] tarditatis, qui in tam illustri scholâ tam parùm profecerim.

---

[1] T. omits *Anglum.*   [2] Quamque T.   [3] T. omits *tamen.*   [4] Se principem T.   [5] T. omits *tuorum.*   [6] Privatorum T.   [7] Me vehementer puderet T.

Itaque literas, literatissima Princeps, tuere ac protege; id est, nobis, qui hic vivimus, nostra privilegia, illis quos emisimus suam dignitatem, sua præmia in republicâ, in ecclesiâ, quod facis, conserva. Academiam utramque novis immunitatibus munire, novis legibus fundare, perge. Utraque, à te ornata, in te ornanda certabit; cæteroqui omni genere laudis pares, hoc[1] nostra fœlicior, quòd tuos vultus iterum intuetur, in cujus oculis habitant Gratiæ, in fronte benignitas, in ore majestas, in pectore sapientia, in manibus liberalitas, in toto corpore pulchritudo & venustas digna principe, digna tantis prognatâ principibus, digna imperio: ut tecum, jam propè parens Natura, redeamus in gratiam, quæ cùm parem, effusis hìc viribus, procreare non posses, neminem voluisti ex tantâ principe disparem superesse.

The Tanner MS. adds this note :—

Transcrib'd from *Sir Ja. Ware's MS. Collections Vol.* 47, being part of Q. Elizabeth's Enterteinment at Oxford 1592, of which see Camden's Annals, part 2, p. 53. And tho' yᵉ later part of what goes before, is indeed (as yᵉ whole is entitled) an Oration to Q. Elizabeth & a just Encomium of her: yet yᵉ former part seems to be yᵉ Determination of 2 questions disputed before yᵉ Queen, (at which Sir H. Savile sat Moderator) yᵉ 1st, Whether Arms, & Letters may flourish together in yᵉ same Kingdom; yᵉ 2d, Whether judicial Astrology be to be tolerated in a well-ordered State.

APPENDIX B².

Reginæ Elisabethæ Oratio Valedictoria ad Oxonienses.
Sept. 28. 1592.

Merita, et gratitudo sic meam rationem captivam duxerunt, ut facere cogant, quæ ratio ipsa negat. Curæ enim Regnorum tam magnum pondus habent, ut potiùs ingenium obtundere, quam memoriam acuere soleant. Addatur etiam hujus linguæ desuetudo,

[1] ps hæc T.
[2] Printed from MS. Bodl. Tanner 461, f. 171ᵇ, where it immediately follows the preceding Speech.

quæ talis, & tam diuturna fuit, ut in tribus annis, credo, vix trige-
sies me usam fuisse meminerim. Sed fracta nunc est glacies: aut
inhærere, aut evadere oportet. Merita vestra non sunt laudes ex-
imiæ, et insignes (sed immeritæ) meæ; non doctrinarum in multis
generibus Exercitia, quæ declarâsse vos cum laude sentio; non rationes multis, & varijs modis eruditè, & insigniter expressæ: sed
aliud quoddam est multò pretiosius, & præstantius, amor scilicet
vester; qualis nec unquam auditus, nec scripto, nec memoriâ hominum notus fuit; cujus exemplo parentes carent, nec inter familiares
cadit, imò nec inter amantes, in quorum sortem non semper fides
incidit, experientiâ ipsâ docente; qualem nec persuasiones, nec
minæ, nec execrationes delere potuerunt; imò in quem tempus
potestatem non habet; quod ferrum consumit, quod scopulos minuit,
id istum separare non potuit. Ista sunt merita; & sunt ejusmodi,
quæ sempiterna futura putarem, si & ego æterna essem: ob quæ,
si mille pro unâ linguas haberem, gratias debitas exprimere non
valerem; tantùm animus concipere potest, quæ exprimere nequit:
In cujus gratitudinem accipite tantùm votum, & consilium.

Ab initio Regni mei summa, & præcipua mea solicitudo, cura, &
vigilia fuit, ut tam ab externis inimicis, quam internis tumultibus
servaretur; ut quod diu, & multis seculis floruisset, sub meis manibus non debilitaretur: post enim animæ meæ tutelam, in hoc solo
meam solicitudinem collocavi. Quod si pro totius salute tam semper
fuerim vigilans cùm & ista Academia pars ejus non minima putetur;
quomodo non & in illam extenditur ista cautio? pro quâ tantâ
diligentiâ usura semper sum, ut nullo stimulo opus sit ad eam ex-
citandam, quæ ex seipsa prompta est ad promovendam, servandam,
& decorandam illam.

Nunc quod ad consilium attinet, tale accipite; quod si sequamini,
haud dubito, quin erit in Dei gloriam, vestram utilitatem, & meum
singulare gaudium. Ut diuturna sit hæc Academia, habeatur inprimis cura, ut Deus colatur; non more omnium opinionum, non secundum, ingenia inquisita, & exquisita; sed ut Lex Divina jubet, &
nostra præcipit. Non enim talem principem habetis, quæ vobis
quicquam præcipiat, quod contra conscientiam vere Christianam
esse deberet: scitote, me priùs morituram, quam tale aliquid fac-
turam, aut quicquam iussuram, quod in Sacris Literis vetatur. Si
enim corporum vestrorum semper curam suscepi, deseramne animarum? Vetet Deus! Animarum ego curam negligam, pro quarum
neglectu anima mea judicabitur? Longè absit. Moneo ergo, ut
non præeatis leges; sequamini. Ne disputetis, num meliora possint

præscribi; sed observetis, quæ Lex Divina iubet, & nostra cogit. Deinde memineritis, ut unusquisque in gradu suo superiori obediat; non præscribendo, quæ esse deberent, sed sequendo, quod præscriptum est: hoc cogitantes, quòd si superiores agere cœperint, quæ non decet, alium superiorem habebunt, à quo regantur, qui illos punire & debeat, & velit. Postremò, sitis unanimes; cùm intelligatis, unita robustiora, separata infirmiora, & citò in ruinam casura.

Ibidem ubi supr.

V

APOLLINIS ET MVSARVM
EIDYLLIA

APOLLINIS ET MVSARVM

'ΕΥΚΤΙΚᾺ 'ΕΙΔΎΛΛΙΑ,

IN SERENISSIMÆ REGINÆ ELIZABETHÆ

auspicatissimum Oxoniam aduentum, *decimo die Calend. Octobris, An:* M.D.LXXXXII

[Arms of the University of Oxford omitted]

OXONIÆ,

Excudebat IOSEPHVS BARNESIVS.

ORNATISSIMO VIRO

D. DOCTORI BONDO, ALMAE

ACADEMIAE INSIGNI PROCANCELLA-

rio, & Collegii Magdalenensis dignissimo Præsidi;

Patrono & Mæcenati suo longè optimo.

ACcipe Mæcenas, cecinit quos nuper Apollo,
    Et quos versiculos turba nouena dedit :
Cùm subijt nostros Princeps augusta penates,
    Viseret vt doctas Elisabetha scholas.
Carmina nos Musis affinximus ista : sed ecce,
    Vilia sunt, tanto nec satis apta choro.
Nec bene tersa satis, nec lœui pumice munda,
    Digna sed vt iaceant sordibus vncta foris.
Qualiacunque sient, nostro sub nomine poni
    Vix patiar, ni sint numine tecta tuo.

Tuæ Dignitati deditissimus

IOANNES SANFORDVS.

IN REGINAE ELIZABETHAE AVSPI-

CATISSIMVM ET EXOPTATISSIMVM

aduentum, Apollinis & Musarum

εὐκτικὰ Εἰδύλλια.

DVm sedet ad Thamesin Parnassi fonte relicto
    Cynthius, hic vitreus lento quà flumine serpit
Isis, & Alfredi doctam vagus alluit vrbem :
Attonitus nouitate loci, cœliíque solique
Temperie, dixit, certum est hic ponere sedes
Musis perpetuas, huius nunc incola terræ
Dicar, & hunc populum nostro celebrabimus ore.
Vos iuga Pierij montis, vos stagna valete,
Gorgonis vnda vale, valeant & Phocidis amnes
Affatusíque suas comites, quàm turpiter, inquit,
Expulsi patriâ, quàm dulcia liquimus arua,
Quàmque per æquoreos fluctus huc paupere cymbâ
Appulimus, scitis, quanquam meminisse doletis,
Hic tamen & syluas, & prata virentia passim,
(Vera fatebor enim) vix concedentia primis
Cernitis, has terras certe Dea magna tuetur.
Hæc dum mirantur stantes in margine ripæ,
Ecce sub illunem noctem feriata per agros
Turba ruens, inflansíque tubas & tinnula sistra,
Clamat adesse deam, proprias vt visat Athenas.
Tum Deus auratâ sumptâ testudine, laudem
Principis aggreditur pulsis ad carmina neruis :
Quem parili studio Musarum turba secuta

A i j

Conci-

Concinuёre, sono vicinia tota rcsultat.

APOLLO.

O Semper querulo carmine barbiton
    Gratum Dijs superis, deliciæ Iouis,
Te posco positis prorsus amoribus
Nunc insigne melos, quale frequens sonas
Inter lauta dapum fercula cœlitum.
Non Daphne capitis nunc decus vnicum
Nostri; non Clymene filia Tethyos;
Non Circes genitrix, nec Chione dolo
Quæ me sensit anum Dædalionia;
Sed ncc Leucathoёs thurea virgula
Nunc cantanda tibi est : fertilior seges
In promptu dabitur carminis aurei.
En Regina suo cincta satellite,
Herôum celebri nobilium choro
Ascito, niueis vecta iugalibus,
Musarum studijs structa palatia
Exoptata subit, quam Procerum cohors
Ambit purpureis splcndida vestibus,
Sublimesǘue citis terga premunt equis.
Quos intcr Tyrio murice virgines
Distinctæ propcrant, colla monilibus,
Ornatæǘue sinus torquibus aureis.
Hos longo sequitur plebs leuis agmine,

Tantæ

Tantæ festa canens iubila Principi.

Huius tu modulis suauibus, & sono

Dulci fac celebres inclyta numina,

Quæ nos hospitio suscipiens nouo

Tutatur, Latij barbarus incola

Quos diris odijs expulit, & vagos

Eiecit patrijs sedibus exules.

CALLIOPE.

TV qui potenti Ioua regis manu

  Poli micantis militiam vagam,

    Qui syderum vultus, minaces

      Comprimis, imperioq́; frænas:

Deterge cœlo nubila tempora,

Tollat nociuum Sirius & iubar

  Hinc vsq́ue ad Afros, nec procellas

    Excitet Æolias Orion.

Obstringe ventos ne rabies Noti,

Imbres furenti depluat impetu:

  Absconde Pleiadas madentes,

    Atq́ue Hyadas pluuiale sydus:

Ne fortè moto turbine, Principis

Tardetur ardor, quo minùs impigrè

  Huc pergat interesse doctis

    Litibus, ac lepido duello.

Dies serenus solis ab exitu

A i i j

Egressus,

Egressus, octo perpetuet vices,

  Spectaculis vt ter bcata

    Elisabeth saturata clamet :

Satis iocorum vidimus vndiq́ ;

Satis scholarum ; risimus & satis ;

  Nil non probamus ; cccc læta,

    Plaudite sæpedato, recedo.

CLIO.

PAnde sublimes age læta portas

  Sede Musarum celebris Calæna,

Vrbis æratæ pateant reuulso

    Cardine valuæ.

Aduenit longâ comitata turmâ

Virgo regali trabeata veste,

Continens sceptrum manibus tremendum

    Elisabetha.

Ite vos ciues date dona Diuæ,

Principi Prætor gladium resignet,

Lictor huic fasces ferat, & secures

    Tradat habendas.

Nos nouem quales deccant sorores,

Promimus sacros codices, scholarum

Aureos fœtus ; damus hæc benignæ

    Pignora mentis.

Munus amborum capiet serenâ

                   Fronte,

Fronte, quòd Marti simul & Mineruæ
Apta, natiuo Genio vtriusque
     Nouerit arma.
Feruet ad pugnas animo virili,
Sicut armatas ruit in cohortes,
Dignior certè meliore sexu
     Volsca Camilla.
Fertur ad pacis studium suapte
Sponte, dū stringit manus vna ferrū:
Alteram sacri tenet occupatam
     Pagina verbi.
Pallas vtrinque est: vacat illa doctis
Literis, & quas faciunt lituras
Bella, subridens probat: Arte, Marte
     Nobilis æquè.
Ergò coniunctis animis precemur
Principi tantæ senium Sibyllæ,
Copias Xerxis, cumulosque Crœsi
     Æris & auri.

THALIA.

SAlue conspicuū decus Brytannûm,
  Tu regum soboles, iubar perenne
Lucis, cura Iouis, fauor deorum.
Te Diuam colimus, Deam canemus
Musis propitiam, benigna cuius

A i i i j

Promit

Promit dextera liberalitatis

Gazas Attalicas opem roganti.

Non ignara mali faues egenis,

Extorres miseros domo paternâ

Tu Regina capis domo patenti.

Olim Sidonis vt vagos Elisa,

Teucros hospitio suo fouebat.

Viuas perpetuo beata regno,

Et votis habeas deum annuentē,

Ciues morigeros: citâ rebelles

Plectantur nece perduelliones,

Qui turbare volunt tuam quietē.

De cœlo tibi Ioua largiatur

Annos Nestoriæ pares senectæ,

Lætos vt videas diu Brytannos,

Læti & te videant diu Brytanni.

EVTERPE.

ERgò ades Elisabeth nostros visura penates,
    Pieridumque domos?

Ergò ades vt spectes exercent qualia nostræ
    Ludicra bella Scholæ?

Hic nobis supremus honos: en erigit omnes
    Nominis aura tui.

Cœlica Diua vides reficit quàm suauiter omnes
    Numinis vmbra tui.

Cer-

Cernis vt ampla cohors iuuenum per cōpita passim
    Densat vtrinĝue vias.

Per vicos glomerata frequens stant ordine longo
    Gens onerata stolis.

Hi tibi gratantes clamant (lectissima Princeps)
    Viuat Elisa diu.

Viuas, & firmâ teneas pro iure precantur
    Regia sceptra manu.

Tu parili studio doctas fœliciter artes
    Dulcis alumna foue.

Præside te nostri florescant rostra Lycæi
    Principe te vigeant.

Sic veniente die subsellia nostra sonabunt,
    Et fugiente canent:

Viuat Elisa diu nobis, post funera semper
    Viuat Elisa Deo.

ERATO.

IOuis cerebro tu Dea
    Prognata, nostræ quæ præes

Turbæ, regisĝue feruidos

Gentis togatæ spiritus:

Suffunde venam fertilem,

Atque inde vires cœlitùs

Ad carmen aureum, tuo

Dignum choro, dignū chely.

Tu mitis inuentrix sacræ

Oliuæ ades, mater bonæ

Pacis, virenti fronte fac

Ornes alumnos obsecro :

Vt prodeamus obuij

  Ramo arboris tuæ, velut

  Caduceo insignes ; adest

  Proles Iouis, Princeps pia.

Virgo diserta, publicæ

  Quietis altus quam subit

Amor, colona scilicet

Fontis Caballini, tuo

Sancto dicati numini :

Tuas Athenas quæ colit,

Et nunc suâ præsentiâ

Exornat artifex proba.

Hîc ergo defigat pedem,

Trahatq́ ; longas hîc moras :

Fausto & recedens te duce,

Iter capessat omine.

POLYHYMNIA.

SIc te, Diua potens, regat

 Tutis auspicijs. Iupiter optimus,

Vt quocunq́ue feras pedem,

 Vites insidias cautiùs anguibus.

Nep-

Neptunusáue maris Deus,

  Sic circum Albionis candida littora

AEstu perpetuo fremat,

  Hostes vt rapidis fluctibus arceat.

Sic Mars veste adamantinâ

  Munitus vigiles excubias agat :

Ne sicarius impio

  Telo virgineum perterebret latus.

Illum ex cautibus editum

  Credo Caucasijs, quē Armenius leo

Scuit, Tigris & vbera

  Admouit genitrix, nutrijt aut lupa :

Cui primo stetit in manu,

  Regalem sitiens pugio sanguinem.

Dij nos foemineum genus

  Tutentur faciles numine prouido.

Vt quas inualidas facit

  Sexus, quas faciunt innocuas pudor,

Candor, casta modestia ;

  Fortes efficiat, fulciat & Deus.

MELPOMENE.

CŒli monarcha, præpotens deûm sator,

  Et rex bonus mortalium,

Cui præpes ales armiger ferox gerit

  Faces coruscas fulmine :

De sede sublimis throni nos despice
   Stratas humi Sororculas,
Et voce supplici rogantes, vt velis
   Anglam beare Principem.
Tu fac auitum hæres diu solium premat
   Prognata virgo regibus;
Diadema fronte, sceptra fac manibus ferat,
   Regatque Gentem bellicam
Pacisq; cum dici parens cupiat bonæ,
   AEuo fruatur optimo.
Et si quod vlcus, publicæ aut pestis rei,
   Tam corneis fibris siet,
Qui fortis ausis impijs, struat scelus
   Tibi sacratæ Virgini:
Tu stringe sulphureum pater telū citò
   In tam feri monstri caput;
Vt mole pressus Aetnæâ Enceladi leuet
   Onus, latusque languidum,
Ne viuus aërem scelesto polluat
   Oris sui contagio.
Aut si superstitem velis, notam gerat
   Quam cædis author, carnifex
Et primus infami tulit maculâ, graue
   In fratre designans nefas,
Vt sic cruces homicîda stigmaticus malæ
   Mentis perennes sentiat.

Terp-

TERPSICHORE.

VOs lanificæ trina Sorores
　　Numina, quarum est texere fatum:
Queis pulchra colus tenui filo
Fundit nostræ stamina vitæ:
Nostris precibus sistite cursum
Vestris digitis: dulcis Elisæ
Tardo currat pollice fusus.
Vos Penelopes æmula turba,
Sedula quicquid fortiter vrget,
Fessa diurno dextra labore:
Rursus tacita nocte retexat.
Et Mygdonij senis ætatem,
Et quos Nestor viderat annos
Per tria sæcula, vatis & ævum
Dircæi, vetulæ siue Sybillæ:
Faciles nostræ apponite Elisæ.
Spargant seri tempora cani,
Nullaque frontem ruga senilis
Aret, aut tremulos fulciat artus
Fractos senio triste bacillum.
Maneat pulchro candor in ore,
Decor & malas roseus tingat
Semper solito more rubentes.
Nūquam (id certè dabitis nunquā)

U　Biij

Pectus

Pectus tantæ Principis, atri

Læthi durus sauciet ictus.

At quia fatum ferre necesse est,

Serò saltem funera curet.

VRANIA.

ILla ego, quâ viuunt orbes, animantur & ignes,
   Cuius mouentur spiritu sydera clara poli :
A Ioue nacta genus, cœlo notissima virgo,
   Cuius coruscâ splendidum nomen ab arce gero :
Signaui, Regina, locos vbi stabis in axe,
   Postquam supremum mors tibi clauserit atra diē.
Est locus Erigonen inter plaustrumǿue Boötæ,
   Cœlo sereno lucidus, conspicuusǿue solo :
Vnde micat rutilum pulchræ Minoïdis astrum,
   Et Iulium sydus cui Roma superba subest.
Hinc tua subiectis radiabit stella Brytannis,
   Et lene nautis Anglicis sparget amica iubar.
Tu Cynosura tuis, Heliceǿ; per æquora vectis
   Hinc nauibus clara feres præuia luce faces.
Duxǿue per ambiguos tractus, ad littoris oras
   Sistes, quiescat vt suo tuta carina vado.
Pone metum, Princeps, sedes tibi certa paratur
   Stellas & æther parturit, iā tibi mundus ouat.
Sera tamen subeas fœlicia regna precabor,
   Vt fulgeas throno diu, celsior inde polo.

HÆC

HAEc cecinere nouē Phœbo præunte sorores

Aönides, plausuq́; dato nemus omne remugit,

Hinc Regina potēs plumatis tracta quadrigis,

Auratíque rotis currus, atque agmine denso

Nobiliū Procerum comitata subintrat Athenas

Virgine de tantâ, de tanta Principe lætas.

Quam solito incedens telis armata tenore,

Solenni de more cohors deducit ad ædes,

Sumptibus Attalicis quas struxit Wolseus olim.

Ædes Christi.

At diuersa petunt venerandi tecta Dynastæ,

Inuisuntque domos alias quas laudibus ornāt,

Miranturque suis cum Fundatoribus arces.

Stat procul à reliquis rediuiui Solis ad ortū,

Nobile Gymnasium Waynfleti; proxima cuius

Vnda lauat muros, vbi tardo labitur amne

Charwellus, lentisq́; intersecat arua fluentis.

Ampla dom', spaciosa loco, speciosa superbas

Ostendit portas; surgunt fastigia pinnis;

Intus & è pictis camerata cubilia tignis,

Fundatoris opes & opus sine voce loquuntur.

Collegium Diuæ Mariæ Magda-lenæ.

Conuocat huc regni Primores, Præses ab aulâ

Principis huc missus, quē tota Academia patrē

Suspiciens reuerēter amat, quem vita probatis

Moribus exornat, quem pagina sacra disertum

Efficit, & grauitas decorat non tetrica frōtem.

Hospitibusque suis epulum facturus opimum,

D. Doctor Bondus almæ Vniuer-sitatis Procancel-larius.

Tantos conuiuas dapibus genialibus explet.

Dulcia vina cado depromit, fercula magnis

Sumptibus accersit; circumstant ordine lōgo,

Qui mēsas onerent famuli qui vina ministrent,

Cœlatosq́; scyphos, aurataque; pocula ponant.

Legatus
Gallicus.

    Discūbunt satrapæ : tū prima sedilia magnus

Augusta grauitate premit Legatus ab oris

Celtarum missus, clari Bourbônis imago,

Bellica magnanimûm quem iactat Gallia regē.

D. Cecilius
magnus
Angliæ
Thesaura-
rius. De
Nestore
*Ouid. li.*12.
Meta-
morph.

    Nobilis à dextra sequitur Cecilius heros,

Vir grauis & doctus, veræ pietatis amator,

Facundusq; senex, *æui prudentia nostri.*

Qui designatus Quæstor primarius, amplo

Præficitur fisco : sapiens vigilansque Senator,

Principis & patriæ grauiora negotia tractat.

Comes Vi-
gorniensis.

    E regione locū tenuit Comes inclytus ille,

Fertilis eximium cui dat Vigornia nomen.

Quū gentile decus, quē laus, & laurea magnæ

Cognitionis, amor patriæ, prosapia, clarum

Efficiunt : geminos cuius de corpore natos,

D. Herbert:
Henr:
Somerset.

Spirantesq́; patris generoso in pectore mores,

Nobilium fratrum par nobile, suscipit alma

Magdaleëna domus, tanto & lætatur alumno.

Comes
Cumbriæ.

    Affuit his epulis generosus Cūbrius heros,

Feruidus ad pugnas, qui ter congressus Iberis,

In quos (nauali bello violenter adortus)

Hor-

Horribili tonitru Vulcania dirigit arma,

Omnibus & gemmis & mercibus exuit Indis,

Lætus & in patriam spolijs remeauit onustus,

Sic fatus socios : En viuis gloria nobis

Se spondet comitem ; sed quid si mersus arenis

Cum duce miles (ait) caderet sine honore sepulchri?

Marmoreo tegitur tumulo qui cōditur vndis.

Ordine tum sequitur Dominus Pembrochius, ipse

Nobilitatis honos, cuius præconia cantat

Cambria, quam dextrè tranquillâ pace gubernat,

Rite secans lites Iudex, ac iurgia Præses.

Quem fauisse pijs, homines coluisse disertos,

Relligiosa fides, & numinis entheus ardor

Edocuit : puer huc patrem comitatus euntem

Sedit conuiuas inter, prænobilis hæres

Indolis egregiæ, sed cui *stat messis in herbâ.*

Proximus accubuit reliquis Essexius heros,

Nobilis & sapiens, superās iuuenilibus annis

Cognitione senes, canosque ætate magistros.

Qui doctos homines miratur, doctior ipse ;

Mæcenasque bonos passis amplectitur vlnis.

In bello pugnax, vir strenuus ὄζος Ἄρηος,

Cuius in Hyspanos res forti pectore gestas,

Sensit ab occiduo Lusitania sole tepescens,

Dum per agros medios ruit acer, & ipse superbæ

Pulsat Vlyxbonæ ferratâ cuspide portas.

Comes
Pem-
brochiæ.

D.Herbert:
filius
Comitis
Pembroch:
cuius illud
est Em-
blema.

Comes
Essexiæ
magister
Equitum.

De
Titaresio
Hesiod in
lib. περὶ
ἀσπίδος τοῦ
ἡρακλέους.

C   Cuius

Cuius & insultus (dum vitæ prodigus ardet

Afflictos Gallos tegere auxiliaribus armis)

Laudibus Armoricæ celebrat gens incola terræ.

Ille cito subuectus equo qui naribus ignes.

Spirat, & indocilis rigidum mordere lupatum

Spumeus exultat, sequitur te Regia Virgo

Clarus eques, milesque ferox, Equitūque magister.

Comes South Hamp- toniæ.

Post hunc insequitur clarâ de stirpe Dynasta,

Iure suo diues quem South-Hamptonia magnum

Vendicat heroem ; quo non formosior alter

Affuit, aut docta iuuenis præstantior arte ;

Ora licet tenerâ vix dum lanugine vernent.

D. Howar- dusmagnus Angliæ Admiral- lius.

Assidet his Satrapis multùm celebratus Houärdus

Corpore procero & reliquos supereminet omnes.

Magna Ducum soboles, proauorum clara propago,

Cui soli Regina fauens de stemmate tanto,

Iussit vt illius tutelæ Regia Classis

Mandaretur, onus non quovis remige dignum,

Sed magnis cautisque viris & pectore forti.

Nec tuus hinc aberat, Comes inclyte, filius hæres,

D. Strange filius Comitis Derbiensis.

Derbia cui paret, quemque Insula Mona salutat

Regem, sed talem qui magnæ iussa capessis

Principis, illius sceptro tua iura resignans :

Qui diadema geris quod nectit bractea plumbi,

Vilior argento, fuluoq ; impurior auro.

Hi sunt (si memini) tua qui conuiuia Præses,

Qui

Qui Waynflete tuos castos adiere penates.

Intererant alij plures de gente minori,

Quos taceo, cunctos quia percensere molestum est.

   Vnus abes Sackville choro dilecte togato,

Maximus vrbis honos, Academia nostra patrono

Quo gauisa suo est, & Mæcenate benigno.

Quæ tibi sic loquitur; cur gaudia nostra moraris,

Vocibus & votis cùm sis mihi mille petitus?

Ostendunt crebri gemitus, querimonia tristis,

Quàm sit dulce frui, quàm te caruisse dolendum.

Hinc tamen ad regni maiora negocia missus

Cogeris, esse procul; quem munia magna fatigant,

Curaq́; sollicitum distringit adesse volentem.

Quod quoniam Regina tui fidissima iussit,

Postulat obsequium; quare parere necesse est.

Hæc, inquam, mihi visa queri; stupor ora deinceps

Occupat, & matris natorum iuncta querela est.

   Hi sedêre Duces, vario sermone trahentes

Tempus, & appositis satiantes corpora mensis.

Ista quibus viuâ dicenda poëmata voce

Si licuisset erant; subitò sed rumor ad omnes

Pertigit, egressam thalamo, tectoque relicto,

Reginam Diuæ properare ad Virginis ædes.

Protinus vt dederant vltrò citròque salutem,

Discedunt; magnas capit hospes ab hospite grates.

D. Buck-
hurstius
summus
Academiæ
Oxon:
Cancel-
larius.

C i j

Con-

Conuiuantibus regijs Conciliarijs pauca quæ
dicenda erant carmina.

Hactenus, egregij Proceres, spectastis honorem
Quem dedit effuso ruris gens incola censu,
Turbaque magnificis epulis generosior auxit.
Nunc, quibus applaudit vobis Academia votis,
Excipit & quantis vrbs vndique læta triumphis
Principis aduentum, festâ plebecula voce
Testatur, vacuas quatiens clamoribus auras.

Nec sua sunt tantùm plaudenti gaudia vulgo,
Verbaque non solùm spirantibus edita fibris
Vocales sparsere sonos: sub turribus altis
Pendula pulsatis tremuerunt ictibus æra.
Muta domus loquitur candenti perlita gypso,
Picta coloratis trabibus; minioque renidens
Clamat Io paries, & mœnia celsa videntur
Submisisse caput, vobisq; assurgere portæ,
Vt vestris meritis reuerentia debita fiat.
Vestit honoratos herôas gloria tanta.

Gaudia sic ciues peragunt, rurisque coloni
Sic partes egere suas: nos, altera turba,
Nos humiles Musæ, tenues humilesq; myricæ
Quas dabimus grates? gratæ quæ munera mentis?
Nulla sub his tectis gemma, aut pretiosa supellex,
Transtulit Eôis qualem mercator ab Indis.

Non

Non Syræ merces, non lamina fulua metalli
Danda venit nobis, non byssina tela, quotannis
Qualia ab arboribus depectunt vellera Seres.
Viuimus hic tenui quadrâ, stat paupere mensâ
Parca Ceres, raro seruent conuiuia Baccho.

Ergò quid è nostro promemus pectore? certe
Vota decent humiles & verba precãtia Musas:
Hæc satis vna placent vobis, si nil damus vltrà,
Cum simus tenues molimur grandia frustrà.
Viuite fœlices, & limina nostra frequenter
Visite, conspicui Proceres, famulantia vestris
Nutibus, has ædes, hæc tecta, has Palladis arces
Structas à vestris proauis, munite fauore.

Eisdem honoratissimis viris.

Romulus, vt fertur, iaculū dum librat in aprū,
   Colle Palatino rasilis hasta stetit.
Et creuit stabilita nouis radicibus arbor,
   Frondescensq; altas ventilat illa comas.
Floruit, & populo miranti præbuit vmbras,
   Donec in Imperio ciuica bella silent.
Post vbi Cæsaream discordia fregerat vrbem,
   Sanguineq; imbuerat plebs furiata manus:
Protinus excussis folijs ruit Itala cornus,
   Aruit, & ramos exuit alta suos.

Romuli hasta in cornum arborem mutata, Ouid. Met. lib. 15. creuit & viruit vsq; ad tēpora belli ciuilis sub Iulio Cæsare, Plut. in vitâ. Romuli.

X   C i i j

Vestris

Vestris (aurati Proceres regnique Senatus)

 Fraxinus auspicijs, consiliisáue viret.

Lancea fit laurus, frameam pacalis oliua

 Vestit, & inducto cortice fronde tegit.

Nos inter Martis lituos fera bella minantes,

 Securos agimus pace vigente dies.

Dumáue ruunt alij strictis in vulnera telis,

 Auspice Reginâ terra Brytanna canit.

Et canet assiduò, tutaáue quiescet in vmbra,

 Si pugnæ vestra sedulitate cadant.

Sin fremat infestis odijs, & concitus œstro,

 Imperio populus libera colla gerat:

Concidet Iliacis subitò gens nostra ruinis;

 Concidet Elisabeth; Curia sacra ruet.

Quæque prius tereti succreuerat arbor ab hastâ

 Cæsa dabit nostræ tela cruenta neci.

Arceat hoc nostris Deus à ceruicibus omen,

 Et pia pro regno sint rata vota velit.

Publica res vigeat, salvū cum Principe vulgus

 Floreat, hostiles nec tremat illa dolos.

Vosáue, quibus regni sunt tota negocia curæ,

 Qui consulta datis, ter generosa cohors:

Promite solertes fæcundi pectoris artes,

 Ferueat vt sacrum Relligionis opus.

Quæ nunc ingenijs malè cōuenientibus acta,

 Litibus innumeris, dissidijsque gemit.

Sic

Sic Deus intererit vestris conatibus, et vos

   Diriget afflatu Spiritus ipse suo.

Sic dabitur semper vestris & fascibus hæres,

   Consulis & proles vestra subibit onus.

Viuite nunc læti, vobis pincerna Deorum,

   Nectaris & succos, Ambrosiamque ferat.

                   Bon prou vous façe.

FINIS.

[*Row of seven ornaments omitted.*]

INDEX.

THE END.